Peterson's

Math
Exercises
for the SAT*

THOMSON

PETERSON'S

Australia • Canada • Mexico • Singapore • Spain • United Kingdom • United States

About Peterson's

Founded in 1966, Peterson's, a division of Thomson Learning, is the nation's largest and most respected provider of lifelong learning resources, both in print and online. The Education Supersite℠ at www.petersons.com—the Internet's most heavily traveled education resource—has searchable databases and interactive tools for contacting U.S.-accredited institutions and programs. In addition, Peterson's delivers unmatched financial aid resources and test-preparation tools. Peterson's serves more than 100 million education consumers annually.

Peterson's is a division of Thomson Learning, one of the world's largest providers of lifelong learning. Thomson Learning serves the needs of individuals, learning institutions, and corporations with products and services for both traditional and distributed learning. Headquartered in Stamford, Connecticut, with offices worldwide, Thomson Learning is a division of The Thomson Corporation (www.thomson.com), one of the world's leading e-information and solutions companies in the business, professional, and education marketplaces. For more information, visit www.thomsonlearning.com.

For more information, contact Peterson's, 2000 Lenox Drive, Lawrenceville, NJ 08648; 800-338-3282; or find us on the World Wide Web at: www.petersons.com/about

ISBN 0-7689-0807-8

Printed in the United States of America
10 9 8 7 6 5 4 3   02

Contents

About the SAT

PURPOSE OF THE SAT

The Scholastic Assessment Test (SAT) is a standardized exam used by many colleges and universities in the United States and Canada to help them make their admissions decisions. The test is developed and administered by Educational Testing Service (ETS) for the College Entrance Examination Board.

The SAT consists of two different types of exams designated SAT I and SAT II. SAT I tests verbal and mathematical reasoning skills — your ability to understand what you read, to use language effectively, to reason clearly, and to apply fundamental mathematical principles to unfamiliar problems. SAT II tests mastery of specific subjects such as Chemistry or French or World History.

TAKING SAT I

SAT I is offered on one Saturday morning in October, November, December, January, March, May, and June. When you apply to a college, find out whether it requires you to take SAT I and if so when scores are due. To make sure your scores arrive in time, sign up for a test date that's at least six weeks before the school's deadline for test scores.

Registration forms for SAT I are available in most high school guidance offices. You can also get registration forms and any other SAT information from:

College Board SAT Program
P.O. Box 6200
Princeton, NJ 08541-6200
609-771-7600

Monday through Friday, 8:30 a.m. to 9:30 p.m. Eastern Time

www.collegeboard.com

or

P.O. Box 1025
Berkeley, CA 94701
415-849-0950

Monday through Friday, 8:15 a.m. to 4:30 p.m. Pacific Time

Along with your registration form you will receive a current *SAT Student Bulletin*. The bulletin includes all necessary information on procedures, exceptions and special arrangements, times and places, and fees.

FORMAT OF SAT I

SAT I is a three-hour, mostly multiple-choice examination divided into sections as shown in the chart below. One of the sections is experimental. Your score on the six nonexperimental sections is the score colleges use to evaluate your application.

The verbal sections of SAT I use Sentence Completions, Analogies, and Critical Reading Questions to test your reading and vocabulary skills.

The mathematical sections use Standard Multiple-Choice Math, Quantitative Comparisons, and Student-Produced Response Questions to test your knowledge of arithmetic, algebra, and geometry. Many of the formulas that you need will be given in the test instructions. You are not required to memorize them. SAT math questions are designed to test your skill in applying basic math principles you already know to unfamiliar situations.

The experimental section of SAT I may test verbal reasoning or mathematical reasoning, and it can occur at any point during the test. This section is used solely by the testmakers to try out questions for use in future tests. Even though the experimental section doesn't count toward your score, you won't know which section it is. So you'll have to do your best on all of the sections.

FORMAT OF A TYPICAL SAT I

Section #/Content		Number of Questions	Time
(1)	Verbal Reasoning	30 or 31	30 min.
	Sentence Completions	9	
	Analogies	6	
	Critical Reading	15	
(2)	Mathematical Reasoning	25	30 min.
	Standard Multiple Choice		
	Mathematics		
(3)	Verbal Reasoning	35 or 36	30 min.
	Sentence Completions	10	
	Analogies	13	
	Critical Reading	12	
(4)	Mathematical Reasoning	25	30 min.
	Quantitative Comparisons	15	
	Grid-Ins	10	
(5)	"Wild Card" Section	varies	30 min.
(6)	Verbal Reasoning	12 or 13	15 min.
	Critical Reading		
(7)	Mathematical Reasoning	10	15 min.
	Standard Multiple Choice		
	Mathematics		

THE SAT I MATH QUESTIONS

The mathematical reasoning sections of SAT I test problem solving in arithmetic, elementary algebra, and geometry using three question types:

- **Standard multiple-choice questions** give you a problem in arithmetic, algebra, or geometry. Then you choose the correct answer from the five choices.

- **Quantitative comparison questions** test your skills in comparing information and in estimating. You'll see two quantities, one in Column A and one in Column B. Your job is to compare the two quantities and decide if one is greater than the other, if they are equal, or if no comparison is possible.

- **Grid-Ins** do not give you answer choices. You have to compute the answer and then use the bubbles on the answer sheet to fill in your solution.

Although calculators are not required to answer any SAT I math questions, students are encouraged to bring a calculator to the test and to use it wherever it is helpful.

Regular Mathematics (35 standard multiple-choice questions) tests your knowledge of arithmetic, algebra, and geometry. You are to select the correct solution to the problem from the five choices given.

Example:

If $(x + y)^2 = 17$, and $xy = 3$, then $x^2 + y^2 =$

- (A) 11
- (B) 14
- (C) 17
- (D) 20
- (E) 23

Solution:

The correct answer is (A).

$$(x+y)^2 = 17$$
$$(x+y)(x+y) = 17$$
$$x^2 + 2xy + y^2 = 17$$

Since $xy = 3$,

$$x^2 + 2(3) + y^2 = 17$$
$$x^2 + 6 + y^2 = 17$$
$$x^2 + y^2 = 17$$

Quantitative Comparisons (15 questions) test your knowledge of equalities, inequalities, and estimation. In general, quantitative comparison questions require less reading and less computation than regular mathematical questions; however, the directions for this question type may be unfamiliar to some students. Each quantitative comparison question consists of two quantities, one in Column A and one in Column B. Information concerning one or both of the quantities to be compared is centered above the two columns. You are to compare the two quantities and determine whether one quantity is greater than the other, whether the two quantities are equal, or whether the relationship cannot be determined from the information given.

Example:

Compare the quantities in Column A and Column B. Mark your answer sheet:

(A)   if the quantity in Column A is greater
(B)   if the quantity in Column B is greater
(C)   if the two quantities are equal
(D)   if the relationship cannot be determined from the information given

<u>Column A</u>	<u>Column B</u>
$\dfrac{4}{\sqrt{2}}$	$\sqrt{2}$

Solution:

The correct answer is (A) (Column A is greater than Column B). To eliminate the division in Column A, multiply both columns by $\sqrt{2}$.

$$\frac{4}{\sqrt{2}} \cdot \sqrt{2} = 4 \qquad\qquad \sqrt{2} \cdot \sqrt{2} = 2$$

Therefore, Column A is greater than Column B.

Student-Produced Responses (10 questions) test your ability to solve mathematical problems when no choices are offered.

Example:

On a map having a scale of $\frac{1}{4}$ inch = 20 miles, how many inches should there be between towns that are 70 miles apart?

Solution:

The correct answer is $\frac{7}{8}$ or .875, depending upon whether you choose to solve the problem using fractions or decimals.

Using fractions	Using decimals
$\dfrac{\frac{1}{4}}{20} = \dfrac{x}{70}$	$\dfrac{.25}{20} = \dfrac{x}{10}$
$20x = \dfrac{70}{4}$	$20x = 17.5$
	$x = .875$
$x = \left(\dfrac{70}{4}\right)\left(\dfrac{1}{20}\right) = \dfrac{7}{8}$	

HOW TO USE THE ANSWER GRID

The answer grid for student-produced response (grid-ins) questions is similar to the grid used for your zip code on the personal information section of your answer sheet. An example of the answer grid is shown below.

The open spaces above the grid are for you to write in the numerical value of your answer. The first row of ovals has only two ovals in the middle with a "/". These allow you to enter numbers in fractional form. Since a fraction must have both a numerator and a denominator, it is not possible that the leftmost or rightmost positions could have a "/". To protect you from yourself, there are no "/s" in those positions. The next row has decimal points. The horizontal bar separates the fraction lines and decimal points from the digits 0 to 9. Record your answers to grid-in questions according to the rules that follow.

GRID RULES

1. **Write your answer in the boxes at the top of the grid.**

   Technically this isn't required by the SAT. Realistically, it gives you something to follow as you fill in the ovals. Do it—it will help you.

2. **Mark the bubbles that correspond to the answer you entered in the boxes.**

   Mark one bubble per column. The machine that scores the test can only read the bubbles, so if you don't fill them in, you won't get credit. Just entering your answer in the boxes is not enough.

3. **Start your answer in any column, if space permits.**

   Unused columns should be left blank. Don't put in zeroes. Look at this example:

Here are two ways to enter an answer of "150."

4. **Work with decimals or fractions.**

    An answer can be expressed as $\frac{3}{4}$ or as .75. Do not put a zero in front of a decimal that is less than 1. Just remember that you have only four spaces to work with and that a decimal point or a fraction slash uses up one of the spaces.

    For decimal answers, be as accurate as possible but keep within the four spaces. Say you get an answer of .1777. Here are your options:

Fractions do not have to be simplified to simplest form unless they don't fit in the answer grid. For example, you can grid $\frac{4}{10}$, but you can't grid $\frac{12}{16}$ because you'd need five spaces. So, you would simplify it and grid $\frac{3}{4}$.

5. **Express a mixed number as a decimal or as an improper fraction.**

   If you tried to grid $1\frac{3}{4}$, it would be read as $\frac{13}{4}$, which would give you a wrong answer. Instead you should grid this answer as 1.75 or as $\frac{7}{4}$.

6. **If more than one answer is possible, grid any one.**

   Sometimes the problems in this section will have more than one correct answer. In such cases, choose one answer and grid it. For example, if a question asks for a prime number between 5 and 13, the answer could be 7 or 11. Grid 7 or grid 11, but don't put in both answers.

CALCULATORS AND THE SAT

Calculators are allowed on the SAT I. You may bring to your exam any of the following types of calculators:

- four-function

- scientific

- graphing

You may not bring calculators of the following types:

- calculators with paper tape or printers

- laptop computers

- pocket organizers

- "hand-held" microcomputers

Make sure that the calculator you bring is one you are thoroughly familiar with.

WHEN TO USE A CALCULATOR

No question requires the use of a calculator. For some questions a calculator may be helpful; for others it may be inappropriate. In general, the calculator may be useful for any question that involves arithmetic computations. Remember, though, that the calculator is only a tool. It can help you avoid inaccuracies in computation, but it cannot take the place of understanding how to set up and solve a mathematical problem.

Here is a sample problem for which a calculator would be useful:

Example:

The cost of two dozen apples is $3.60. At this rate, what is the cost of 10 apples?

(A) $1.75
(B) $1.60
(C) $1.55
(D) $1.50
(E) $1.25

Solution:

The correct answer is (D).
Make a ratio of apples to dollars:

$$\frac{\textbf{apples}}{\textbf{dollars}} : \frac{24}{3.60} = \frac{10}{x}$$

$$24x = 36$$

$$x = \frac{36}{24} = \$1.50$$

A calculator would be useful in solving this problem. Although the calculations are fairly simple, the calculator can improve your speed and accuracy.

Here is a problem for which a calculator would not be useful:

Example:

Joshua travels a distance of d miles in t - 6 hours. At this rate, how many miles will he travel in t^2 - 36 hours?

(A) $d(t + 6)$
(B) $d(t - 6)$
(C) $\dfrac{d}{t+6}$
(D) $\dfrac{d}{t-6}$
(E) $\dfrac{t+6}{d}$

Solution:

The correct answer is (A).

$$\textbf{rate} = \frac{\textbf{distance}}{\textbf{time}}$$

$$\textbf{Joshua's rate} = \frac{d}{t-6}$$

To calculate his new distance, use distance = rate x time

$$\textbf{Distance} = \left(\frac{d}{t-6}\right)\left(t^2 - 36\right)$$

$$= \left(\frac{d}{t-6}\right)(t+6)(t-6)$$

$$= d(t+6)$$

This is an algebra problem. Using a calculator would not be helpful.

SCORING SAT I

Every correct answer is worth one point. If you leave an answer blank, you score no point. For incorrect answers to all verbal questions and to regular mathematics questions, you lose one-fourth of a point. For incorrect answers to quantitative comparisons, you lose one-third of a point. For incorrect answers to student-produced responses, there is no penalty. The penalties for wrong answers are intended to discourage random guessing.

Regardless of the number of questions on the test, all SAT I scores are reported on a scale of 200 to 800. The scores are based on the nonexperimental sections and are broken down into separate math and verbal scores.

Five or six weeks after the exam, your scores will be sent to the colleges you have named on your registration form, to your high school, and to you.

HOW TO USE THIS BOOK

The math review that follows is designed as a self-teaching text to help you prepare for the mathematics sections of the SAT I. At the beginning of each chapter, you will find a ten-question diagnostic test. Try this test before you read the chapter. Check your answers with the solutions provided at the end of the chapter. If you get eight to ten questions right, you may skip that chapter and go right on to the next diagnostic test at the beginning of the following chapter. Or you may prefer to skim the instructional material anyway, just for review, but not bother with the practice exercises. If you get five to seven questions right, you might do the practice exercises only in the sections dealing with problems you missed. If you get fewer than five questions right, you should work carefully through the entire chapter.

At the end of each chapter you will find a retest that is similar to the diagnostic test. After working through the chapter, you should do better on the retest. If not, go back and review any instructional material dealing with errors you made before proceeding to the next chapter.

Working diligently through each chapter in this manner will strengthen your weaknesses and prepare you to get your best score on the three Practice SAT Math Tests at the end of this book—and on your actual SAT I.

Operations with Whole Numbers and Decimals

1

DIAGNOSTIC TEST

Directions: Work out each problem. Circle the letter that appears before your answer.

Answers are at the end of the chapter.

1. Find the sum of 683, 72, and 5429.

    (A) 5184
    (B) 6184
    (C) 6183
    (D) 6193
    (E) 6284

2. Subtract 417 from 804.

    (A) 287
    (B) 388
    (C) 397
    (D) 387
    (E) 288

3. Find the product of 307 and 46.

    (A) 3070
    (B) 14,082
    (C) 13,922
    (D) 13,882
    (E) 14,122

4. Divide 38,304 by 48.

    (A) 787
    (B) 798
    (C) 824
    (D) 1098
    (E) 1253

5. Add 6.43 + 46.3 + .346.

    (A) 14.52
    (B) 53.779
    (C) 53.392
    (D) 53.076
    (E) 1452

6. Subtract 81.763 from 145.1.

    (A) 64.347
    (B) 64.463
    (C) 63.463
    (D) 63.337
    (E) 63.347

7. Multiply 3.47 by 2.3.

    (A) 79.81
    (B) 7.981
    (C) 6.981
    (D) 7.273
    (E) 7.984

8. Divide 2.163 by .03.

    (A) 7210
    (B) 721
    (C) 72.1
    (D) 7.21
    (E) 0.721

9. Find $3 - 16 \div 8 + 4 \times 2$.

    (A) 9
    (B) $2\frac{1}{3}$
    (C) 10
    (D) 18
    (E) $\frac{2}{3}$

10. Which of the following is closest to $\dfrac{8317 \times 91}{217 \times .8}$?

    (A) 4
    (B) 40
    (C) 400
    (D) 4000
    (E) 40,000

In preparing for the mathematics section of your college entrance examination, it is most important to overcome any fear of mathematics. The level of this examination extends no further than relatively simple geometry. Most problems can be solved using only arithmetic. By reading this chapter carefully, following the sample problems, and then working on the practice problems in each section, you can review important concepts and vocabulary, as well as familiarize yourself with various types of questions. Since arithmetic is basic to any further work in mathematics, this chapter is extremely important and should not be treated lightly. By doing these problems carefully and reading the worked-out solutions, you can build the confidence needed to do well.

1. ADDITION OF WHOLE NUMBERS

In the process of addition, the numbers to be added are called *addends*. The answer is called the *sum*. In writing an addition problem, put one number underneath the other, being careful to keep columns straight with the units' digits one below the other. If you find a sum by adding from top to bottom, you can check it by adding from bottom to top.

Example:

Find the sum of 403, 37, 8314, and 5.

Solution:

```
   403
    37
  8314
+    5
  8759
```

Exercise 1

1. Find the sum of 360, 4352, 87, and 205.
    - (A) 5013
    - (B) 5004
    - (C) 5003
    - (D) 6004
    - (E) 6013

2. Find the sum of 4321, 2143, 1234, and 3412.
    - (A) 12,110
    - (B) 11,011
    - (C) 11,101
    - (D) 11,111
    - (E) 11,110

3. Add 56 + 321 + 8 + 42.
    - (A) 427
    - (B) 437
    - (C) 517
    - (D) 417
    - (E) 527

4. Add 99 + 88 + 77 + 66 + 55.
    - (A) 384
    - (B) 485
    - (C) 385
    - (D) 375
    - (E) 376

5. Add 1212 + 2323 + 3434 + 4545 + 5656.
    - (A) 17,171
    - (B) 17,170
    - (C) 17,160
    - (D) 17,280
    - (E) 17,270

2. SUBTRACTION OF WHOLE NUMBERS

The number from which we subtract is called the *minuend*. The number which we take away is called the *subtrahend*. The answer in subtraction is called the *difference*.

If 5 is subtracted from 11, the minuend is 11, the subtrahend is 5, and the difference is 6.

Since we cannot subtract a larger number from a smaller one, we often must borrow in performing a subtraction. Remember that when we borrow, because of our base 10 number system, we reduce the digit to the left by 1, but increase the right-hand digit by 10.

Example:

$$\begin{array}{r} 54 \\ -\,38 \\ \hline \end{array}$$

Since we cannot subtract 8 from 4, we borrow 1 from 5 and change the 4 to 14. We are really borrowing 1 from the tens column and, therefore, add 10 to the ones column. Then we can subtract.

Solution:

$$\begin{array}{r} 4\,^{1}4 \\ -\,3\;8 \\ \hline 1\;6 \end{array}$$

Sometimes we must borrow across several columns.

Example:

$$\begin{array}{r} 503 \\ -267 \\ \hline \end{array}$$

We cannot subtract 7 from 3 and cannot borrow from 0. Therefore we reduce the 5 by one and make the 0 into a 10. Then we can borrow 1 from the 10, making it a 9. This makes the 3 into 13.

Solution:

$$\begin{array}{r} 4\,^{1}0\;\;3 \quad 4\;9\,^{1}3 \\ -2\;\;6\;\;7 \quad -2\;6\;7 \\ \hline 2\;3\;6 \end{array}$$

Exercise 2

1. Subtract 803 from 952.
   (A) 248
   (B) 148
   (C) 249
   (D) 149
   (E) 147

2. From the sum of 837 and 415, subtract 1035.
   (A) 217
   (B) 216
   (C) 326
   (D) 227
   (E) 226

3. From 1872 subtract the sum of 76 and 43.
   (A) 1754
   (B) 1838
   (C) 1753
   (D) 1839
   (E) 1905

4. Find the difference between 237 and 732.
   (A) 496
   (B) 495
   (C) 486
   (D) 405
   (E) 497

5. By how much does the sum of 612 and 315 exceed the sum of 451 and 283?
   (A) 294
   (B) 1661
   (C) 293
   (D) 197
   (E) 193

3. MULTIPLICATION OF WHOLE NUMBERS

The answer to a multiplication problem is called the *product*. The numbers being multiplied are called factors of the product.

When multiplying by a number containing two or more digits, place value is extremely important when writing partial products. When we multiply 537 by 72, for example, we multiply first by 2 and then by 7. However, when we multiply by 7, we are really multiplying by 70 and therefore leave a 0 at the extreme right before we proceed with the multiplication.

Example:

$$
\begin{array}{r}
537 \\
\times \ \ 72 \\
\hline
1074 \\
+ \ \ 37590 \\
\hline
38664
\end{array}
$$

If we multiply by a three-digit number, we leave one zero on the right when multiplying by the tens digit and two zeros on the right when multiplying by the hundreds digit.

Example:

$$
\begin{array}{r}
372 \\
\times \ \ 461 \\
\hline
372 \\
22320 \\
+148800 \\
\hline
171492
\end{array}
$$

Exercise 3

Find the following products.

1. 526 multiplied by 317
    - (A) 156,742
    - (B) 165,742
    - (C) 166,742
    - (D) 166,748
    - (E) 166,708

2. 8347 multiplied by 62
    - (A) 517,514
    - (B) 517,414
    - (C) 517,504
    - (D) 517,114
    - (E) 617,114

3. 705 multiplied by 89
    - (A) 11,985
    - (B) 52,745
    - (C) 62,705
    - (D) 62,745
    - (E) 15,121

4. 437 multiplied by 607
    - (A) 265,259
    - (B) 265,219
    - (C) 265,359
    - (D) 265,059
    - (E) 262,059

5. 798 multiplied by 450
    - (A) 358,600
    - (B) 359,100
    - (C) 71,820
    - (D) 358,100
    - (E) 360,820

4. DIVISION OF WHOLE NUMBERS

The number being divided is called the *dividend*. The number we are dividing by is called the *divisor*. The answer to the division is called the *quotient*. When we divide 18 by 6, 18 is the dividend, 6 is the divisor, and 3 is the quotient. If the quotient is not an integer, we have a *remainder*. The remainder when 20 is divided by 6 is 2, because 6 will divide 18 evenly, leaving a remainder of 2. The quotient in this case is $6\frac{2}{6}$. Remember that in writing the fractional part of a quotient involving a remainder, the remainder becomes the numerator and the divisor the denominator.

When dividing by a single-digit divisor, no long division procedures are needed. Simply carry the remainder of each step over to the next digit and continue.

Example:

$$6)\overline{5\ 8^4\ 3^1\ 4^2\ 4}$$
$$9\ 7\ 2\ 4$$

Exercise 4

1. Divide 391 by 23.

    (A) 170
    (B) 16
    (C) 17
    (D) 18
    (E) 180

2. Divide 49,523,436 by 9.

    (A) 5,502,605
    (B) 5,502,514
    (C) 5,502,604
    (D) 5,502,614
    (E) 5,502,603

3. Find the remainder when 4832 is divided by 15.

    (A) 1
    (B) 2
    (C) 3
    (D) 4
    (E) 5

4. Divide 42,098 by 7.

    (A) 6014
    (B) 6015
    (C) 6019
    (D) 6011
    (E) 6010

5. Which of the following is the quotient of 333,180 and 617?

    (A) 541
    (B) 542
    (C) 549
    (D) 540
    (E) 545

5. ADDITION OR SUBTRACTION OF DECIMALS

The most important thing to watch for in adding or subtracting decimals is to keep all decimal points underneath one another. The proper placement of the decimal point in the answer will be in line with all the decimal points above.

Example:

Find the sum of 8.4, .37, and 2.641

Solution:

$$
\begin{array}{r}
8.4 \\
.37 \\
\underline{2.641} \\
11.411
\end{array}
$$

Example:

From 48.3 subtract 27.56

Solution:

$$
\begin{array}{r}
4\,8.\,\overset{7}{\cancel{8}}\,\overset{12}{\cancel{3}}^{1}0 \\
\underline{2\,7.5\,6} \\
2\,0.\,7\,4
\end{array}
$$

In subtraction, the upper decimal must have as many decimal places as the lower, so we must fill in zeros where needed.

Exercise 5

1. From the sum of .65, 4.2, 17.63, and 8, subtract 12.7.
   - (A) 9.78
   - (B) 17.68
   - (C) 17.78
   - (D) 17.79
   - (E) 18.78

2. Find the sum of .837, .12, 52.3, and .354.
   - (A) 53.503
   - (B) 53.611
   - (C) 53.601
   - (D) 54.601
   - (E) 54.611

3. From 561.8 subtract 34.75.
   - (A) 537.05
   - (B) 537.15
   - (C) 527.15
   - (D) 527.04
   - (E) 527.05

4. From 53.72 subtract the sum of 4.81 and 17.5.
   - (A) 31.86
   - (B) 31.41
   - (C) 41.03
   - (D) 66.41
   - (E) 41.86

5. Find the difference between 100 and 52.18.
   - (A) 37.82
   - (B) 47.18
   - (C) 47.92
   - (D) 47.82
   - (E) 37.92

6. MULTIPLICATION OF DECIMALS

In multiplying decimals, we proceed as we do with integers, using the decimal points only as an indication of where to place a decimal point in the product. The number of decimal places in the product is equal to the sum of the number of decimal places in the numbers being multiplied.

Example:

Multiply .375 by .42

Solution:

$$
\begin{array}{r}
.375 \\
\times\ .42 \\
\hline
750 \\
+\ 15000 \\
\hline
.15750
\end{array}
$$

Since the first number being multiplied contains three decimal places and the second number contains two decimal places, the product will contain five decimal places.

To multiply a decimal by 10, 100, 1000, etc., we need only to move the decimal point to the right the proper number of places. In multiplying by 10, move one place to the right (10 has one zero), by 100 move two places to the right (100 has two zeros), by 1000 move three places to the right (1000 has three zeros), and so forth.

Example:

The product of .837 and 100 is 83.7

Exercise 6

Find the following products.

1. 437 x .24 =
    (A)   1.0488
    (B)   10.488
    (C)   104.88
    (D)   1048.8
    (E)   10,488

2. 5.06 x .7 =
    (A)   .3542
    (B)   .392
    (C)   3.92
    (D)   3.542
    (E)   35.42

3. 83 x 1.5 =
    (A)   12.45
    (B)   49.8
    (C)   498
    (D)   124.5
    (E)   1.245

4. .7314 x 100 =
    (A)   .007314
    (B)   .07314
    (C)   7.314
    (D)   73.14
    (E)   731.4

5. .0008 x 4.3 =
    (A)   .000344
    (B)   .00344
    (C)   .0344
    (D)   0.344
    (E)   3.44

7. DIVISION OF DECIMALS

When dividing by a decimal, always change the decimal to a whole number by moving the decimal point to the end of the divisor. Count the number of places you have moved the decimal point and move the dividend's decimal point the same number of places. The decimal point in the quotient will be directly above the one in the dividend.

Example:

Divide 2.592 by .06

Solution:

$$.06\overline{)2.592}^{\,43.2}$$

To divide a decimal by 10, 100, 1000, etc., we move the decimal point the proper number of places to the *left*. The number of places to be moved is always equal to the number of zeros in the divisor.

Example:

Divide 43.7 by 1000

Solution:

The decimal point must be moved three places (there are three zeros in 1000) to the left. Therefore our quotient is .0437

Sometimes division can be done in fraction form. Always remember to move the decimal point to the end of the divisor (denominator) and then the same number of places in the dividend (numerator).

Example:

Divide: $\dfrac{.0175}{.05} = \dfrac{1.75}{5} = .35$

Exercise 7

1. Divide 4.3 by 100.
   - (A) .0043
   - (B) 0.043
   - (C) 0.43
   - (D) 43
   - (E) 430

2. Find the quotient when 4.371 is divided by .3.
   - (A) 0.1457
   - (B) 1.457
   - (C) 14.57
   - (D) 145.7
   - (E) 1457

3. Divide .64 by .4.
   - (A) .0016
   - (B) 0.016
   - (C) 0.16
   - (D) 1.6
   - (E) 16

4. Find $.12 \div \dfrac{2}{.5}$.
   - (A) 4.8
   - (B) 48
   - (C) .03
   - (D) 0.3
   - (E) 3

5. Find $\dfrac{10.2}{.03} \div \dfrac{1.7}{.1}$.
   - (A) .02
   - (B) 0.2
   - (C) 2
   - (D) 20
   - (E) 200

8. THE LAWS OF ARITHMETIC

Addition and multiplication are *commutative* operations, as the order in which we add or multiply does not change an answer.

Example:

$$4 + 7 = 7 + 4$$
$$5 \cdot 3 = 3 \cdot 5$$

Subtraction and division are not commutative, as changing the order does change the answer.

Example:

$$5 - 3 \neq 3 - 5$$
$$20 \div 5 \neq 5 \div 20$$

Addition and multiplication are *associative*, as we may group in any manner and arrive at the same answer.

Example:

$$(3+4)+5 = 3+(4+5)$$
$$(3 \cdot 4) \cdot 5 = 3 \cdot (4 \cdot 5)$$

Subtraction and division are not associative, as regrouping changes an answer.

Example:

$$(5-4)-3 \neq 5-(4-3)$$
$$(100 \div 20) \div 5 \neq 100 \div (20 \div 5)$$

Multiplication is *distributive* over addition. If a sum is to be multiplied by a number, we may multiply each addend by the given number and add the results. This will give the same answer as if we had added first and then multiplied.

Example:

$3(5 + 2 + 4)$ is either $15 + 6 + 12$ or $3(11)$.

The *identity for addition* is 0 since any number plus 0, or 0 plus any number, is equal to the given number.

The *identity for multiplication* is 1 since any number times 1, or 1 times any number, is equal to the given number.

There are no identity elements for subtraction or division. Although $5 - 0 = 5$, $0 - 5 \neq 5$. Although $8 \div 1 = 8$, $1 \div 8 \neq 8$.

When several operations are involved in a single problem, parentheses are usually included to make the order of operations clear. If there are no parentheses, multiplication and division are always performed prior to addition and subtraction.

Example:

Find $5 \cdot 4 + 6 \div 2 - 16 \div 4$

Solution:

The + and - signs indicate where groupings should begin and end. If we were to insert parentheses to clarify operations, we would have $(5 \cdot 4) + (6 \div 2) - (16 \div 4)$, giving $20 + 3 - 4 = 19$.

10   **Chapter 1**

Exercise 8

1. Find $8 + 4 \div 2 + 6 \cdot 3 - 1$.

   (A) 35
   (B) 47
   (C) 43
   (D) 27
   (E) 88

2. $16 \div 4 + 2 \cdot 3 + 2 - 8 \div 2$.

   (A) 6
   (B) 8
   (C) 2
   (D) 4
   (E) 10

3. Match each illustration in the left-hand column with the law it illustrates from the right-hand column.

   a. $475 \cdot 1 = 475$ u. Identity for Addition
   b. $75 + 12 = 12 + 75$ v. Associative Law of Addition
   c. $32(12 + 8) = 32(12) + 32(8)$ w. Associative Law of Multiplication
   d. $378 + 0 = 378$ x. Identity for Multiplication
   e. $(7 \cdot 5) \cdot 2 = 7 \cdot (5 \cdot 2)$ y. Distributive Law of Multiplication
                                                          over Addition
                                                      z. Commutative Law of Addition

9. ESTIMATING ANSWERS

On a competitive examination, where time is an important factor, it is essential that you be able to estimate an answer. Simply round off all answers to the nearest multiples of 10 or 100 and estimate with the results. On multiple-choice tests, this should enable you to pick the correct answer without any time-consuming computation.

Example:

The product of 498 and 103 is

   (A) 5124
   (B) 501,294
   (C) 51,294
   (D) 31,674
   (E) 817,324

Solution:

498 is about 500. 103 is about 100. Therefore the product is about (500) (100) or 50,000 (just move the decimal point two places to the right when multiplying by 100). Therefore the correct answer is (C).

Example:

Which of the following is closest to the value of $4831 \cdot \dfrac{710}{2314}$?

   (A) 83
   (B) 425
   (C) 1600
   (D) 3140
   (E) 6372

Solution:

Estimating, we have $\left(\dfrac{(5000)(700)}{2000} \right)$. Dividing numerator and denominator by 1000, we have $\dfrac{5(700)}{2}$ or $\dfrac{3500}{2}$, which is about 1750. Therefore we choose answer (C).

Exercise 9

Choose the answer closest to the exact value of each of the following problems. Use estimation in your solutions. No written computation should be needed. Circle the letter before your answer.

1. $\dfrac{483+1875}{119}$

    (A) 2
    (B) 10
    (C) 20
    (D) 50
    (E) 100

2. $\dfrac{6017 \cdot 312}{364+618}$

    (A) 18
    (B) 180
    (C) 1800
    (D) 18,000
    (E) 180,000

3. $\dfrac{783+491}{1532-879}$

    (A) .02
    (B) .2
    (C) 2
    (D) 20
    (E) 200

RETEST

1. Find the sum of 86, 4861, and 205.

    (A) 5142
    (B) 5132
    (C) 5152
    (D) 5052
    (E) 4152

2. From 803 subtract 459.

    (A) 454
    (B) 444
    (C) 354
    (D) 344
    (E) 346

3. Find the product of 65 and 908.

    (A) 59,020
    (B) 9988
    (C) 58,920
    (D) 58,020
    (E) 59,920

4. Divide 66,456 by 72.

    (A) 903
    (B) 923
    (C) 911
    (D) 921
    (E) 925

5. Find the sum of .361 + 8.7 + 43.17.

    (A) 52.078
    (B) 51.538
    (C) 51.385
    (D) 52.161
    (E) 52.231

6. Subtract 23.17 from 50.9.

    (A) 26.92
    (B) 27.79
    (C) 27.73
    (D) 37.73
    (E) 37.79

7. Multiply 8.35 by .43.

    (A) 3.5805
    (B) 3.5905
    (C) 3.5915
    (D) 35.905
    (E) .35905

8. Divide 2.937 by .11.

    (A) .267
    (B) 2.67
    (C) 26.7
    (D) 267
    (E) 2670

9. Find $8 + 10 \div 2 + 4 \cdot 2 - 21 \div 7$.

    (A) 17
    (B) 23
    (C) 18
    (D) 14
    (E) $\dfrac{5}{7}$

10. Which of the following is closest to $\dfrac{2875+932}{\dfrac{5817}{29}}$?

    (A) .2
    (B) 2
    (C) 20
    (D) 200
    (E) 2000

SOLUTIONS TO PRACTICE EXERCISES

Diagnostic Test

1. (B)
$$\begin{array}{r} 683 \\ 72 \\ +\ 5429 \\ \hline 6184 \end{array}$$

2. (D)
$$\begin{array}{r} {}^{7\,9}\!80^{1}4 \\ -\ \ \ 417 \\ \hline 387 \end{array}$$

3. (E)
$$\begin{array}{r} 307 \\ \times\ \ \ 46 \\ \hline 1842 \\ 12280 \\ \hline 14{,}122 \end{array}$$

4. (B)
$$\begin{array}{r} 798 \\ 48\overline{)38304} \\ \underline{336} \\ 470 \\ \underline{432} \\ 384 \\ 384 \end{array}$$

5. (D)
$$\begin{array}{r} 6.43 \\ 46.3 \\ +\ \ .346 \\ \hline 53.076 \end{array}$$

6. (D)
$$\begin{array}{r} {}^{4}\ {}^{10}\ 9\\ 14\,\overset{}{5}.\,\overset{}{1}\ 0^{1}0 \\ -\ \ 81\,.\,7\,6\,3 \\ \hline 63.\,3\,3\,7 \end{array}$$

7. (B)
$$\begin{array}{r} 3.47 \\ \times\ \ 2.3 \\ \hline 1041 \\ 6940 \\ \hline 7.981 \end{array}$$

8. (C)
$$\begin{array}{r} 72.1 \\ .03\overline{)2.163} \end{array}$$

9. (A) $3 - (16 \div 8) + (4 \times 2) = 3 - 2 + 8 = 9$

10. (D) Estimate $\dfrac{8000 \cdot 100}{200 \cdot 1} = 4000$

Exercise 1

1. (B)
$$\begin{array}{r} 360 \\ 4352 \\ 87 \\ +\ 205 \\ \hline 5004 \end{array}$$

2. (E)
$$\begin{array}{r} 4321 \\ 2143 \\ 1234 \\ +\ 3412 \\ \hline 11{,}110 \end{array}$$

3. (A)
$$\begin{array}{r} 56 \\ 321 \\ 8 \\ +\ 42 \\ \hline 427 \end{array}$$

4. (C)
$$\begin{array}{r} 99 \\ 88 \\ 77 \\ 66 \\ +\ 55 \\ \hline 385 \end{array}$$

5. (B)
$$\begin{array}{r} 1212 \\ 2323 \\ 3434 \\ 4545 \\ +\ 5656 \\ \hline 17{,}170 \end{array}$$

Exercise 2

1. (D)
$$9\overset{4}{\cancel{5}}{}^{1}2$$
$$-\;8\;0\;3$$
$$\overline{1\;4\;9}$$

2. (A)
$$837$$
$$+\;415$$
$$\overline{125\overset{4}{\cancel{1}}{}^{1}2}$$
$$-\;10\;\;3\;\;5$$
$$\overline{217}$$

3. (C)
$$76$$
$$+\;\;43$$
$$\overline{119}$$

$$18\overset{6}{\cancel{7}}{}^{1}2$$
$$-\;\;119$$
$$\overline{1753}$$

4. (B)
$$7\overset{6}{\cancel{3}}\overset{12}{\cancel{3}}{}^{1}2$$
$$-\;2\;3\;7$$
$$\overline{4\;9\;5}$$

5. (E)
$$612$$
$$+\;315$$
$$\overline{927}$$
$$451$$
$$+\;283$$
$$\overline{734}$$
$$\overset{8}{\cancel{9}}{}^{1}27$$
$$-\;7\;3\;4$$
$$\overline{1\;9\;3}$$

Exercise 3

1. (C)
$$526$$
$$\times\;\;317$$
$$\overline{3682}$$
$$5260$$
$$157800$$
$$\overline{166,742}$$

2. (A)
$$8347$$
$$\times\;\;\;\;62$$
$$\overline{16694}$$
$$500820$$
$$\overline{517,514}$$

3. (D)
$$705$$
$$\times\;\;\;89$$
$$\overline{6345}$$
$$56400$$
$$\overline{62,745}$$

4. (A)
$$437$$
$$\times\;\;607$$
$$\overline{3059}$$
$$262200$$
$$\overline{265,259}$$

5. (B)
$$798$$
$$\times\;\;450$$
$$\overline{39900}$$
$$319200$$
$$\overline{359,100}$$

Exercise 4

1. (C)

$$23\overline{)391} \quad \overset{17}{}$$

$$\begin{array}{r} 23 \\ \hline 161 \\ 161 \end{array}$$

2. (C)

$$9\overline{)49,523,436} \quad \overset{5,502,604}{}$$

3. (B)

$$15\overline{)4832} \quad \overset{322 \text{ Remainder } 2}{}$$

$$\begin{array}{r} 45 \\ \hline 33 \\ 30 \\ \hline 32 \\ 30 \\ \hline 2 \end{array}$$

4. (A)

$$7\overline{)42098} \quad \overset{6014}{}$$

5. (D) Since the quotient, when multiplied by 617, must give 333,180 as an answer, the quotient must end in a number which, when multiplied by 617, will end in 0. This can only be (D), since 617 times (A) would end in 7, (B) would end in 4, (C) in 3, and (E) in 5.

Exercise 5

1. (C)

$$\begin{array}{r} .65 \\ 4.2 \\ 17.63 \\ + \ 8. \\ \hline 30.48 \end{array}$$

$$\begin{array}{r} 30.48 \\ - \ 12.70 \\ \hline 17.78 \end{array}$$

2. (B)

$$\begin{array}{r} .837 \\ .12 \\ 52.3 \\ + \ .354 \\ \hline 53.611 \end{array}$$

3. (E)

$$\begin{array}{r} 5\ 6\ 1\ 7\ 0 \\ - \ 3\ 4.\ 7\ 5 \\ \hline 5\ 2\ 7.\ 0\ 5 \end{array}$$

4. (B)

$$\begin{array}{rr} 4.81 & 53.72 \\ +17.5 & -22.31 \\ \hline 22.31 & 31.41 \end{array}$$

5. (D)

$$\begin{array}{r} 1\ 0\ 0.\ 0\ 0 \\ - \ 5\ 2.\ 1\ 8 \\ \hline 4\ 7.\ 8\ 2 \end{array}$$

Exercise 6

1. (C)
$$\begin{array}{r} 437 \\ \times\ .24 \\ \hline 1748 \\ 8740 \\ \hline 104.88 \end{array}$$

2. (D)
$$\begin{array}{r} 5.06 \\ \times\ .7 \\ \hline 3.542 \end{array}$$

3. (D)
$$\begin{array}{r} 83 \\ \times\ 1.5 \\ \hline 415 \\ 830 \\ \hline 124.5 \end{array}$$

4. (D)
$$\begin{array}{r} .7314 \\ \times\ 100 \\ \hline 73.14 \end{array}$$
Just move the decimal point two places to the right.

5. (B)
$$\begin{array}{r} .0008 \\ \times\ 4.3 \\ \hline 24 \\ 320 \\ \hline .00344 \end{array}$$

Exercise 7

1. (B) Just move decimal point two places to left, giving .043 as the answer.

2. (C) $.3\overline{)4.371}$ giving 14.57

3. (D) $.4\overline{).64}$ giving 1.6

4. (C) $.12 \div \dfrac{2.0}{.5} = .12 \div 4 = .03$

5. (D) $\dfrac{10.20}{.03} \div \dfrac{1.7}{.1} = 340 \div 17 = 20$

Exercise 8

1. (D) $8 + (4 \div 2) + (6 \cdot 3) - 1 = 8 + 2 + 18 - 1 = 27$

2. (B) $(16 \div 4) + (2 \cdot 3) + 2 - (8 \div 2) = 4 + 6 + 2 - 4 = 8$

3. $(a, x)(b, z)(c, y)(d, u)(e, w)$

Exercise 9

1. (C) **Estimate** $\dfrac{500 + 2000}{100} = \dfrac{2500}{100} = 25,$ **closest to 20**

2. (C) **Estimate** $\dfrac{6000 \cdot 300}{400 + 600} = \dfrac{1,800,000}{1000} = 1800$

3. (C) **Estimate** $\dfrac{800 + 500}{1500 - 900} = \dfrac{1300}{600} =$ **about 2**

Retest

1. (C)
$$
\begin{array}{r}
86 \\
4861 \\
+\ 205 \\
\hline
5152
\end{array}
$$

2. (D)
$$
\begin{array}{r}
{}^{7}8\ {}^{9}0^{1}\ 3 \\
-\ 4\ 5\ 9 \\
\hline
3\ 4\ 4
\end{array}
$$

3. (A)
$$
\begin{array}{r}
908 \\
\times\ \ 65 \\
\hline
4540 \\
54480 \\
\hline
59{,}020
\end{array}
$$

4. (B)
$$
\begin{array}{r}
923 \\
72\overline{)66456} \\
648 \\
\hline
165 \\
144 \\
\hline
216 \\
216
\end{array}
$$

5. (E)
$$
\begin{array}{r}
.361 \\
8.7 \\
+\ 43.17 \\
\hline
52.231
\end{array}
$$

6. (C)
$$
\begin{array}{r}
{}^{4}\cancel{5}\ {}^{1}0.\ {}^{8}\cancel{9}^{1}\ 0 \\
-\ 2\ 3.1\ 7 \\
\hline
2\ 7.7\ 3
\end{array}
$$

7. (B)
$$
\begin{array}{r}
8.35 \\
\times\ \ .43 \\
\hline
2505 \\
33400 \\
\hline
3.5905
\end{array}
$$

8. (C)
$$
\begin{array}{r}
26.7 \\
.11\overline{)2.937} \\
22 \\
\hline
73 \\
66 \\
\hline
77 \\
77
\end{array}
$$

9. (C) $8 + (10 \div 2) + (4 \cdot 2) - (21 \div 7) = 8 + 5 + 8 - 3 = 18$

10. (C) **Estimate** $\dfrac{\frac{3000 + 1000}{6000}}{30} = \dfrac{4000}{200} = 20$

Operations with Fractions

2

DIAGNOSTIC TEST

Directions: Work out each problem. Circle the letter that appears before your answer.

Answers are at the end of the chapter.

1. The sum of $\frac{3}{5}$, $\frac{2}{3}$, and $\frac{1}{4}$ is

   (A) $\frac{1}{2}$

   (B) $\frac{27}{20}$

   (C) $\frac{3}{2}$

   (D) $\frac{91}{60}$

   (E) $1\frac{5}{12}$

2. Subtract $\frac{3}{4}$ from $\frac{9}{10}$.

   (A) $\frac{3}{20}$

   (B) 1

   (C) $\frac{3}{5}$

   (D) $\frac{3}{40}$

   (E) $\frac{7}{40}$

3. The number 582,354 is divisible by

   (A) 4
   (B) 5
   (C) 8
   (D) 9
   (E) 10

4. $\frac{5}{6} \div \left(\frac{4}{3} \cdot \frac{5}{4} \right)$ is equal to

   (A) 2

   (B) $\frac{50}{36}$

   (C) $\frac{1}{2}$

   (D) $\frac{36}{50}$

   (E) $\frac{7}{12}$

5. Subtract $32\frac{3}{5}$ from 57.

   (A) $24\frac{2}{5}$

   (B) $25\frac{3}{5}$

   (C) $25\frac{2}{5}$

   (D) $24\frac{3}{5}$

   (E) $24\frac{1}{5}$

6. Divide $4\dfrac{1}{2}$ by $1\dfrac{1}{8}$.

   (A) $\dfrac{1}{4}$

   (B) 4

   (C) $\dfrac{8}{9}$

   (D) $\dfrac{9}{8}$

   (E) $3\dfrac{1}{2}$

7. Which of the following fractions is the largest?

   (A) $\dfrac{1}{2}$

   (B) $\dfrac{11}{16}$

   (C) $\dfrac{5}{8}$

   (D) $\dfrac{21}{32}$

   (E) $\dfrac{3}{4}$

8. Which of the following fractions is closest to $\dfrac{2}{3}$?

   (A) $\dfrac{11}{15}$

   (B) $\dfrac{7}{10}$

   (C) $\dfrac{4}{5}$

   (D) $\dfrac{1}{2}$

   (E) $\dfrac{5}{6}$

9. Simplify $\dfrac{4-\dfrac{9}{10}}{\dfrac{2}{3}+\dfrac{1}{2}}$.

   (A) $\dfrac{93}{5}$

   (B) $\dfrac{93}{35}$

   (C) $\dfrac{147}{35}$

   (D) $\dfrac{147}{5}$

   (E) $\dfrac{97}{35}$

10. Find the value of $\dfrac{\dfrac{1}{a}+\dfrac{1}{b}}{\dfrac{1}{a}-\dfrac{1}{b}}$ when $a = 3, b = 4$.

    (A) 7

    (B) 2

    (C) 1

    (D) $\dfrac{1}{7}$

    (E) $\dfrac{2}{7}$

1. ADDITION AND SUBTRACTION

To add or subtract fractions, they must have the same *denominator*. To add several fractions, this common denominator will be the least number into which each given denominator will divide evenly.

Example:

Add $\dfrac{1}{2} + \dfrac{1}{3} + \dfrac{1}{4} + \dfrac{1}{5}$

Solution:

The common denominator must contain two factors of 2 to accommodate the 4, and also a factor of 3 and one of 5. That makes the least common denominator 60. Rename each fraction to have 60 as the denominator by dividing the given denominator into 60 and multiplying the quotient by the given numerator.

$$\frac{30}{60} + \frac{20}{60} + \frac{15}{60} + \frac{12}{60} = \frac{77}{60} = 1\frac{17}{60}$$

When only two fractions are being added, a shortcut method can be used: $\dfrac{a}{b} + \dfrac{c}{d} = \dfrac{ad + bc}{bd}$. That is, in order to add two fractions, add the two cross products and place this sum over the product of the given denominators.

Example:

$\dfrac{4}{5} + \dfrac{7}{12}$

Solution:

$$\frac{4(12) + 5(7)}{5(12)} = \frac{48 + 35}{60} = \frac{83}{60} = 1\frac{23}{60}$$

A similar shortcut applies to the subtraction of two fractions:

$$\frac{a}{b} - \frac{c}{d} = \frac{ad - bc}{bd}$$

Example:

$$\frac{4}{5} - \frac{7}{12} = \frac{4(12) - 5(7)}{5(12)} = \frac{48 - 35}{60} = \frac{13}{60}$$

Exercise 1

Work out each problem. Circle the letter that appears before your answer.

1. The sum of $\dfrac{1}{2} + \dfrac{2}{3} + \dfrac{3}{4}$ is

    (A) $\dfrac{6}{9}$

    (B) $\dfrac{23}{12}$

    (C) $\dfrac{23}{36}$

    (D) $\dfrac{6}{24}$

    (E) $2\dfrac{1}{3}$

2. The sum of $\dfrac{5}{17}$ and $\dfrac{3}{15}$ is

    (A) $\dfrac{126}{255}$

    (B) $\dfrac{40}{255}$

    (C) $\dfrac{8}{32}$

    (D) $\dfrac{40}{32}$

    (E) $\dfrac{126}{265}$

3. From the sum of $\dfrac{3}{4}$ and $\dfrac{5}{6}$ subtract the sum of $\dfrac{1}{4}$ and $\dfrac{2}{3}$.

    (A) 2

    (B) $\dfrac{1}{2}$

    (C) $\dfrac{36}{70}$

    (D) $\dfrac{2}{3}$

    (E) $\dfrac{5}{24}$

4. Subtract $\dfrac{3}{5}$ from $\dfrac{9}{11}$.

    (A) $-\dfrac{12}{55}$

    (B) $\dfrac{12}{55}$

    (C) 1

    (D) $\dfrac{3}{8}$

    (E) $\dfrac{3}{4}$

5. Subtract $\dfrac{5}{8}$ from the sum of $\dfrac{1}{4}$ and $\dfrac{2}{3}$.

    (A) 2

    (B) $\dfrac{3}{2}$

    (C) $\dfrac{11}{24}$

    (D) $\dfrac{8}{15}$

    (E) $\dfrac{7}{24}$

2. MULTIPLICATION AND DIVISION

In multiplying fractions, always try to divide out any common factor of any denominator with any numerator to keep your numbers as small as possible. Remember that if all numbers divide out in the numerator, you are left with a numerator of 1. The same goes for the denominator. If all numbers in both numerator and denominator divide out, you are left with $\frac{1}{1}$ or 1.

Example:

Multiply $\frac{3}{5} \cdot \frac{15}{33} \cdot \frac{11}{45}$

Solution:

$$\frac{\cancel{3}}{5} \cdot \frac{\cancel{15}^3}{\cancel{33}_3} \cdot \frac{\cancel{11}}{\cancel{45}_3} = \frac{1}{15}$$

In dividing fractions, we multiply by the multiplicative inverse.

Example:

Divide $\frac{5}{18}$ by $\frac{5}{9}$

Solution:

$$\frac{\cancel{5}}{_2\cancel{18}} \cdot \frac{\cancel{9}}{\cancel{5}} = \frac{1}{2}$$

Exercise 2

Work out each problem. Circle the letter that appears before your answer.

1. Find the product of $\frac{3}{2}$, 6, $\frac{4}{9}$, and $\frac{1}{12}$.

    (A) 3

    (B) $\frac{1}{3}$

    (C) $\frac{14}{23}$

    (D) $\frac{1}{36}$

    (E) $\frac{5}{12}$

2. Find $\frac{7}{8} \cdot \frac{2}{3} \div \frac{1}{8}$.

    (A) $\frac{3}{14}$

    (B) $\frac{7}{96}$

    (C) $\frac{21}{128}$

    (D) $\frac{14}{3}$

    (E) $\frac{8}{3}$

3. $\dfrac{3}{5} \div \left(\dfrac{1}{2} \cdot \dfrac{3}{10} \right)$ is equal to

    (A) 4

    (B) $\dfrac{1}{4}$

    (C) $\dfrac{12}{5}$

    (D) $\dfrac{5}{12}$

    (E) $\dfrac{12}{15}$

4. Find $\dfrac{2}{3}$ of $\dfrac{7}{12}$.

    (A) $\dfrac{7}{8}$

    (B) $\dfrac{7}{9}$

    (C) $\dfrac{8}{7}$

    (D) $\dfrac{8}{9}$

    (E) $\dfrac{7}{18}$

5. Divide 5 by $\dfrac{5}{12}$.

    (A) $\dfrac{25}{12}$

    (B) $\dfrac{1}{12}$

    (C) $\dfrac{5}{12}$

    (D) 12

    (E) $\dfrac{12}{5}$

3. SIMPLIFYING FRACTIONS

All fractional answers should be left in simplest form. There should be no factor that can still be divided into numerator and denominator. In simplifying fractions involving very large numbers, it is helpful to tell at a glance whether or not a given number will divide evenly into both numerator and denominator. Certain tests for divisibility assist with this.

If a number is divisible by	Then
2	its last digit is 0, 2, 4, 6, or 8
3	the sum of the digits is divisible by 3
4	the number formed by the last 2 digits is divisible by 4
5	the last digit is 5 or 0
6	the number meets the tests for divisibility by 2 and 3
8	the number formed by the last 3 digits is divisible by 8
9	the sum of the digits is divisible by 9

Example:

By what single digit number should we simplify $\dfrac{135,492}{428,376}$?

Solution:

Since both numbers are even, they are at least divisible by 2. The sum of the digits in the numerator is 24. The sum of the digits in the denominator is 30. Since these sums are both divisible by 3, each number is divisible by 3. Since these numbers meet the divisibility tests for 2 and 3, they are each divisible by 6.

Example:

Simplify to simplest form: $\dfrac{43,672}{52,832}$

Solution:

Since both numbers are even, they are at least divisible by 2. However, to save time, we would like to divide by a larger number. The sum of the digits in the numerator is 22, so it is not divisible by 3. The number formed by the last two digits of each number is divisible by 4, making the entire number divisible by 4. The numbers formed by the last three digits of each number is divisible by 8.

Therefore, each number is divisible by 8. Dividing by 8, we have $\dfrac{5459}{6604}$. Since these numbers are no longer even and divisibility by 3 was ruled out earlier, there is no longer a single digit factor common to numerator and denominator. It is unlikely, at the level of this examination, that you will be called on to divide by a two-digit number.

Exercise 3

Work out each problem. Circle the letter that appears before your answer.

1. Which of the following numbers is divisible by 5 and 9?

   (A) 42,235
   (B) 34,325
   (C) 46,505
   (D) 37,845
   (E) 53,290

2. Given the number 83,21*p*, in order for this number to be divisible by 3, 6, and 9, *p* must be

   (A) 4
   (B) 5
   (C) 6
   (D) 0
   (E) 9

3. If *n!* means $n(n-1)(n-2) \ldots (4)(3)(2)(1)$, so that $4! = (4)(3)(2)(1) = 24$, then 19! is divisible by

   I.   17
   II. 54
   III. 100
   IV. 39

   (A) I and II only
   (B) I only
   (C) I and IV only
   (D) I, II, III, and IV
   (E) none of the above

4. The fraction $\dfrac{432}{801}$ can be simplified by dividing numerator and denominator by

    (A) 2
    (B) 4
    (C) 6
    (D) 8
    (E) 9

5. The number 6,862,140 is divisible by

    I.   3
    II.   4
    III. 5

    (A) I only
    (B) I and III only
    (C) II and III only
    (D) I, II, and III
    (E) III only

4. OPERATIONS WITH MIXED NUMBERS

To add or subtract mixed numbers, it is again important to find common denominators. If it is necessary to borrow in subtraction, you must borrow in terms of the common denominator.

Example:

$$23\frac{1}{3} - 6\frac{2}{5}$$

Solution:

$$23\frac{1}{3} = 23\frac{5}{15}$$

$$-6\frac{2}{5} = -6\frac{6}{15}$$

Since we cannot subtract $\dfrac{6}{15}$ from $\dfrac{5}{15}$, we borrow $\dfrac{15}{15}$ from 23 and rewrite our problem as

$$22\frac{20}{15}$$
$$-6\frac{6}{15}$$

In this form, subtraction is possible, giving us an answer of $16\dfrac{14}{15}$.

Example:

Add $17\dfrac{3}{4}$ to $43\dfrac{3}{5}$

Solution:

Again we first rename the fractions to have a common denominator. This time it will be 20.

$$17\frac{3}{4} = 17\frac{15}{20}$$

$$+43\frac{3}{5} = +43\frac{12}{20}$$

When adding, we get a sum of $60\dfrac{27}{20}$, which we change to $61\dfrac{7}{20}$.

To multiply or divide mixed numbers, always rename them as improper fractions first.

Example:

Multiply $3\frac{3}{5} \cdot 1\frac{1}{9} \cdot 2\frac{3}{4}$

Solution:

$$\frac{^2\cancel{18}}{\cancel{5}} \cdot \frac{\cancel{10}^2}{9} \cdot \frac{11}{\cancel{4}_2} = 11$$

Example:

Divide $3\frac{3}{4}$ by $5\frac{5}{8}$

Solution:

$$\frac{15}{4} \div \frac{45}{8} = \frac{\cancel{15}}{4} \cdot \frac{\cancel{8}^2}{\cancel{45}_3} = \frac{2}{3}$$

Exercise 4

Work out each problem. Circle the letter that appears before your answer.

1. Find the sum of $1\frac{1}{16}, 2\frac{2}{3}$, and $3\frac{3}{4}$.

    (A) $7\frac{5}{12}$

    (B) $6\frac{6}{13}$

    (C) $7\frac{7}{12}$

    (D) $6\frac{1}{3}$

    (E) $7\frac{1}{12}$

2. Subtract $45\frac{5}{12}$ from 61.

    (A) $15\frac{7}{12}$

    (B) $15\frac{5}{12}$

    (C) $16\frac{7}{12}$

    (D) $16\frac{5}{12}$

    (E) $17\frac{5}{12}$

3. Find the product of $32\frac{1}{2}$ and $5\frac{1}{5}$.

    (A) 26

    (B) 13

    (C) 169

    (D) $160\frac{1}{10}$

    (E) $160\frac{2}{7}$

4. Divide $17\frac{1}{2}$ by 70.

    (A) $\frac{1}{4}$

    (B) 4

    (C) $\frac{1}{2}$

    (D) $4\frac{1}{2}$

    (E) $\frac{4}{9}$

5. Find $1\frac{3}{4} \cdot 12 \div 8\frac{2}{5}$.

    (A) $\frac{2}{5}$

    (B) $\frac{5}{288}$

    (C) $2\frac{1}{5}$

    (D) $\frac{1}{2}$

    (E) $2\frac{1}{2}$

5. COMPARING FRACTIONS

There are two methods by which fractions may be compared to see which is larger (or smaller).

Method I—Rename the fractions to have the same denominator. When this is done, the fraction with the larger numerator is the larger fraction.

Example:

Which is larger, $\frac{5}{6}$ or $\frac{8}{11}$?

Solution:

The least common denominator is 66.

$$\frac{5}{6} = \frac{55}{66} \qquad \frac{8}{11} = \frac{48}{66}$$

Therefore, $\frac{5}{6}$ is the larger fraction.

Method II—To compare $\frac{a}{b}$ with $\frac{c}{d}$, compare the cross products as follows:

If $ad > bc$, then $\frac{a}{b} > \frac{c}{d}$

If $ad < bc$, then $\frac{a}{b} < \frac{c}{d}$

If $ad = bc$, then $\frac{a}{b} = \frac{c}{d}$

Using the example above, to compare $\frac{5}{6}$ with $\frac{8}{11}$, compare $5 \cdot 11$ with $6 \cdot 8$. Since $5 \cdot 11$ is greater, $\frac{5}{6}$ is the larger fraction.

Sometimes, a combination of these methods must be used in comparing a series of fractions. When a common denominator can be found easily for a series of fractions, Method I is easier. When a common denominator would result in a very large number, Method II is easier.

Example:

Which of the following fractions is the largest?

(A) $\frac{3}{5}$

(B) $\frac{21}{32}$

(C) $\frac{11}{16}$

(D) $\frac{55}{64}$

(E) $\frac{7}{8}$

Solution:

To compare the last four, we can easily use a common denominator of 64.

$$\frac{21}{32} = \frac{42}{64} \qquad \frac{11}{16} = \frac{44}{64} \qquad \frac{55}{64} \qquad \frac{7}{8} = \frac{56}{64}$$

The largest of these is $\frac{7}{8}$. Now we compare $\frac{7}{8}$ with $\frac{3}{5}$ using Method II. $7 \cdot 5 > 8 \cdot 3$, therefore $\frac{7}{8}$ is

the greatest fraction.

Exercise 5

Work out each problem. Circle the letter that appears before your answer.

1. Arrange these fractions in order of size, from largest to smallest: $\frac{4}{15}, \frac{2}{5}, \frac{1}{3}$.

    (A) $\frac{4}{15}, \frac{2}{5}, \frac{1}{3}$

    (B) $\frac{4}{15}, \frac{1}{3}, \frac{2}{5}$

    (C) $\frac{2}{5}, \frac{1}{3}, \frac{4}{15}$

    (D) $\frac{1}{3}, \frac{4}{15}, \frac{2}{5}$

    (E) $\frac{1}{3}, \frac{2}{5}, \frac{4}{15}$

2. Which of the following fractions is the smallest?

    (A) $\frac{3}{4}$

    (B) $\frac{5}{6}$

    (C) $\frac{7}{8}$

    (D) $\frac{19}{24}$

    (E) $\frac{13}{15}$

3. Which of the following fractions is the largest?

    (A) $\frac{3}{5}$

    (B) $\frac{7}{10}$

    (C) $\frac{5}{8}$

    (D) $\frac{3}{4}$

    (E) $\frac{13}{20}$

4. Which of the following fractions is closest to $\frac{3}{4}$?

    (A) $\frac{1}{2}$

    (B) $\frac{7}{12}$

    (C) $\frac{5}{6}$

    (D) $\frac{11}{12}$

    (E) $\frac{19}{24}$

5. Which of the following fractions is closest to $\frac{1}{2}$?

    (A) $\frac{5}{12}$

    (B) $\frac{8}{15}$

    (C) $\frac{11}{20}$

    (D) $\frac{31}{60}$

    (E) $\frac{7}{15}$

6. COMPLEX FRACTIONS

To simplify complex fractions, fractions that contain fractions within them, multiply every term by the smallest number needed to clear all fractions in the given numerator and denominator.

Example:

$$\frac{\dfrac{1}{6}+\dfrac{1}{4}}{\dfrac{1}{2}+\dfrac{1}{3}}$$

Solution:

The smallest number into which 6, 4, 2, and 3 will divide is 12. Therefore, multiply every term of the fraction by 12 to simplify the fraction.

$$\frac{2+3}{6+4}=\frac{5}{10}=\frac{1}{2}$$

Example:

$$\frac{\dfrac{3}{4}-\dfrac{2}{3}}{1+\dfrac{1}{2}}$$

Solution:

Again, we multiply every term by 12. Be sure to multiply the 1 by 12 also.

$$\frac{9-8}{12+6}=\frac{1}{18}$$

Exercise 6

Work out each problem. Circle the letter that appears before your answer.

1. Write as a fraction in simplest form: $\dfrac{\dfrac{2}{3}+\dfrac{1}{6}+\dfrac{1}{4}}{\dfrac{2}{3}-\dfrac{1}{2}}$

(A) $\dfrac{13}{2}$

(B) $\dfrac{7}{2}$

(C) $\dfrac{13}{4}$

(D) $\dfrac{4}{13}$

(E) $\dfrac{49}{12}$

2. Simplify: $\dfrac{\dfrac{5}{6}-\dfrac{2}{3}}{\dfrac{5}{12}-\dfrac{1}{6}}$

(A) $\dfrac{5}{12}$

(B) $\dfrac{5}{6}$

(C) $\dfrac{2}{3}$

(D) $\dfrac{1}{6}$

(E) $\dfrac{7}{12}$

3. Find the value of $\dfrac{\dfrac{1}{a}+\dfrac{1}{b}}{\dfrac{1}{ab}}$ when $a = 2$ and $b = 3$.

(A) $\dfrac{5}{6}$

(B) 5

(C) $4\dfrac{1}{6}$

(D) $1\dfrac{1}{5}$

(E) $2\dfrac{2}{5}$

4. Find the value of $\dfrac{\dfrac{1}{a}+\dfrac{1}{b}}{\dfrac{1}{ab}}$ when $a = \dfrac{1}{2}$ and $b = \dfrac{1}{3}.$

(A) $\dfrac{5}{6}$

(B) 5

(C) $4\dfrac{1}{6}$

(D) $1\dfrac{1}{5}$

(E) $2\dfrac{2}{5}$

5. Find the value of $\dfrac{2\dfrac{1}{3}}{5\dfrac{1}{2}+3\dfrac{1}{3}}.$

(A) $\dfrac{4}{17}$

(B) $\dfrac{21}{25}$

(C) $\dfrac{7}{6}$

(D) $\dfrac{12}{51}$

(E) $\dfrac{14}{53}$

RETEST

Work out each problem. Circle the letter that appears before your answer.

1. The sum of $\dfrac{4}{5}$, $\dfrac{3}{4}$, and $\dfrac{1}{3}$ is

(A) $\dfrac{8}{12}$

(B) $\dfrac{113}{60}$

(C) $\dfrac{1}{5}$

(D) $\dfrac{10}{9}$

(E) $\dfrac{11}{6}$

2. Subtract $\dfrac{2}{3}$ from $\dfrac{11}{15}$.

(A) $\dfrac{3}{4}$

(B) $\dfrac{7}{5}$

(C) $\dfrac{5}{7}$

(D) $\dfrac{1}{15}$

(E) $\dfrac{1}{3}$

3. If $52,34p$ is divisible by 9, the digit represented by p must be
(A) 1
(B) 2
(C) 3
(D) 4
(E) 5

4. $\left(\dfrac{3}{5}+\dfrac{1}{4}\right)\div\dfrac{34}{15}$ is equal to

   (A) $\dfrac{5}{3}$

   (B) $\dfrac{5}{8}$

   (C) $\dfrac{8}{3}$

   (D) $\dfrac{8}{5}$

   (E) $\dfrac{3}{8}$

5. Subtract $62\dfrac{2}{3}$ from 100.

   (A) $37\dfrac{1}{3}$

   (B) $38\dfrac{1}{3}$

   (C) $37\dfrac{2}{3}$

   (D) $38\dfrac{2}{3}$

   (E) $28\dfrac{2}{3}$

6. Divide $2\dfrac{2}{5}$ by $4\dfrac{8}{10}$.

   (A) 2

   (B) $\dfrac{1}{2}$

   (C) $\dfrac{288}{25}$

   (D) $\dfrac{25}{288}$

   (E) $2\dfrac{1}{4}$

7. Which of the following fractions is the smallest?

   (A) $\dfrac{7}{12}$

   (B) $\dfrac{8}{15}$

   (C) $\dfrac{11}{20}$

   (D) $\dfrac{5}{6}$

   (E) $\dfrac{2}{3}$

8. Which of the following fractions is closest to $\dfrac{1}{4}$?

   (A) $\dfrac{4}{15}$

   (B) $\dfrac{3}{10}$

   (C) $\dfrac{3}{20}$

   (D) $\dfrac{1}{5}$

   (E) $\dfrac{1}{10}$

9. Simplify: $\dfrac{\dfrac{5}{2}+\dfrac{2}{3}}{\dfrac{3}{4}+\dfrac{5}{6}}$

   (A) 2

   (B) $\dfrac{1}{2}$

   (C) 12

   (D) $\dfrac{1}{4}$

   (E) 4

10. Find the value of $\dfrac{\dfrac{1}{ab}}{\dfrac{1}{a}+\dfrac{1}{b}}$ when $a=4, b=5$.

    (A) 9

    (B) 20

    (C) $\dfrac{1}{9}$

    (D) $\dfrac{1}{20}$

    (E) $\dfrac{9}{40}$

SOLUTIONS TO PRACTICE EXERCISES

Diagnostic Test

1. (D) Change all fractions to sixtieths.

$$\frac{36}{60} + \frac{40}{60} + \frac{15}{60} = \frac{91}{60}$$

2. (A) $\dfrac{9}{10} - \dfrac{3}{4} = \dfrac{36-60}{40} = \dfrac{6}{40} = \dfrac{3}{20}$

3. (D) The sum of the digits is 27, which is divisible by 9.

4. (C) $\dfrac{5}{6} \div \left(\dfrac{4}{3} \cdot \dfrac{5}{4} \right) = \dfrac{5}{6} \div \dfrac{5}{3} = \dfrac{5}{6_2} \cdot \dfrac{3}{5} = \dfrac{1}{2}$

5. (A) $57 = 56\dfrac{5}{5}$

$$32\dfrac{3}{5} = 32\dfrac{3}{5}$$

$$24\dfrac{2}{5}$$

6. (B) $\dfrac{9}{2} \div \dfrac{9}{8} = \dfrac{9}{2} \cdot \dfrac{8^4}{9} = 4$

7. (E) Use a common denominator of 32.

$$\dfrac{1}{2} = \dfrac{16}{32} \quad \dfrac{11}{16} = \dfrac{22}{32} \quad \dfrac{5}{8} = \dfrac{20}{32} \quad \dfrac{21}{32}$$

$$\dfrac{3}{4} = \dfrac{24}{32}$$

Of these, $\dfrac{3}{4}$ is the largest.

8. (B) Use a common denominator of 30.

$$\dfrac{11}{15} = \dfrac{22}{30} \quad \dfrac{7}{10} = \dfrac{21}{30} \quad \dfrac{4}{5} = \dfrac{24}{30}$$

$$\dfrac{1}{2} = \dfrac{15}{30} \quad \dfrac{5}{6} = \dfrac{25}{30}$$

Since $\dfrac{2}{3} = \dfrac{20}{30}$, the answer closest to $\dfrac{2}{3}$ is $\dfrac{7}{10}$.

9. (B) Multiply every term of the fraction by 30.

$$\dfrac{120-27}{20+15} = \dfrac{93}{35}$$

10. (A) $\dfrac{\dfrac{1}{3} + \dfrac{1}{4}}{\dfrac{1}{3} - \dfrac{1}{4}}$

Multiply every term by 12.

$$\dfrac{4+3}{4-3} = 7$$

Exercise 1

1. (B) Change all fractions to twelfths.

$$\dfrac{6}{12} + \dfrac{8}{12} + \dfrac{9}{12} = \dfrac{23}{12}$$

2. (A) Use the cross product method.

$$\dfrac{5(15)+17(3)}{17(15)} = \dfrac{75+51}{255} = \dfrac{126}{255}$$

3. (D) $\dfrac{3}{4} + \dfrac{5}{6} = \dfrac{18+20}{24} = \dfrac{38}{24} = \dfrac{19}{12}$

$$\dfrac{1}{4} + \dfrac{2}{3} = \dfrac{3+8}{12} = \dfrac{11}{12}$$

$$\dfrac{19}{12} - \dfrac{11}{12} = \dfrac{8}{12} = \dfrac{2}{3}$$

4. (B) $\dfrac{9}{11} - \dfrac{3}{5} = \dfrac{45-33}{55} = \dfrac{12}{55}$

5. (E) $\dfrac{1}{4} + \dfrac{2}{3} = \dfrac{3+8}{12} = \dfrac{11}{12}$

$$\dfrac{11}{12} - \dfrac{5}{8} = \dfrac{88-60}{96} = \dfrac{28}{96} = \dfrac{7}{24}$$

Exercise 2

1. (B) $\dfrac{\cancel{3}}{2} \cdot \dfrac{6}{1} \cdot \dfrac{\cancel{4}^{2}}{\cancel{9}_{3}} = \dfrac{1}{\cancel{12}_{2}} = \dfrac{1}{3}$

2. (D) $\dfrac{7}{8} \cdot \dfrac{2}{3} \cdot \dfrac{8}{1} = \dfrac{14}{3}$

3. (A) $\dfrac{\dfrac{3}{5} \div \dfrac{3}{20}}{\dfrac{\cancel{3}}{\cancel{5}} \cdot \dfrac{\cancel{20}^{4}}{\cancel{3}}} = 4$

4. (E) $\dfrac{2}{3} \cdot \dfrac{7}{\cancel{12}_{6}} = \dfrac{7}{18}$

5. (D) $\dfrac{\cancel{5}}{1} \cdot \dfrac{12}{\cancel{5}} = 12$

Exercise 3

1. (D) The digits must add to a number divisible by 9. All answers are divisible by 5. 3 + 7 + 8 + 4 + 5 = 27, which is divisible by 9.

2. (A) The sum of the digits must be divisible by 9, and the digit must be even. 8 + 3 + 2 + 1 = 14. Therefore, we choose (A) because 14 + 4 = 18, which is divisible by 9.

3. (D) 19! = 19 · 18 · 17 · 16 ... 3 · 2 · 1. This is divisible by 17, since it contains a factor of 17. It is divisible by 54, since it contains factors of 9 and 6. It is divisible by 100, since it contains factors of 10, 5, and 2. It is divisible by 39, since it contains factors of 13 and 3.

4. (E) The sum of the digits in both the numerator and denominator are divisible by 9.

5. (D) The sum of the digits is 27, which is divisible by 3. The number formed by the last two digits is 40, which is divisible by 4. The number ends in 0 and is therefore divisible by 5.

Exercise 4

1. (C) $1\dfrac{1}{6} = 1\dfrac{2}{12}$

   $2\dfrac{2}{3} = 2\dfrac{8}{12}$

   $3\dfrac{3}{4} = 3\dfrac{9}{12}$

   $\overline{\quad\quad 6\dfrac{19}{12} = 7\dfrac{7}{12}}$

2. (A) $\begin{array}{r} 61 \quad = 60\dfrac{12}{12} \\ 45\dfrac{5}{12} = 45\dfrac{5}{12} \\ \hline 15\dfrac{7}{12} \end{array}$

3. (C) $\dfrac{\cancel{65}^{13}}{2} \cdot \dfrac{26}{\cancel{5}}^{13} = 169$

4. (A) $17\dfrac{1}{2} \div 70 = \dfrac{35}{2} \div 70 = \dfrac{35}{2} \cdot \dfrac{1}{\cancel{70}_{2}} = \dfrac{1}{4}$

5. (E) $\dfrac{7}{4} \cdot \dfrac{\cancel{12}^{3}}{1} \cdot \dfrac{5}{\cancel{42}_{\underset{2}{6}}} = \dfrac{5}{2} = 2\dfrac{1}{2}$

Exercise 5

1. (C) $\dfrac{2}{5}=\dfrac{6}{15}$ $\quad$ $\dfrac{1}{3}=\dfrac{5}{15}$

2. (A) To compare (A), (B), (C), and (D), use a common denominator of 24.

    $$\dfrac{3}{4}=\dfrac{18}{24} \quad \dfrac{5}{6}=\dfrac{20}{24} \quad \dfrac{7}{8}=\dfrac{21}{24} \quad \dfrac{19}{24}$$

    Of these, $\dfrac{3}{4}$ is the smallest. To compare $\dfrac{3}{4}$ with $\dfrac{13}{15}$, use cross products. Since $(3)(15)<(4)(14)$, $\dfrac{3}{4}<\dfrac{13}{15}$. Therefore, (A) is the smallest.

3. (D) To compare (A), (B), (D), and (E), use a common denominator of 20.

    $$\dfrac{3}{5}=\dfrac{12}{20} \quad \dfrac{7}{10}=\dfrac{14}{20} \quad \dfrac{3}{4}=\dfrac{15}{20} \quad \dfrac{13}{20}$$

    Of these, $\dfrac{3}{4}$ is the largest. To compare $\dfrac{3}{4}$ with $\dfrac{5}{8}$, use cross products. Since $(3)(8)>(4)(5)$, $\dfrac{3}{4}$ is the larger fraction.

4. (E) Use a common denominator of 24.

    $$\dfrac{1}{2}=\dfrac{12}{24} \quad \dfrac{7}{12}=\dfrac{14}{24} \quad \dfrac{5}{6}=\dfrac{20}{24} \quad \dfrac{11}{12}=\dfrac{22}{24}$$

    $$\dfrac{19}{24}$$

    Since $\dfrac{3}{4}=\dfrac{18}{24}$, the answer closest to $\dfrac{3}{4}$ is (E), $\dfrac{19}{24}$.

5. (D) Use a common denominator of 60.

    $$\dfrac{5}{12}=\dfrac{25}{60} \quad \dfrac{8}{15}=\dfrac{32}{60} \quad \dfrac{11}{20}=\dfrac{33}{60} \quad \dfrac{31}{60}$$

    $$\dfrac{7}{15}=\dfrac{28}{60}$$

    Since $\dfrac{1}{2}=\dfrac{30}{60}$, the answer closest to $\dfrac{1}{2}$ is (D), $\dfrac{31}{60}$.

Exercise 6

1. (A) Multiply every term of the fraction by 12.

    $$\dfrac{8+2+3}{8-6}=\dfrac{13}{2}$$

2. (C) Multiply every term of the fraction by 12.

    $$\dfrac{10-8}{5-2}=\dfrac{2}{3}$$

3. (B) $\dfrac{\dfrac{1}{2}+\dfrac{1}{3}}{\dfrac{1}{6}}$ Multiply every term by 6.

    $$\dfrac{3+2}{1}=5$$

4. (A) $\dfrac{1}{\frac{1}{2}}=2 \quad \dfrac{1}{\frac{1}{3}}=3 \quad \dfrac{1}{\frac{1}{6}}=6$

    $$\dfrac{2+3}{6}=\dfrac{5}{6}$$

5. (E) $\dfrac{\dfrac{7}{3}}{\dfrac{11}{2}+\dfrac{10}{3}}$ Multiply every term by 6.

    $$\dfrac{14}{33+20}=\dfrac{14}{53}$$

Retest

1. (B) Rename all fractions as sixtieths.

$$\frac{48}{60} + \frac{45}{60} + \frac{20}{60} = \frac{113}{60}$$

2. (D) $\dfrac{11}{15} - \dfrac{2}{3} = \dfrac{11}{15} - \dfrac{10}{15} = \dfrac{1}{15}$

3. (D) The sum of the digits must be divisible by 9.
    $5 + 2 + 3 + 4 + 4 = 18$, which is divisible by 9.

4. (E) $\dfrac{17}{20} \div \dfrac{34}{15}$

$$\frac{^{1}17}{_{4}20} \cdot \frac{15^{3}}{34_{2}} = \frac{3}{8}$$

5. (A) $100 = 99\dfrac{3}{3}$

$$\dfrac{-62\dfrac{2}{3} = 62\dfrac{2}{3}}{37\dfrac{1}{3}}$$

6. (B) $\dfrac{12}{5} \div \dfrac{48}{10} = \dfrac{^{1}12}{_{1}5} \cdot \dfrac{10^{2}}{48_{4}} = \dfrac{2}{4} = \dfrac{1}{2}$

7. (B) Use a common denominator of 60.

$$\frac{7}{12} = \frac{35}{60} \quad \frac{8}{15} = \frac{32}{60} \quad \frac{11}{20} = \frac{33}{60} \quad \frac{5}{6} = \frac{50}{60}$$

$$\frac{2}{3} = \frac{40}{60}$$

Of these, $\dfrac{8}{15}$ is the smallest.

8. (A) Use a common denominator of 60.

$$\frac{4}{15} = \frac{16}{60} \quad \frac{3}{10} = \frac{18}{60} \quad \frac{3}{20} = \frac{9}{60} \quad \frac{1}{5} = \frac{12}{60}$$

$$\frac{1}{10} = \frac{6}{60}$$

Since $\dfrac{1}{4} = \dfrac{15}{60}$, the answer closest to $\dfrac{1}{4}$ is $\dfrac{4}{15}$.

9. (A) Multiply every term of the fraction by 12.

$$\frac{30 + 8}{9 + 10} = \frac{38}{19} = 2$$

10. (C) $\dfrac{\dfrac{1}{20}}{\dfrac{1}{4} + \dfrac{1}{5}}$

Multiply every term by 20.

$$\frac{1}{5 + 4} = \frac{1}{9}$$

Verbal Problems Involving Fractions

DIAGNOSTIC TEST

Directions: Work out each problem. Circle the letter that appears before your answer.

Answers are at the end of the chapter.

1. On Monday evening, Channel 2 scheduled 2 hours of situation comedy, 1 hour of news, and 3 hours of movies. What part of the evening's programming was devoted to situation comedy?

   (A) $\dfrac{1}{3}$

   (B) $\dfrac{2}{3}$

   (C) $\dfrac{1}{2}$

   (D) $\dfrac{1}{6}$

   (E) $\dfrac{2}{5}$

2. What part of a gallon is 2 qt. 1 pt.?

   (A) $\dfrac{3}{4}$

   (B) $\dfrac{3}{10}$

   (C) $\dfrac{1}{2}$

   (D) $\dfrac{5}{8}$

   (E) $\dfrac{3}{8}$

3. Michelle spent $\dfrac{1}{2}$ of her summer vacation at camp, $\dfrac{1}{5}$ of her vacation babysitting, and $\dfrac{1}{4}$ visiting her grandmother. What part of her vacation was left to relax at home?

   (A) $\dfrac{1}{5}$

   (B) $\dfrac{1}{20}$

   (C) $\dfrac{1}{3}$

   (D) $\dfrac{3}{20}$

   (E) $\dfrac{1}{6}$

4. After doing $\frac{1}{3}$ of the family laundry before breakfast, Mrs. Strauss did $\frac{3}{4}$ of the remainder before lunch. What part of the laundry was left for the afternoon?

   (A) $\frac{1}{2}$

   (B) $\frac{1}{4}$

   (C) $\frac{2}{3}$

   (D) $\frac{1}{5}$

   (E) $\frac{1}{6}$

5. Glenn spent $\frac{2}{5}$ of his allowance on a hit record. He then spent $\frac{2}{3}$ of the remainder on a gift.

   What part of his allowance did he have left?

   (A) $\frac{1}{5}$

   (B) $\frac{1}{3}$

   (C) $\frac{2}{5}$

   (D) $\frac{3}{20}$

   (E) $\frac{1}{10}$

6. Barbara's car has a gasoline tank that holds 20 gallons. When her gauge reads $\frac{1}{4}$ full, how many gallons are needed to fill the tank?

   (A) 5
   (B) 10
   (C) 15
   (D) 12
   (E) 16

7. 42 seniors voted to hold the prom at the Copacabana. This represents $\frac{2}{9}$ of the senior class. How many seniors did not vote for the Copacabana?

   (A) 147
   (B) 101
   (C) 189
   (D) 105
   (E) 126

8. Steve needs M hours to mow the lawn. After working for X hours, what part of the job remains to be done?

   (A) $\frac{M - X}{M}$

   (B) $M - \frac{X}{X}$

   (C) $M - X$

   (D) $X - M$

   (E) $\frac{X}{M}$

9. Of D dogs in Mrs. Pace's kennel, $\dfrac{1}{3}$ are classified as large dogs and $\dfrac{1}{4}$ of the remainder are classified as medium-sized. How many of the dogs are classified as small?

(A) $\dfrac{1}{2}D$

(B) $\dfrac{1}{6}D$

(C) $\dfrac{5}{6}D$

(D) $\dfrac{2}{3}D$

(E) $\dfrac{1}{3}D$

10. A bookshelf contains A autobiographies and B biographies. What part of these books are biographies?

(A) $\dfrac{B}{A}$

(B) $\dfrac{B}{A+B}$

(C) $\dfrac{A}{A}+B$

(D) $\dfrac{A}{B}$

(E) $\dfrac{B}{A}-B$

1. PART OF A WHOLE

A fraction represents a part of a whole. In dealing with fractional problems, we are usually dealing with a part of a quantity.

Example:

Andrea and Danny ran for president of the Math Club. Andrea got 15 votes, while Danny got the other 10. What part of the votes did Andrea receive?

Solution:

Andrea got 15 votes out of 25. That is $\dfrac{15}{25}$ or $\dfrac{3}{5}$ of the votes.

Exercise 1

Work out each problem. Circle the letter that appears before your answer.

1. In a class there are 18 boys and 12 girls. What part of the class is girls?

   (A) $\dfrac{2}{3}$

   (B) $\dfrac{3}{5}$

   (C) $\dfrac{2}{5}$

   (D) $\dfrac{1}{15}$

   (E) $\dfrac{3}{2}$

2. A team played 40 games and lost 6. What part of the games played did it win?

   (A) $\dfrac{3}{20}$

   (B) $\dfrac{3}{17}$

   (C) $\dfrac{14}{17}$

   (D) $\dfrac{17}{20}$

   (E) $\dfrac{7}{8}$

3. What part of an hour elapses between 3:45 P.M. and 4:09 P.M.?

   (A) $\dfrac{6}{25}$

   (B) $\dfrac{2}{5}$

   (C) $\dfrac{5}{12}$

   (D) $\dfrac{1}{24}$

   (E) 24

4. A camp employs 4 men, 6 women, 12 girls, and 8 boys. In the middle of the summer, 3 girls are fired and replaced by women. What part of the staff is then made up of women?

   (A) $\dfrac{1}{5}$

   (B) $\dfrac{2}{9}$

   (C) $\dfrac{1}{3}$

   (D) $\dfrac{3}{10}$

   (E) $\dfrac{1}{2}$

5. There are three times as many seniors as juniors at a high school Junior-Senior dance. What part of the students present are juniors?

   (A) $\dfrac{2}{5}$

   (B) $\dfrac{3}{5}$

   (C) $\dfrac{2}{3}$

   (D) $\dfrac{3}{4}$

   (E) $\dfrac{1}{4}$

6. What part of a yard is 1 ft. 3 in.?

   (A) $\dfrac{5}{12}$

   (B) $\dfrac{1}{3}$

   (C) $\dfrac{1}{2}$

   (D) $\dfrac{5}{8}$

   (E) $\dfrac{4}{9}$

7. Manorville High had a meeting of the Student Senate, which was attended by 10 freshmen, 8 sophomores, 15 juniors, and 7 seniors. What part of the students present at the meeting were sophomores?

(A) $\dfrac{1}{4}$

(B) $\dfrac{5}{8}$

(C) $\dfrac{7}{40}$

(D) $\dfrac{1}{5}$

(E) $\dfrac{1}{3}$

8. The Dobkin family budgets its monthly income as follows: $\dfrac{1}{3}$ for food, $\dfrac{1}{4}$ for rent, $\dfrac{1}{10}$ for clothing, and $\dfrac{1}{5}$ for savings. What part is left for other expenses?

(A) $\dfrac{3}{7}$

(B) $\dfrac{1}{6}$

(C) $\dfrac{7}{60}$

(D) $\dfrac{2}{15}$

(E) $\dfrac{3}{20}$

2. FINDING FRACTIONS OF FRACTIONS

Many problems require you to find a fractional part of a fractional part, such as $\dfrac{3}{5}$ of $\dfrac{2}{3}$. This involves multiplying the fractions together, $\dfrac{3}{4}$ of $\dfrac{2}{3}$ is $\dfrac{1}{2}$.

Example:

$\dfrac{1}{4}$ of the employees of Mr. Brown's firm earn over $20,000 per year. $\dfrac{1}{2}$ of the remainder earn between $15,000 and $20,000. What part of the employees earns less than $15,000 per year?

Solution:

$\dfrac{1}{4}$ earn over $20,000. $\dfrac{1}{2}$ of $\dfrac{3}{4}$ or $\dfrac{3}{8}$ earn between $15,000 and $20,000. That accounts for $\dfrac{1}{4} + \dfrac{3}{8}$ or $\dfrac{5}{8}$ of all employees. Therefore the other $\dfrac{3}{8}$ earn less than $15,000.

Example:

A full bottle of isopropyl alcohol is left open in the school laboratory. If $\dfrac{1}{3}$ of the isopropyl alcohol evaporates in the first 12 hours and $\dfrac{2}{3}$ of the remainder evaporates in the second 12 hours, what part of the bottle is full at the end of 24 hours?

Solution:

$\dfrac{1}{3}$ evaporates during the first 12 hours. $\dfrac{2}{3}$ of $\dfrac{2}{3}$ or $\dfrac{4}{9}$ evaporates during the second 12 hours. This accounts for $\dfrac{7}{9}$ of the isopropyl alcohol. Therefore $\dfrac{2}{9}$ of the bottle is still full.

Exercise 2

Work out each problem. Circle the letter that appears before your answer.

1. Mrs. Natt spent $\dfrac{2}{3}$ of the family income one year and divided the remainder between 4 different savings banks. If she put $2000 into each bank, what was the amount of her family income that year?

    (A) $8000
    (B) $16,000
    (C) $24,000
    (D) $32,000
    (E) $6000

2. After selling $\dfrac{2}{5}$ of the suits in his shop before Christmas, Mr. Gross sold the remainder of the suits at the same price per suit after Christmas for $4500. What was the income from the entire stock?

    (A) $3000
    (B) $7500
    (C) $1800
    (D) $2700
    (E) $8000

3. Of this year's graduating seniors at South High, $\dfrac{9}{10}$ will be going to college. Of these, $\dfrac{4}{5}$ will go to four-year colleges, while the rest will be going to two-year colleges. What part of the class will be going to two-year colleges?

    (A) $\dfrac{9}{50}$

    (B) $\dfrac{1}{5}$

    (C) $\dfrac{4}{5}$

    (D) $\dfrac{36}{50}$

    (E) $\dfrac{4}{25}$

4. Sue and Judy drove from New York to San Francisco, a distance of 3000 miles. They covered $\dfrac{1}{10}$ of the distance the first day and $\dfrac{2}{9}$ of the remaining distance the second day. How many miles were left to be driven?

    (A) 600
    (B) 2000
    (C) 2400
    (D) 2100
    (E) 2700

5. 800 employees work for the Metropolitan Transportation Company. $\dfrac{1}{4}$ of these are college graduates, while $\dfrac{5}{6}$ of the remainder are high school graduates. What part of the employees never graduated from high school?

    (A) $\dfrac{1}{6}$

    (B) $\dfrac{1}{8}$

    (C) $\dfrac{7}{8}$

    (D) $\dfrac{1}{12}$

    (E) $\dfrac{3}{4}$

3. FINDING WHOLE NUMBERS

When a fractional part of a number is given and we wish to find the number representing the whole, it is often easiest to translate the words into mathematical symbols and solve the resulting equation.

Example:

Norman buys a used car for $2400, which is $\frac{2}{5}$ of the original price. Find the original price.

Solution:

$$2400 = \frac{2}{5}x \quad \text{Multiply by 5.}$$

$$12000 = 2x$$

$$\$6000 = x$$

Example:

The gas gauge on Mary's car reads $\frac{1}{8}$ full. She asks the gasoline attendant to fill the tank and finds she needs 21 gallons. What is the capacity of her gas tank?

Solution: $\frac{7}{8}$ of the tank is empty and requires 21 gallons to fill.

$$\frac{7}{8}x = 21$$

Multiply by 8.

$$7x = 168$$

$$x = 24$$

Exercise 3

Work out each problem. Circle the letter that appears before your answer.

1. Daniel spent $4.50 for a ticket to the movies.

   This represents $\frac{3}{4}$ of his allowance for the week.

   What did he have left that week for other

   expenses?

   (A) $6.00
   (B) $4.00
   (C) $3.39
   (D) $1.13
   (E) $1.50

2. 350 seniors attended the prom. This represents $\frac{7}{9}$ of the class. How many seniors did not attend the prom?

   (A) 50
   (B) 100
   (C) 110
   (D) 120
   (E) 450

3. A resolution was passed by a ratio of 5:4. If 900 people voted for the resolution, how many voted against it?

   (A) 500
   (B) 400
   (C) 720
   (D) 600
   (E) 223

4. Mr. Rich owns $\frac{2}{7}$ of a piece of property. If the value of his share is $14,000, what is the total value of the property?

    (A) $70,000
    (B) $49,000
    (C) $98,000
    (D) $10,000
    (E) $35,000

5. The Stone family spends $500 per month for rent. This is $\frac{4}{15}$ of their total monthly income. Assuming that salaries remain constant, what is the Stone family income for one year?

    (A) $1875
    (B) $6000
    (C) $60,000
    (D) $22,500
    (E) $16,000

4. SOLVING WITH LETTERS

When problems use letters in place of numbers, the same principles discussed earlier apply. If you are not sure which operations to use, replace the letters with numbers to determine the steps needed in the solution.

Example:

It takes Mr. Cohen X days to paint his house. If he works for D days, what part of his house must still be painted?

Solution:

He has $X - D$ days of painting left to do out of a total of X days, therefore $\frac{X-D}{X}$ is the correct answer.

Example:

Sue buys 500 stamps. X of these are 10-cent stamps. $\frac{1}{3}$ of the remainder are 15-cent stamps. How many 15-cent stamps does she buy?

Solution:

She buys 500 - X stamps that are not 10-cents stamps. $\frac{1}{3}$ of these are 15-cent stamps. Therefore, she buys $\frac{1}{3}(500 - X)$ or $\frac{500-X}{3}$ 15-cent stamps.

Example:

John spent $$X$ on the latest hit record album. This represents $\frac{1}{M}$ of his weekly allowance. What is his weekly allowance?

Solution:

Translate the sentence into an algebraic equation.

$$X = \frac{1}{M} \cdot A \quad \text{Multiply by } M.$$
$$MX = A$$

Exercise 4

Work out each problem. Circle the letter that appears before your answer.

1. A class contains B boys and G girls. What part of the class is boys?

   (A) $\dfrac{B}{G}$

   (B) $\dfrac{G}{B}$

   (C) $\dfrac{B}{B+G}$

   (D) $\dfrac{B+G}{B}$

   (E) $\dfrac{B}{B-G}$

2. M men agreed to rent a ski lodge for a total of D dollars. By the time they signed the contract, the price had increased by $100. Find the amount each man had to contribute as his total share.

   (A) $\dfrac{D}{M}$

   (B) $\dfrac{D}{M}+100$

   (C) $\dfrac{D+100}{M}$

   (D) $\dfrac{M}{D}+100$

   (E) $\dfrac{M+100}{D}$

3. Of S students in Bryant High, $\dfrac{1}{3}$ study French. $\dfrac{1}{4}$ of the remainder study Italian. How many of the students study Italian?

   (A) $\dfrac{1}{6}S$

   (B) $\dfrac{1}{4}S$

   (C) $\dfrac{2}{3}S$

   (D) $\dfrac{1}{12}S$

   (E) $\dfrac{3}{7}S$

4. Mr. and Mrs. Feldman took t dollars in travelers checks with them on a trip. During the first week, they spent $\dfrac{1}{5}$ of their money. During the second week, they spent $\dfrac{1}{3}$ of the remainder. How much did they have left at the end of the second week?

   (A) $\dfrac{4t}{15}$

   (B) $\dfrac{t}{15}$

   (C) $\dfrac{7t}{15}$

   (D) $\dfrac{11t}{15}$

   (E) $\dfrac{8t}{15}$

5. Frank's gas tank was $\dfrac{1}{4}$ full. After putting in G gallons of gasoline, the tank was $\dfrac{7}{8}$ full. What was the capacity of the tank.

   (A) $\dfrac{5G}{8}$

   (B) $\dfrac{8G}{5}$

   (C) $\dfrac{8G}{7}$

   (D) $\dfrac{7G}{8}$

   (E) $4G$

RETEST

Work out each problem. Circle the letter that appears before your answer.

1. The All Star Appliance Shop sold 10 refrigerators, 8 ranges, 12 freezers, 12 washing machines, and 8 clothes dryers during January. Freezers made up what part of the appliances sold in January?

    (A) $\dfrac{12}{50}$

    (B) $\dfrac{12}{25}$

    (C) $\dfrac{1}{2}$

    (D) $\dfrac{12}{40}$

    (E) $\dfrac{12}{60}$

2. What part of a day is 4 hours 20 minutes?

    (A) $\dfrac{1}{6}$

    (B) $\dfrac{13}{300}$

    (C) $\dfrac{1}{3}$

    (D) $\dfrac{13}{72}$

    (E) $\dfrac{15}{77}$

3. Mrs. Brown owns X books. $\dfrac{1}{3}$ of these are novels, $\dfrac{2}{5}$ of the remainder are poetry, and the rest are nonfiction. How many nonfiction books does Mrs. Brown own?

    (A) $\dfrac{4}{15}X$

    (B) $\dfrac{2}{5}X$

    (C) $\dfrac{2}{3}X$

    (D) $\dfrac{3}{5}X$

    (E) $\dfrac{7}{15}X$

4. After typing $\dfrac{1}{4}$ of a term paper on Friday, Richard completed $\dfrac{2}{3}$ of the remainder on Saturday. If he wanted to finish the paper that weekend, what part was left to be typed on Sunday?

    (A) $\dfrac{1}{4}$

    (B) $\dfrac{2}{3}$

    (C) $\dfrac{1}{3}$

    (D) $\dfrac{1}{2}$

    (E) $\dfrac{5}{6}$

5. What part of an hour elapses between 6:51 P.M. and 7:27 P.M.?

   (A) $\dfrac{1}{2}$

   (B) $\dfrac{2}{3}$

   (C) $\dfrac{3}{5}$

   (D) $\dfrac{17}{30}$

   (E) $\dfrac{7}{12}$

6. Laurie spent 8 hours reading a novel. If she finished $\dfrac{2}{5}$ of the book, how many more hours will she need to read the rest of the book?

   (A) 20
   (B) 12
   (C) $3\dfrac{1}{5}$
   (D) 18
   (E) 10

7. Mrs. Bach spent $\dfrac{2}{7}$ of her weekly grocery money on produce. If she spent $28 on produce, what was her total grocery bill that week?

   (A) $70
   (B) $80
   (C) $56
   (D) $90
   (E) $98

8. After working on a new roof for X hours on Saturday, Mr. Goldman finished the job by working Y hours on Sunday. What part of the total job was done on Sunday?

   (A) $\dfrac{Y}{X+Y}$

   (B) $\dfrac{Y}{X}$

   (C) $\dfrac{X}{X+Y}$

   (D) $\dfrac{Y}{X-Y}$

   (E) $\dfrac{Y}{Y-X}$

9. $\dfrac{1}{2}$ of the women in the Spring Garden Club are over 60 years old. $\dfrac{1}{4}$ of the remainder are under 40. What part of the membership is between 40 and 60 years old?

   (A) $\dfrac{1}{4}$

   (B) $\dfrac{3}{8}$

   (C) $\dfrac{3}{4}$

   (D) $\dfrac{1}{8}$

   (E) $\dfrac{5}{8}$

10. A residential city block contains R one-family homes, S two-family homes, and T apartment houses. What part of the buildings on this block is made up of one or two family houses?

   (A) $\dfrac{R}{T}+\dfrac{S}{T}$

   (B) $\dfrac{RS}{R+S+T}$

   (C) $\dfrac{R+S}{R+S+T}$

   (D) $\dfrac{R+S}{RST}$

   (E) $R+S$

SOLUTIONS TO PRACTICE EXERCISES

Diagnostic Test

1. (A) There was a total of 6 hours of programming time. $\dfrac{2}{6} = \dfrac{1}{3}$

2. (D) Change all measurements to pints. One gallon is 8 pints. 2 qt. 1 pt. = 5 pints = $\dfrac{5}{8}$ gallon.

3. (B) $\dfrac{1}{2} + \dfrac{1}{5} + \dfrac{1}{4} = \dfrac{10}{20} + \dfrac{4}{20} + \dfrac{5}{20} = \dfrac{19}{20}$. Therefore, $\dfrac{1}{20}$ was left to relax.

4. (E) $\dfrac{3}{4}$ of $\dfrac{2}{3}$ or $\dfrac{1}{2}$ of the laundry was done before lunch. Since $\dfrac{1}{3}$ was done before breakfast, $\dfrac{1}{3} + \dfrac{1}{2}$ or $\dfrac{5}{6}$ was done before the afternoon, leaving $\dfrac{1}{6}$ for the afternoon.

5. (A) $\dfrac{2}{3}$ of $\dfrac{3}{5}$ or $\dfrac{2}{5}$ of Glenn's allowance was spent on a gift. Since $\dfrac{2}{5}$ was spent on a hit record, $\dfrac{2}{5} + \dfrac{2}{5}$ or $\dfrac{4}{5}$ was spent, leaving $\dfrac{1}{5}$.

6. (C) The tank contained $\dfrac{1}{4} \cdot 20$ or 5 gallons, leaving 15 gallons to fill the tank.

7. (A) $42 = \dfrac{2}{9}x$ Multiply by 9. Divide by 2.

   $378 = 2x$

   $189 = x$

   This is the number of seniors. Since 42 seniors voted for the Copacabana, 147 did not.

8. (A) After working for X hours, $M - X$ hours are left out of a total of M hours.

9. (A) $\dfrac{1}{3}D$ dogs are large. $\dfrac{1}{4}$ of $\dfrac{2}{3}D$ or $\dfrac{1}{6}D$ are medium. The total of these dogs is

   $\dfrac{1}{3}D + \dfrac{1}{6}D$, leaving $\dfrac{1}{2}D$ small dogs.

10. (B) There are $A + B$ books. B out of $A + B$ are biographies.

Exercise 1

1. (C) There are 30 pupils in the class, of which 12 are girls. Therefore, $\dfrac{12}{30}$ or $\dfrac{2}{5}$ of the class is made up of girls.

2. (D) The team won 34 games out of 40 or $\dfrac{34}{40}$ of its games. This simplifies to $\dfrac{17}{20}$.

3. (B) 24 minutes is $\dfrac{24}{60}$ or $\dfrac{2}{5}$ of an hour.

4. (D) The number of staff members is still 30. Of these, 9 are now women. Therefore $\dfrac{9}{30}$ or $\dfrac{3}{10}$ of the staff are women.

5. (E) Let x = the number of juniors at the dance. $3x$ = the number of seniors at the dance. Then $4x$ = the number of students at the dance. x out of these $4x$ are juniors.

    That is $\dfrac{x}{4x}$ or $\dfrac{1}{4}$ of the students present are juniors.

6. (A) Change all measurements to inches. One yard is 36 inches. 1 ft. 3 in. is 15 inches. $\dfrac{15}{36} = \dfrac{5}{12}$

7. (D) There were 40 students at the meeting. $\dfrac{8}{40} = \dfrac{1}{5}$

8. (C)

    $$\frac{1}{3} + \frac{1}{4} + \frac{1}{10} + \frac{1}{5} = \frac{20}{60} + \frac{15}{60} + \frac{6}{60} + \frac{12}{60} = \frac{53}{60}$$

    Therefore, $\dfrac{7}{60}$ is left for other expenses.

Exercise 2

1. (C) She put $8000 into savings banks.
    $$800 = \frac{1}{3}x \qquad \text{Multiply by 3.}$$
    $24,000 = x$

2. (B) $4500 = \dfrac{3}{5}x$ Multiply by $\dfrac{5}{3}$.
    $7500 = x$

3. (A) Since $\dfrac{4}{5}$ of $\dfrac{9}{10}$ will go to four-year colleges, $\dfrac{1}{5}$ of $\dfrac{9}{10}$ or $\dfrac{9}{50}$ will go to two-year colleges.

4. (D) They covered $\dfrac{1}{10} \cdot 3000$ or 300 miles the first day, leaving 2700 miles still to drive. They covered $\dfrac{2}{9} \cdot 2700$ or 600 miles the second day, leaving 2100 miles still to drive.

5. (B) $\dfrac{5}{6}$ of $\dfrac{3}{4}$ or $\dfrac{5}{8}$ are high school graduates. Since $\dfrac{1}{4}$ are college graduates, $\dfrac{1}{4} + \dfrac{5}{8}$ or $\dfrac{7}{8}$ of the employees graduated from high school, leaving $\dfrac{1}{8}$ who did not.

Exercise 3

1. (E) $4.50 = \dfrac{3}{4}x$ Multiply by 4. Divide by 3.

   $18.00 = 3x$

   $x = \$6.00$, his allowance for the week. $6.00 - $4.50 = $1.50 left for other expenses.

2. (B) $350 = \dfrac{7}{9}x$ Multiply by 9. Divide by 7.

   $3150 = 7x$

   $450 = x$

   This is the number of students in the class. If 350 attend the prom, 100 do not.

3. (C) $\dfrac{5}{9}$ of the voters voted for the resolution.

   $900 = \dfrac{5}{9}x$ Multiply by 9. Divide by 5.

   $8100 = 5x$

   $1620 = x$

   1620 - 900 = 720 voted against the resolution.

4. (B) $\dfrac{2}{7}x = 14,000$ Multiply by 7. Divide by 2.

   $2x = 98,000$

   $x = \$49,000$

5. (D) $\dfrac{4}{15}x = 500$ Multiply by 15. Divide

   $4x = 7500$ by 4. This is their

   $x = \$1875$ *monthly* income.

   Multiply by 12 to find yearly income: $22,500.

Exercise 4

1. (C) There are $B + G$ students in the class. B out of $B + G$ are boys.

2. (C) The total cost is $D + 100$, which must be divided by the number of men to find each share.

3. (A) $\dfrac{1}{3}S$ students study French.

   $\dfrac{1}{4}$ of $\dfrac{2}{3}S$ or $\dfrac{1}{6}S$ study Italian.

4. (E) They spent $\dfrac{1}{5}t$ the first week. They spent

   $\dfrac{1}{3}$ of $\dfrac{4}{5}t$ or $\dfrac{4}{15}t$ the second week. During

   these two weeks they spent a total of

   $\dfrac{1}{5}t + \dfrac{4}{15}t$ or $\dfrac{7}{15}t$, leaving $\dfrac{8}{15}t$.

5. (B) The G gallons fill $\dfrac{7}{8} - \dfrac{1}{4}$ or $\dfrac{5}{8}$ of the tank.

   $\dfrac{5}{8}x = G$ Multiply by $\dfrac{8}{5}$.

   $x = \dfrac{8G}{5}$

Retest

1. (A) There were 50 appliances sold in January;

   $\frac{12}{50}$ were freezers.

2. (D) Change all measurements to minutes. One

   day is $60 \cdot 24$ or 1440 minutes. 4 hr. 20 min. =

   260 min. $\frac{260}{1440} = \frac{13}{72}$

3. (B) $\frac{1}{3}X$ books are novels.

   $\frac{2}{5}$ of $\frac{2}{3}X$ or $\frac{4}{15}X$ are poetry. The total of

   these books is $\frac{1}{3}X + \frac{4}{15}X$ or $\frac{9}{15}X$, leaving

   $\frac{6}{15}X$ or $\frac{2}{5}X$ books which are nonfiction.

4. (A) $\frac{2}{3}$ of $\frac{3}{4}$ or $\frac{1}{2}$ of the term paper was

   completed on Saturday. Since $\frac{1}{4}$ was

   completed on Friday, $\frac{1}{4} + \frac{1}{2}$ or $\frac{3}{4}$ was

   completed before Sunday, leaving $\frac{1}{4}$ to be

   typed on Sunday.

5. (C) 36 minutes is $\frac{36}{60}$ or $\frac{3}{5}$ of an hour.

6. (B) $8 = \frac{2}{5}x$ Multiply by 5. Divide by 2.

    $40 = 2x$

    $20 = x$

   This is the total number of hours needed to read
   the book. Since Laurie already read for 8 hours,
   she will need 12 more hours to finish the book.

7. (E) $\frac{2}{7}x = 28$ Multiply by 7. Divide by 2.

    $2x = 196$

    $x = \$98$

8. (A) Mr. Goldman worked a total of $X + Y$
    hours. Y out of $X + Y$ was done on Sunday.

9. (B) $\frac{1}{4}$ of $\frac{1}{2}$ or $\frac{1}{8}$ are under 40. Since

   $\frac{1}{2} + \frac{1}{8}$ or $\frac{5}{8}$ are over 60 or under 40, $\frac{3}{8}$ are

   between 40 and 60.

10. (C) There is a total of $R + S + T$ buildings on
     the block. $R + S$ out of $R + S + T$ are one or two
     family houses.

Variation

4

DIAGNOSTIC TEST

Directions: Work out each problem. Circle the letter that appears before your answer.

Answers are at the end of the chapter.

1. Solve for x: $\dfrac{2x}{3} = \dfrac{x+5}{4}$

   (A) 2
   (B) 3
   (C) 4
   (D) $4\dfrac{1}{2}$
   (E) 5

2. Solve for x if $a = 7$, $b = 8$, $c = 5$: $\dfrac{a-3}{x} = \dfrac{b+2}{4c}$

   (A) 4
   (B) 5
   (C) 6
   (D) 7
   (E) 8

3. A map is drawn using a scale of 2 inches = 25 miles. How far apart in miles are two cities which are $5\dfrac{2}{5}$ inches apart on the map?

   (A) 60
   (B) 65
   (C) $67\dfrac{1}{2}$
   (D) 69
   (E) 70

4. How many apples can be bought for c cents if n apples cost d cents?

   (A) $\dfrac{nc}{d}$
   (B) $\dfrac{nd}{c}$
   (C) $\dfrac{cd}{n}$
   (D) $\dfrac{d}{c}$
   (E) nc

5. Ms. Dehn drove 7000 miles during the first 5 months of the year. At this rate, how many miles will she drive in a full year?

   (A) 16,000
   (B) 16,800
   (C) 14,800
   (D) 15,000
   (E) 16,400

6. A gear having 20 teeth turns at 30 revolutions per minute and is meshed with another gear having 25 teeth. At how many revolutions per minute is the second gear turning?

   (A) 35
   (B) $37\dfrac{1}{2}$
   (C) $22\dfrac{1}{2}$
   (D) 30
   (E) 24

7. A boy weighing 90 pounds sits 3 feet from the fulcrum of a seesaw. His younger brother weighs 50 pounds. How far on the other side of the fulcrum should he sit to balance the seesaw?

    (A) $5\dfrac{3}{4}$ ft.

    (B) $5\dfrac{2}{5}$ ft.

    (C) $1\dfrac{2}{3}$ ft.

    (D) $1\dfrac{1}{3}$ ft.

    (E) $4\dfrac{1}{2}$ ft.

8. Alan has enough dog food to last his two dogs for three weeks. If a neighbor asks him to feed her dog as well, how long will the dog food last, assuming that all three dogs eat the same amount?

    (A) 10 days
    (B) 12 days
    (C) 14 days
    (D) 16 days
    (E) 18 days

9. A newspaper can be printed by m machines in h hours. If 2 of the machines are not working, how many hours will it take to print the paper?

    (A) $\dfrac{mh - 2h}{m}$

    (B) $\dfrac{m - 2}{mh}$

    (C) $\dfrac{mh + 2h}{m}$

    (D) $\dfrac{mh}{m - 2}$

    (E) $\dfrac{mh}{m + 2}$

10. An army platoon has enough rations to last 20 men for 6 days. If 4 more men join the group, for how many fewer days will the rations last?

    (A) 5
    (B) 2
    (C) 1
    (D) 1.8
    (E) 4

1. RATIO AND PROPORTION

A ratio is a comparison between two quantities. In making this comparison, both quantities must be expressed in terms of the same units.

Example:

Express the ratio of 1 hour to 1 day.

Solution:

A day contains 24 hours. The ratio is $\dfrac{1}{24}$, which can also be written 1 : 24.

Example:

Find the ratio of the shaded portion to the unshaded portion.

Solution:

There are 5 squares shaded out of 9. The ratio of the shaded portion to unshaded portion is $\dfrac{5}{4}$.

A proportion is a statement of equality between two ratios. The denominator of the first fraction and the numerator of the second are called the means of the proportion. The numerator of the first fraction and the denominator of the second are called the extremes. In solving a proportion, we use the theorem that states the product of the means is equal to the product of the extremes. We refer to this as *cross multiplying*.

Example:

Solve for x: $\dfrac{x+3}{5} = \dfrac{8-x}{6}$

Solution:

Cross multiply. $6x + 18 = 40 - 5x$

$$11x = 22$$

$$x = 2$$

Example:

Solve for x: $4 : x = 9 : 18$

Solution:

Rewrite in fraction form. $\dfrac{4}{x} = \dfrac{9}{18}$

Cross multiply. $9x = 72$

$$x = 8$$

If you observe that the second fraction is equal to $\dfrac{1}{2}$, then the first must also be equal to $\dfrac{1}{2}$. Therefore the missing denominator must be 8. Observation often saves valuable time.

Exercise 1

Work out each problem. Circle the letter that appears before your answer.

1. Find the ratio of 1 ft. 4 in. to 1 yd.
   (A) 1 : 3
   (B) 2 : 9
   (C) 4 : 9
   (D) 3 : 5
   (E) 5 : 12

2. A team won 25 games in a 40 game season. Find the ratio of games won to games lost.
   (A) $\dfrac{5}{8}$
   (B) $\dfrac{3}{8}$
   (C) $\dfrac{3}{5}$
   (D) $\dfrac{5}{3}$
   (E) $\dfrac{3}{2}$

3. In the proportion $a : b = c : d$, solve for d in terms of a, b and c.
   (A) $\dfrac{ac}{b}$
   (B) $\dfrac{bc}{a}$
   (C) $\dfrac{ab}{c}$
   (D) $\dfrac{a}{bc}$
   (E) $\dfrac{bc}{d}$

4. Solve for x: $\dfrac{x+1}{8} = \dfrac{28}{32}$
    (A) $6\dfrac{1}{2}$
    (B) 5
    (C) 4
    (D) 7
    (E) 6

5. Solve for y: $\dfrac{2y}{9} = \dfrac{y-1}{3}$
    (A) 3
    (B) $\dfrac{1}{3}$
    (C) $\dfrac{9}{15}$
    (D) $\dfrac{9}{4}$
    (E) $\dfrac{4}{9}$

2. DIRECT VARIATION

Two quantities are said to vary directly if they change in the same direction. As the first increases, the second does also. As the first decreases, the second does also.

For example, the distance you travel at a constant rate varies directly as the time spent traveling. The number of pounds of apples you buy varies directly as the amount of money you spend. The number of pounds of butter you use in a cookie recipe varies directly as the number of cups of sugar you use.

Whenever two quantities vary directly, a problem can be solved using a proportion. We must be very careful to compare quantities in the same order and in terms of the same units in both fractions. If we compare miles with hours in the first fraction, we must compare miles with hours in the second fraction.

You must always be sure that as one quantity increases or decreases, the other changes in the same direction before you try to solve using a proportion.

Example:

If 4 bottles of milk cost $2, how many bottles of milk can you buy for $8?

Solution:

The more milk you buy, the more it will cost. This is *direct*. We are comparing the number of bottles with cost.

$$\frac{4}{2} = \frac{x}{8}$$

If we cross multiply, we get $2x = 32$ or $x = 16$.

A shortcut in the above example would be to observe what change takes place in the denominator and apply the same change to the numerator. The denominator of the left fraction was multiplied by 4 to give the denominator of the right fraction. Therefore we multiply the numerator by 4 as well to maintain the equality. This method often means a proportion can be solved at sight with no written computation at all, saving valuable time.

Example:

If b boys can deliver n newspapers in one hour, how many newspapers can c boys deliver in the same time?

Solution:

The more boys, the more papers will be delivered. This is *direct*. We are comparing the number of boys with the number of newspapers.

$$\frac{b}{n} = \frac{c}{x}$$ Cross multiply and solve for x.

$$bx = cn$$

$$x = \frac{cn}{b}$$

Exercise 2

Work out each problem. Circle the letter that appears before your answer.

1. Find the cost, in cents, of 8 books if 3 books of the same kind cost D dollars.

   (A) $\dfrac{8D}{3}$

   (B) $\dfrac{3}{800D}$

   (C) $\dfrac{3}{8D}$

   (D) $\dfrac{800D}{3}$

   (E) $\dfrac{108D}{3}$

2. On a map $\dfrac{1}{2}$ inch = 10 miles. How many miles apart are two towns that are $2\dfrac{1}{4}$ inches apart on the map?

   (A) $11\dfrac{1}{4}$

   (B) 45

   (C) $22\dfrac{1}{2}$

   (D) $40\dfrac{1}{2}$

   (E) 42

3. The toll on the Intercoastal Thruway is 8¢ for every 5 miles traveled. What is the toll for a trip of 115 miles on this road?

   (A) $9.20
   (B) $1.70
   (C) $1.84
   (D) $1.64
   (E) $1.76

4. Mark's car uses 20 gallons of gas to drive 425 miles. At this rate, approximately how many gallons of gas will he need for a trip of 1000 miles?

   (A) 44
   (B) 45
   (C) 46
   (D) 47
   (E) 49

5. If r planes can carry p passengers, how many planes are needed to carry m passengers?

   (A) $\dfrac{rm}{p}$

   (B) $\dfrac{rp}{m}$

   (C) $\dfrac{p}{rm}$

   (D) $\dfrac{pm}{r}$

   (E) $\dfrac{m}{rp}$

3. INVERSE VARIATION

Two quantities are said to vary inversely if they change in opposite directions. As the first increases, the second decreases. As the first decreases, the second increases.

Whenever two quantities vary inversely, their product remains constant. Instead of dividing one quantity by the other and setting their quotients equal as we did in direct variation, we multiply one quantity by the other and set the products equal.

There are several situations that are good examples of inverse variation.

A) The number of teeth in a meshed gear varies inversely as the number of revolutions it makes per minute. The more teeth a gear has, the fewer revolutions it will make per minute. The less teeth it has, the more revolutions it will make per minute. The product of the number of teeth and the revolutions per minute remains constant.

B) The distance a weight is placed from the fulcrum of a balanced lever varies inversely as its weight. The heavier the object, the shorter must be its distance from the fulcrum. The lighter the object, the greater must be the distance. The product of the weight of the object and its distance from the fulcrum remains constant.

C) When two pulleys are connected by a belt, the diameter of a pulley varies inversely as the number of revolutions per minute. The larger the diameter, the smaller the number of revolutions per minute. The smaller the diameter, the greater the number of revolutions per minute. The product of the diameter of a pulley and the number of revolutions per minute remains constant.

D) The number of people hired to work on a job varies inversely as the time needed to complete the job. The more people working, the less time it will take. The fewer people working, the longer it will take. The product of the number of people and the time worked remains constant.

E) How long food, or any commodity, lasts varies inversely as the number of people who consume it. The more people, the less time it will last. The fewer people, the longer it will last. The product of the number of people and the time it will last remains constant.

Example:

If 3 men can paint a house in 2 days, how long will it take 2 men to do the same job?

Solution:

The fewer men, the more days. This is *inverse*.

$$3 \cdot 2 = 2 \cdot x$$
$$6 = 2x$$
$$x = 3 \text{ days}$$

Exercise 3

Work out each problem. Circle the letter that appears before your answer.

1. A field can be plowed by 8 machines in 6 hours. If 3 machines are broken and cannot be used, how many hours will it take to plow the field?

    (A) 12

    (B) $9\dfrac{3}{5}$

    (C) $3\dfrac{3}{4}$

    (D) 4

    (E) 16

2. Camp Starlight has enough milk to feed 90 children for 4 days. If 10 of the children do not drink milk, how many days will the supply last?

    (A) 5

    (B) 6

    (C) $4\dfrac{1}{2}$

    (D) $4\dfrac{1}{8}$

    (E) $5\dfrac{1}{3}$

3. A pulley revolving at 200 revolutions per minute has a diameter of 15 inches. It is belted to a second pulley which revolves at 150 revolutions per minute. Find the diameter, in inches, of the second pulley.

    (A) 11.2

    (B) 20

    (C) 18

    (D) 16.4

    (E) 2

4. Two boys weighing 60 pounds and 80 pounds balance a seesaw. How many feet from the fulcrum must the heavier boy sit if the lighter boy is 8 feet from the fulcrum?

    (A) 10

    (B) $10\dfrac{2}{3}$

    (C) 9

    (D) $7\dfrac{1}{2}$

    (E) 6

5. A gear with 20 teeth revolving at 200 revolutions per minute is meshed with a second gear turning at 250 revolutions per minute. How many teeth does this gear have?

    (A) 16

    (B) 25

    (C) 15

    (D) 10

    (E) 24

In solving variation problems, you must decide whether the two quantities involved change in the same direction, in which case it is direct variation and should be solved by means of proportions. If the quantities change in opposite directions, it is inverse variation, solved by means of constant products. In the following exercises, decide carefully whether each is an example of direct or inverse variation.

Exercise 4

Work out each problem. Circle the letter that appears before your answer.

1. A farmer has enough chicken feed to last 30 chickens for 4 days. If 10 more chickens are added, how many days will the feed last?

   (A) 3

   (B) $1\frac{1}{3}$

   (C) 12

   (D) $2\frac{2}{3}$

   (E) $5\frac{1}{3}$

2. At c cents per can, what is the cost of p cases of soda if there are 12 cans in a case?

   (A) $12cp$

   (B) $\dfrac{cp}{12}$

   (C) $\dfrac{12}{cp}$

   (D) $\dfrac{12p}{c}$

   (E) $\dfrac{12c}{p}$

3. If m boys can put up a fence in d days, how many days will it take to put up the fence if two of the boys cannot participate?

   (A) $\dfrac{d}{-2}$

   (B) $\dfrac{d(m-2)}{m}$

   (C) $\dfrac{md}{m-2}$

   (D) $\dfrac{m-2}{md}$

   (E) $\dfrac{m(m-2)}{d}$

4. A recipe calls for $\frac{3}{4}$ lb. of butter and 18 oz. of sugar. If only 10 oz. of butter are available, how many ounces of sugar should be used?

   (A) $13\frac{1}{2}$

   (B) 23

   (C) 24

   (D) 14

   (E) 15

5. If 3 kilometers are equal to 1.8 miles, how many kilometers are equal to 100 miles?

   (A) 60

   (B) $166\frac{2}{3}$

   (C) 540

   (D) $150\frac{1}{2}$

   (E) 160.4

RETEST

Work out each problem. Circle the letter that appears before your answer.

1. Solve for x: $\dfrac{3x}{8} = \dfrac{x+7}{12}$

    (A) $\dfrac{7}{28}$

    (B) 2

    (C) 4

    (D) $2\dfrac{3}{4}$

    (E) 1

2. Solve for x if $a = 5$, $b = 8$, and $c = 3$:

    $$\dfrac{a-3}{x} = \dfrac{b+2}{5c}$$

    (A) 5
    (B) 20
    (C) 2
    (D) 3
    (E) 6

3. A map is drawn to a scale of $\dfrac{1}{2}$ inch = 20 miles. How many miles apart are two cities that are $3\dfrac{1}{4}$ inches apart on the map?

    (A) 70
    (B) 130
    (C) 65
    (D) $32\dfrac{1}{2}$
    (E) 35

4. Mr. Weiss earned $12,000 during the first 5 months of the year. If his salary continues at the same rate, what will his annual income be that year?

    (A) $60,000
    (B) $28,000
    (C) $27,000
    (D) $30,000
    (E) $28,800

5. How many pencils can be bought for D dollars if n pencils cost c cents?

    (A) $\dfrac{nD}{c}$

    (B) $\dfrac{nD}{100c}$

    (C) $\dfrac{100D}{nc}$

    (D) $\dfrac{100nD}{c}$

    (E) $\dfrac{nc}{100D}$

6. Ten boys agree to paint the gym in 5 days. If five more boys join in before the work begins, how many days should the painting take?

    (A) $3\dfrac{1}{3}$

    (B) $3\dfrac{1}{2}$

    (C) 10

    (D) $2\dfrac{1}{2}$

    (E) $2\dfrac{3}{4}$

7. A weight of 120 pounds is placed five feet from the fulcrum of a lever. How far from the fulcrum should a 100 pound weight be placed in order to balance the lever?

    (A) 6 ft.

    (B) $4\dfrac{1}{6}$ ft.

    (C) $5\dfrac{1}{2}$ ft.

    (D) $6\dfrac{1}{2}$ ft.

    (E) $6\dfrac{2}{3}$ ft.

8. A photograph negative measures $1\frac{7}{8}$ inches by $2\frac{1}{2}$ inches. The printed picture is to have its longer dimension be 4 inches. How long should the shorter dimension be?

    (A) $2\frac{3}{8}''$

    (B) $2\frac{1}{2}''$

    (C) 3"

    (D) $3\frac{1}{8}''$

    (E) $3\frac{3}{8}''$

9. A gear with 60 teeth is meshed to a gear with 40 teeth. If the larger gear revolves at 20 revolutions per minute, how many revolutions does the smaller gear make in a minute?

    (A) $13\frac{1}{3}$
    (B) 3
    (C) 300
    (D) 120
    (E) 30

10. How many gallons of paint must be purchased to paint a room containing 820 square feet of wall space, if one gallon covers 150 square feet?

    (A) 4
    (B) 5
    (C) 6
    (D) 7
    (E) 8

SOLUTIONS TO PRACTICE EXERCISES

Diagnostic Test

1. (B) $2x(4) = 3(x+5)$

$$8x = 3x + 15$$
$$5x = 15$$
$$x = 3$$

2. (E) $\dfrac{4}{x} = \dfrac{10}{20}$ Cross multiply.

$$80 = 10x$$
$$x = 8$$

3. (C) We compare inches to miles.

$$\dfrac{2}{25} = \dfrac{5\frac{2}{5}}{x}$$ Cross multiply.

$$2x = 135$$
$$x = 67\frac{1}{2}$$

4. (A) We compare apples to cents.

$$\dfrac{x}{c} = \dfrac{n}{d}$$ Cross multiply.

$$dx = nc$$
$$x = \dfrac{nc}{d}$$

5. (B) We compare miles to months.

$$\dfrac{5}{7000} = \dfrac{12}{x}$$

$$5x = 84,000$$
$$x = 16,800$$

6. (E) Number of teeth times speed remains constant.

$$20 \cdot 30 = x \cdot 25$$
$$600 = 25x$$
$$x = 24$$

7. (B) Weight times distance from the fulcrum remains constant.

$$90 \cdot 3 = 50 \cdot x$$
$$270 = 50x$$
$$x = 5\frac{2}{5} \text{ ft.}$$

8. (C) The more dogs, the fewer days. This is inverse variation.

$$2 \cdot 3 = 3 \cdot x$$
$$6 = 3x$$
$$x = 2 \text{ weeks} = 14 \text{ days}$$

9. (D) Number of machines times hours needed remains constant.

$$m \cdot h = (m-2) \cdot x$$
$$x = \dfrac{mh}{m-2}$$

10. (C) The more men, the fewer days. This is inverse variation.

$$20 \cdot 6 = 24 \cdot x$$
$$120 = 24x$$
$$x = 5$$

The rations will last 1 day less.

Exercise 1

1. (C) 1 ft. 4 in. $= 16$ in.

   1 yd. $= 36$ in.

   $$\frac{16}{36} = \frac{4}{9}$$

2. (D) The team won 25 games and lost 15.

   $$\frac{25}{15} = \frac{5}{3}$$

3. (B) $\dfrac{a}{b} = \dfrac{c}{d}$ Cross multiply. Divide by a.

   $ad = bc$

   $d = \dfrac{bc}{a}$

4. (E) $32(x + 1) = 28(8)$

   $32x + 32 = 224$

   $32x = 192$

   $x = 6$

5. (A) $9(y - 1) = 2y(3)$

   $9y - 9 = 6y$

   $3y = 9$

   $y = 3$

Exercise 2

1. (D) We compare books with cents. D dollars is equivalent to $100D$ cents.

   $$\frac{3}{100D} = \frac{8}{x}$$

   $3x = 800D$

   $x = \dfrac{800D}{3}$

2. (B) We compare inches to miles.

   $\dfrac{\frac{1}{2}}{10} = \dfrac{2\frac{1}{4}}{x}$ Cross multiply. Multiply by 2.

   $\dfrac{1}{2}x = 22\dfrac{1}{2}$

   $x = 45$

3. (C) We compare cents to miles.

   $\dfrac{8}{5} = \dfrac{x}{115}$ Cross multiply.

   $5x = 920$

   $x = \$1.84$

4. (D) We compare gallons to miles.

   $\dfrac{20}{425} = \dfrac{x}{1000}$ Cross multiply. To avoid large numbers, divide by 25.

   $425x = 20{,}000$

   $17x = 800$

   $x = 47\dfrac{1}{17}$

5. (A) We compare planes to passengers.

   $\dfrac{r}{p} = \dfrac{x}{m}$

   $px = rm$ Cross multiply. Divide by p.

   $x = \dfrac{rm}{p}$

Exercise 3

1. (B) Number of machines times hours needed remains constant.

$$8 \cdot 6 = 5 \cdot x$$
$$5x = 48$$
$$x = 9\frac{3}{5}$$

2. (C) Number of children times days remains constant.

$$90 \cdot 4 = 80 \cdot x$$
$$80x = 360$$
$$x = 4\frac{1}{2}$$

3. (B) Diameter times speed remains constant.

$$15 \cdot 200 = x \cdot 150$$
$$3000 = 150x$$
$$x = 20$$

4. (E) Weight times distance from fulcrum remains constant.

$$80 \cdot x = 60 \cdot 8$$
$$80x = 480$$
$$x = 6$$

5. (A) Number of teeth times speed remains constant.

$$20 \cdot 200 = x \cdot 250$$
$$250x = 4000$$
$$x = 16$$

Exercise 4

1. (A) The more chickens, the fewer days. This is *inverse*.

$$30 \cdot 4 = 40 \cdot x$$
$$40x = 120$$
$$x = 3$$

2. (A) The more cases, the more cents. This is *direct*. We compare cents with cans. In p cases there will be $12p$ cans.

$$\frac{c}{1} = \frac{x}{12p}$$
$$x = 12cp$$

3. (C) The fewer boys, the more days. This is *inverse*.

$$m \cdot d = (m - 2) \cdot x$$
$$\frac{md}{m - 2} = x$$

4. (E) The less butter, the less sugar. This is *direct*. Change $\frac{3}{4}$ lb. to 12 oz.

$$\frac{12}{18} = \frac{10}{x}$$
$$12x = 180$$
$$x = 15$$

5. (B) The more kilometers, the more miles. This is *direct*.

$$\frac{3}{1.8} = \frac{x}{100}$$
$$1.8x = 300$$
$$18x = 3000$$
$$x = 166\frac{2}{3}$$

Retest

1. (B) $3x(12) = 8(x + 7)$

$$36x = 8x + 56$$
$$28x = 56$$
$$x = 2$$

2. (D) $\dfrac{2}{x} = \dfrac{10}{15}$ Cross multiply.

$$30 = 10x$$
$$x = 3$$

3. (B) We compare inches to miles.

$$\dfrac{\frac{1}{2}}{20} = \dfrac{3\frac{1}{4}}{x}$$

$\dfrac{1}{2}x = 65$ Cross multiply. Multiply by 2.

$$x = 130$$

4. (E) We compare dollars to months.

$$\dfrac{12,000}{5} = \dfrac{x}{12}$$

$144,000 = 5x$ Cross multiply.

$$x = \$28,800$$

5. (D) We compare pencils to dollars. The cost of

n pencils is $\dfrac{c}{100}$ dollars.

$\dfrac{x}{D} = \dfrac{n}{\frac{c}{100}}$ Cross multiply.

$\dfrac{cx}{100} = nD$ Multiply by $\dfrac{100}{c}$.

$$x = \dfrac{100nD}{c}$$

6. (A) The more boys, the fewer days. This is *inverse*.

$$10 \cdot 5 = 15 \cdot x$$
$$50 = 15x$$
$$x = 3\dfrac{1}{3}$$

7. (A) Weight times distance from the fulcrum remains constant.

$$120 \cdot 5 = 100 \cdot x$$
$$600 = 100x$$
$$x = 6 \text{ ft.}$$

8. (C)

$$\dfrac{2\frac{1}{2}}{4} = \dfrac{1\frac{7}{8}}{x}$$

$\dfrac{5}{2}x = \dfrac{15}{2}$ Cross multiply. Multiply by 2.

$$5x = 15$$
$$x = 3''$$

9. (E) Number of teeth times speed remains constant.

$$60 \cdot 20 = 40 \cdot x$$
$$1200 = 40x$$
$$x = 30$$

10. (C) We compare gallons to square feet.

$\dfrac{x}{820} = \dfrac{1}{150}$ Cross multiply.

$$150x = 820$$

$x = 5.47$, which means 6 gallons must be purchased

Percent

5

DIAGNOSTIC TEST

Directions: Work out each problem. Circle the letter that appears before your answer.

Answers are at the end of the chapter.

1. Write as a fraction: 4.5%

   (A) $\dfrac{9}{2}$

   (B) $\dfrac{9}{20}$

   (C) $\dfrac{9}{200}$

   (D) $\dfrac{9}{2000}$

   (E) $\dfrac{4.5}{10}$

2. Write $\dfrac{2}{5}\%$ as a decimal.

   (A) .40
   (B) .04
   (C) 40.0
   (D) .004
   (E) 4.00

3. What is $62\dfrac{1}{2}\%$ of 80?

   (A) 5000
   (B) 500
   (C) 50
   (D) 5
   (E) .5

4. Find 6% of b.

   (A) .6b
   (B) .06b
   (C) $\dfrac{b}{6}$
   (D) $\dfrac{b}{.06}$
   (E) $\dfrac{100b}{6}$

5. 80 is 40% of what number?

   (A) 3200
   (B) 320
   (C) 32
   (D) 200
   (E) 20

6. c is $83\dfrac{1}{3}\%$ of what number?

   (A) $\dfrac{5c}{6}$
   (B) $\dfrac{6c}{5}$
   (C) $\dfrac{7c}{8}$
   (D) $\dfrac{8c}{7}$
   (E) $\dfrac{2c}{3}$

Peterson's Math Exercises for the SAT   65   *www.petersons.com*

7. How many sixteenths are there in $87\frac{1}{2}\%$?
    (A) 7
    (B) 8
    (C) 10
    (D) 12
    (E) 14

8. What percent of 40 is 16?
    (A) $2\frac{1}{2}$
    (B) 25
    (C) 30
    (D) 40
    (E) 45

9. Find 112% of 80.
    (A) 92
    (B) 89.6
    (C) 88
    (D) 70.5
    (E) 91

10. What percent of 60 is 72?
    (A) 105
    (B) 125
    (C) 120
    (D) $83\frac{1}{3}$
    (E) 110

1. FRACTIONAL AND DECIMAL EQUIVALENTS OF PERCENTS

Percent means "out of 100." If you understand this concept, it then becomes very easy to change a percent to an equivalent decimal or fraction.

Example:

5% means 5 out of 100 or $\frac{5}{100}$, which is equal to .05

3.4% means 3.4 out of 100 or $\frac{3.4}{100}$, which is equivalent to $\frac{34}{1000}$ or .034

c% means c out of 100 or $\frac{c}{100}$, which is equivalent to $\frac{1}{100} \cdot c$ or .01c

$\frac{1}{4}\%$ means $\frac{1}{4}$ out of 100 or $\frac{\frac{1}{4}}{100}$, which is equivalent to $\frac{1}{100} \cdot .25$ or .0025

To change a percent to a decimal, therefore, we must move the decimal point two places to the *left*, as we are dividing by 100.

Example:

62% = .62

.4% = .004

3.2% = .032

To change a decimal to a percent, we must reverse the above steps. We multiply by 100, which has the effect of moving the decimal point two places to the *right*, and insert the percent sign.

Example:

.27 = 27%

.012 = 1.2%

.003 = .3%

To change a percent to a fraction, we remove the percent sign and divide by 100. This has the effect of putting the percent over 100 and then simplifying the resulting fraction.

Example:

$$25\% = \frac{25}{100} = \frac{1}{4}$$

$$70\% = \frac{70}{100} = \frac{7}{10}$$

$$.5\% = \frac{.5}{100} = \frac{5}{1000} = \frac{1}{200}$$

To change a fraction to a percent, we must reverse the above steps. We multiply by 100 and insert the percent sign.

Example:

$$\frac{4}{5} = \frac{4}{\cancel{5}} \cdot \overset{20}{\cancel{100}}\% = 80\%$$

$$\frac{3}{8} = \frac{3}{\underset{2}{\cancel{8}}} \cdot \overset{25}{\cancel{100}}\% = \frac{75}{2}\% = 37\frac{1}{2}\%$$

Some fractions do not convert easily, as the denominator does not divide into 100. Such fractions must be changed to decimals first by dividing the numerator by the denominator. Then convert the decimal to a percent as explained on the previous page. Divide to two places only, unless it clearly comes out even in one or two additional places.

Example:

$$\frac{8}{17} = 17\overline{)8.00}^{.47} = 47\frac{1}{17}\%$$

$$\frac{6\ 8}{1\ 20}$$
$$\frac{1\ 19}{1}$$

$$\frac{4}{125} = 125\overline{)4.000}^{.032} = 3.2\%$$

$$\frac{3\ 75}{250}$$
$$\frac{250}{}$$

Certain fractional and decimal equivalents of common percents occur frequently enough so that they should be memorized. Learning the values in the following table will make your work with percent problems much easier.

PERCENT	DECIMAL	FRACTION
50%	.5	$\frac{1}{2}$
25%	.25	$\frac{1}{4}$
75%	.75	$\frac{3}{4}$
10%	.1	$\frac{1}{10}$
30%	.3	$\frac{3}{10}$
70%	.7	$\frac{7}{10}$
90%	.9	$\frac{9}{10}$
$33\frac{1}{3}\%$	$.3\overline{3}$	$\frac{1}{3}$
$66\frac{2}{3}\%$	$.6\overline{6}$	$\frac{2}{3}$
$16\frac{2}{3}\%$	$.1\overline{6}$	$\frac{1}{6}$
$83\frac{1}{3}\%$	$.8\overline{3}$	$\frac{5}{6}$
20%	.2	$\frac{1}{5}$
40%	.4	$\frac{2}{5}$
60%	.6	$\frac{3}{5}$
80%	.8	$\frac{4}{5}$
$12\frac{1}{2}\%$	.125	$\frac{1}{8}$
$37\frac{1}{2}\%$	.375	$\frac{3}{8}$
$62\frac{1}{2}\%$	.625	$\frac{5}{8}$
$87\frac{1}{2}\%$	.875	$\frac{7}{8}$

Exercise 1

Work out each problem. Circle the letter that appears before your answer.

1. $3\frac{1}{2}\%$ may be written as a decimal as
   (A) 3.5
   (B) .35
   (C) .035
   (D) .0035
   (E) 3.05

2. Write as a fraction in simplest form: 85%.
   (A) $\frac{13}{20}$
   (B) $\frac{17}{20}$
   (C) $\frac{17}{10}$
   (D) $\frac{19}{20}$
   (E) $\frac{17}{2}$

3. Write 4.6 as a percent.
   (A) 4.6%
   (B) .46%
   (C) .046%
   (D) 46%
   (E) 460%

4. Write $\frac{5}{12}$ as an equivalent percent.
   (A) 41%
   (B) 41.6%
   (C) $41\frac{2}{3}\%$
   (D) 4.1%
   (E) $.41\frac{2}{3}\%$

5. Write $\frac{1}{2}\%$ as a decimal.
   (A) .5
   (B) .005
   (C) 5.0
   (D) 50.0
   (E) .05

2. FINDING A PERCENT OF A NUMBER

Most percentage problems can be solved by using the proportion

$$\frac{\%}{100} = \frac{\text{part}}{\text{whole}}.$$

Although this method will work, it often yields unnecessarily large numbers that make for difficult computation. As we look at different types of percent problems, we will compare methods of solution. In finding a percent of a number, it is usually easier to change the percent to an equivalent decimal or fraction and multiply by the given number.

Example:

Find 32% of 84.

Proportion Method

$$\frac{32}{100} = \frac{x}{84}$$
$$100x = 2688$$
$$x = 26.88$$

Decimal Method

Change 32% to .32 and multiply.

$$\begin{array}{r} 84 \\ \times\,.32 \\ \hline 168 \\ 252 \\ \hline 26.88 \end{array}$$

Example:

Find $12\frac{1}{2}\%$ of 112.

Proportion Method   *Decimal Method*   *Fraction Method*

$$\frac{12\frac{1}{2}}{100} = \frac{x}{112}$$

$$
\begin{array}{r}
112 \\
\times\,.125 \\
\hline
5\ 60 \\
2\ 24 \\
11\ 2 \\
\hline
14.000
\end{array}
$$

Change $12\frac{1}{2}\%$ to $\frac{1}{8}$

$100x = 1400$

$x = 14$

$\frac{1}{8} \cdot \overset{14}{\cancel{112}} = 14$

Which method do you think is the easiest? When the fractional equivalent of the required percent is among those given in the previous chart, the fraction method is by far the least time-consuming. It really pays to memorize those fractional equivalents.

Exercise 2

Work out each problem. Circle the letter that appears before your answer.

1. What is 40% of 40?

    (A) .16
    (B) 1.6
    (C) 16
    (D) 160
    (E) 1600

2. What is 42% of 67?

    (A) 2814
    (B) 281.4
    (C) 2.814
    (D) .2814
    (E) 28.14

3. Find $16\frac{2}{3}\%$ of 120.

    (A) 20
    (B) 2
    (C) 200
    (D) 16
    (E) 32

4. What is $\frac{1}{5}\%$ of 40?

    (A) 8
    (B) .8
    (C) .08
    (D) .008
    (E) .0008

5. Find $r\%$ of s.

    (A) $\dfrac{100s}{r}$

    (B) $\dfrac{rs}{100}$

    (C) $\dfrac{100r}{s}$

    (D) $\dfrac{r}{100s}$

    (E) $\dfrac{s}{100r}$

3. FINDING A NUMBER WHEN A PERCENT OF IT IS GIVEN

This type of problem may be solved using the proportion method, although this may again result in the unnecessary use of time. It is often easier to translate the words of such a problem into an algebraic statement, using decimal or fractional equivalents for the percents involved. Then it will become evident that we divide the given number by the given percent to solve.

Example:

7 is 5% of what number?

Proportion Method

$$\frac{5}{100} = \frac{7}{x}$$
$$5x = 700$$
$$x = 140$$

Equation Method

$$7 = .05x$$
$$700 = 5x$$
$$140 = x$$

Example:

40 is $66\frac{2}{3}\%$ of what number?

Proportion Method

$$\frac{66\frac{2}{3}}{100} = \frac{40}{x}$$
$$66\frac{2}{3}x = 4000$$
$$\frac{200}{3}x = 4000$$
$$200x = 12000$$
$$2x = 120$$
$$x = 60$$

Equation Method

$$40 = \frac{2}{3}x$$
$$120 = 2x$$
$$60 = x$$

Just think of the amount of time you will save and the extra problems you will get to do if you know that $66\frac{2}{3}\%$ is $\frac{2}{3}$ and use the equation method. Are you convinced that the common fraction equivalents in the previously given chart should be memorized?

Exercise 3

Work out each problem. Circle the letter that appears before your answer.

1. 72 is 12% of what number?

    (A)   6
    (B)   60
    (C)   600
    (D)   86.4
    (E)   8.64

2. 80 is $12\frac{1}{2}\%$ of what number?

    (A)   10
    (B)   100
    (C)   64
    (D)   640
    (E)   6400

3. $37\frac{1}{2}\%$ of what number is 27?

    (A)   72

    (B) $10\frac{1}{8}$

    (C)   90

    (D)   101.25

    (E)   216

4. m is $p\%$ of what number?

    (A) $\dfrac{mp}{100}$

    (B) $\dfrac{100p}{m}$

    (C) $\dfrac{m}{100p}$

    (D) $\dfrac{p}{100m}$

    (E) $\dfrac{100m}{p}$

5. 50% of what number is r?

    (A) $\dfrac{1}{2}r$

    (B) $5r$

    (C) $10r$

    (D) $2r$

    (E) $100r$

4. TO FIND WHAT PERCENT ONE NUMBER IS OF ANOTHER

This type of problem may also be solved using the proportion method. However, this may again result in the use of an unnecessary amount of time. It is often easier to put the part over the whole, simplify the resulting fraction, and multiply by 100.

Example:

30 is what percent of 1500?

Proportion Method

$$\frac{x}{100} = \frac{30}{1500}$$
$$1500x = 3000$$
$$x = 2\%$$

Fraction Method

$$\frac{30}{1500} = \frac{3}{150} = \frac{1}{50} \cdot 100 = 2\%$$

Example:

12 is what percent of 72?

Proportion Method

$$\frac{x}{100} = \frac{12}{72}$$
$$72x = 1200$$

Fraction Method

$$\frac{12}{72} = \frac{1}{6} = 16\frac{2}{3}\%$$

Time consuming long division is needed to find $x = 16\frac{2}{3}\%$. If you have memorized the fractional equivalents of common percents, this method requires only a few seconds.

Example:

What percent of 72 is 16?

Proportion Method

$$\frac{x}{100} = \frac{16}{72}$$
$$72x = 1600$$
$$x = 22\frac{2}{9}\%$$

Fraction Method

$$\frac{16}{72} = \frac{2}{9} \cdot 100 = \frac{200}{9} = 22\frac{2}{9}\%$$

Exercise 4

Work out each problem. Circle the letter that appears before your answer.

1. 4 is what percent of 80?
   - (A) 20
   - (B) 2
   - (C) 5
   - (D) .5
   - (E) 40

2. $\frac{1}{2}$ of 6 is what percent of $\frac{1}{4}$ of 60?
   - (A) 5
   - (B) 20
   - (C) 10
   - (D) 25
   - (E) 15

3. What percent of 96 is 12?
   - (A) $16\frac{2}{3}$
   - (B) $8\frac{1}{3}$
   - (C) $37\frac{1}{2}$
   - (D) 8
   - (E) $12\frac{1}{2}$

4. What percent of 48 is 48?
   - (A) 1
   - (B) 10
   - (C) 100
   - (D) 48
   - (E) 0

5. What percent of y is x?
   - (A) $\frac{x}{y}$
   - (B) $\frac{x}{100y}$
   - (C) $\frac{xy}{100}$
   - (D) $\frac{100x}{y}$
   - (E) $\frac{100y}{x}$

5. PERCENTS GREATER THAN 100

When the percentage involved in a problem is greater than 100, the same methods apply. Remember that $100\% = 1$; $200\% = 2$; $300\% = 3$ and so forth. Therefore 150% will be equal to $100\% + 50\%$ or $1\frac{1}{2}$. Let us look at one example of each previously discussed problem, using percents greater than 100.

Example:

Find 175% of 60

Proportion Method   *Decimal Method*   *Fraction Method*

$$\frac{175}{100} = \frac{x}{60}$$

$$100x = 10500$$

$$x = 105$$

$$\begin{array}{r} 60 \\ \times 1.75 \\ \hline 300 \\ 4200 \\ 6000 \\ \hline 105.00 \end{array}$$

$$1\frac{3}{4} \cdot 60$$

$$\frac{7}{4} \cdot \overset{15}{60} = 105$$

Example:

80 is 125% of what number?

Proportion Method   *Decimal Method*   *Fraction Method*

$$\frac{125}{100} = \frac{80}{x}$$

$$125x = 8000$$

$$x = 64$$

$$80 = 1.25x$$

$$8000 = 125x$$

$$x = 64$$

$$80 = 1\frac{1}{4}x$$

$$80 = \frac{5}{4}x$$

$$320 = 5x$$

$$x = 64$$

Example:

40 is what percent of 30?

Proportion Method   *Fraction Method*

$$\frac{x}{100} = \frac{40}{30}$$

$$30x = 4000$$

$$x = 133\frac{1}{3}\%$$

$$\frac{40}{30} = \frac{4}{3} = 1\frac{1}{3} = 133\frac{1}{3}\%$$

Exercise 5

Work out each problem. Circle the letter that appears before your answer.

1. 36 is 150% of what number?

   (A) 24
   (B) 54
   (C) 26
   (D) 12
   (E) 48

2. What is 300% of 6?

   (A) 2
   (B) 3
   (C) 12
   (D) 18
   (E) 24

3. What percent of 90 is 120?

   (A) 75

   (B) $133\frac{1}{3}$

   (C) 125

   (D) 120

   (E) $1\frac{1}{3}$

4. 500 is 200% of what number?

   (A) 250
   (B) 1000
   (C) 100
   (D) 750
   (E) 300

5. To multiply a number by $137\frac{1}{2}\%$, the number should be multiplied by

   (A) 137.5
   (B) 13750
   (C) 1.375
   (D) 13.75
   (E) .1375

RETEST

Work out each problem. Circle the letter that appears before your answer.

1. Write as a fraction in lowest terms: .25%.

   (A) $\frac{1}{4}$

   (B) $\frac{1}{40}$

   (C) $\frac{1}{400}$

   (D) $\frac{1}{4000}$

   (E) $\frac{1}{25}$

2. Write $\frac{3}{4}\%$ as a decimal.

   (A) .75
   (B) 75.0
   (C) .075
   (D) .0075
   (E) 7.5

3. Find 12% of 80.

   (A) 10
   (B) .96
   (C) .096
   (D) 960
   (E) 9.6

4. 18 is 20% of what number?

   (A) 3.6
   (B) 90
   (C) 72
   (D) 21.6
   (E) 108

5. What is $b\%$ of 6?

   (A) $\frac{3b}{50}$

   (B) $\frac{3}{50b}$

   (C) $\frac{50b}{3}$

   (D) $\frac{50}{3b}$

   (E) $\frac{b}{150}$

6. m is $62\dfrac{1}{2}\%$ of what number?

    (A) $\dfrac{5m}{8}$

    (B) $\dfrac{8m}{5}$

    (C) $8m$

    (D) $\dfrac{5}{8m}$

    (E) $\dfrac{8}{5m}$

7. What percent of 12 is 2?

    (A) 600

    (B) $12\dfrac{1}{2}$

    (C) $16\dfrac{2}{3}$

    (D) $6\dfrac{2}{3}$

    (E) 6

8. What is 140% of 70?

    (A) 9800
    (B) 980
    (C) .98
    (D) 9.8
    (E) 98

9. How many fifths are there in 280%?

    (A) 28
    (B) 1.4
    (C) 14
    (D) 56
    (E) 2.8

10. What percent of 12 is 16?

    (A) $133\dfrac{1}{3}$

    (B) 125

    (C) 75

    (D) 80

    (E) $1\dfrac{1}{4}$

SOLUTIONS TO PRACTICE EXERCISES

Diagnostic Test

1. (C) $4.5\% = \dfrac{4.5}{100} = \dfrac{45}{1000} = \dfrac{9}{200}$

2. (D) $\dfrac{2}{5}\% = .4\% = .004$

3. (C) $62\dfrac{1}{2}\% = \dfrac{5}{8}$ $\dfrac{5}{\cancel{8}} \cdot \overset{10}{\cancel{80}} = 50$

4. (B) $6\% = .06$ $.06 \cdot b = .06b$

5. (D) $80 = .40x$ Divide by .40
   $200 = x$

6. (B) $83\dfrac{1}{3}\% = \dfrac{5}{6}$ Multiply by 6. Divide by 5.

   $c = \dfrac{5}{6}x$

   $6c = 5x$

   $\dfrac{6c}{5} = x$

7. (E) $87\dfrac{1}{2}\% = \dfrac{7}{8} = \dfrac{14}{16}$

8. (D) $\dfrac{16}{40} = \dfrac{2}{5} = 40\%$

9. (B) $112\% = 1.12$
   $1.12 \cdot 80 = 89.6$

10. (C) $\dfrac{72}{60} = \dfrac{6}{5} = 120\%$

Exercise 1

1. (C) $3\dfrac{1}{2}\% = 3.5\% = .035$ To change a percent
   to a decimal, move the decimal point two
   places to the *left*.

2. (B) $85\% = \dfrac{85}{100} = \dfrac{17}{20}$

3. (E) To change a decimal to a percent, move the
   decimal point two places to the *right*.

4. (C) $\dfrac{5}{\underset{3}{\cancel{12}}} \cdot \overset{25}{\cancel{100}} = \dfrac{125}{3} = 41\dfrac{2}{3}\%$

   To change a fraction to a percent, multiply by 100

5. (B) $\dfrac{1}{2}\% = .5\% = .005$

Exercise 2

1. (C) $40\% = \dfrac{2}{5}$

    $\dfrac{2}{\cancel{5}} \cdot \cancel{40}^{8} = 16$

2. (E)
$$
\begin{array}{r}
67 \\
\times .42 \\
\hline
1\ 34 \\
26\ 80 \\
\hline
28.14
\end{array}
$$

3. (A) $16\dfrac{2}{3}\% = \dfrac{1}{6}$

    $\dfrac{1}{\cancel{6}} \cdot \cancel{120}^{20} = 20$

4. (C) $\dfrac{1}{5}\% = .2\% = .002$

$$
\begin{array}{r}
40 \\
\times .002 \\
\hline
.0800
\end{array}
$$

5. (B) $r\% = \dfrac{r}{100}$

    $\dfrac{r}{100} \cdot s = \dfrac{rs}{100}$

Exercise 3

1. (C) $72 = .12x$

    $7200 = 12x$

    $x = 600$

2. (D) $80 = \dfrac{1}{8}x$

    $640 = x$

3. (A) $\dfrac{3}{8}x = 27$

    $3x = 216$

    $x = 72$

4. (E) $m = \dfrac{p}{100} \cdot x$

    $100m = px$

    $\dfrac{100m}{p} = x$

5. (D) $\dfrac{1}{2}x = r$

    $x = 2r$

Exercise 4

1. (C) $\dfrac{4}{80} = \dfrac{1}{\cancel{20}} \cdot \cancel{100}^{5} = 5\%$

2. (B)
    $\dfrac{1}{2}$ of 6 $\qquad = 3$

    $\dfrac{1}{4}$ of 60 $\qquad = 15$

    $\dfrac{3}{15} = \dfrac{1}{5} \qquad = 20\%$

3. (E) $\dfrac{12}{96} = \dfrac{1}{8} = 12\dfrac{1}{2}\%$

4. (C) $\dfrac{48}{48} = 1 = 100\%$

5. (D) $\dfrac{x}{y} \cdot 100 = \dfrac{100x}{y}$

Exercise 5

1. (A) $36 = 1\frac{1}{2}x$

$$36 = \frac{3}{2}x$$
$$72 = 3x$$
$$x = 24$$

2. (D) $300\% = 3$

$$6 \cdot 3 = 18$$

3. (B) $\dfrac{120}{90} = \dfrac{4}{3} = 133\frac{1}{3}\%$

4. (A) $500 = 2x$

$$250 = x$$

5. (C) $137.5\% = 1.375$

Retest

1. (C) $.25\% = \dfrac{.25}{100} = \dfrac{25}{10,000} = \dfrac{1}{400}$

2. (D) $\dfrac{3}{4}\% = .75\% = .0075$

3. (E) $\quad 12\% = .12$

$$.12 \cdot 80 = 9.6$$

4. (B) $18 = .20x$ Divide by .20.

$$90 = x$$

5. (A) $b\% = \dfrac{b}{100} \qquad \dfrac{b}{\underset{50}{100}} \cdot \overset{3}{6} = \dfrac{3b}{50}$

6. (B)

$$62\frac{1}{2}\% = \frac{5}{8} \qquad \text{Multiply by 8. Divide by 5.}$$
$$m = \frac{5}{8}x$$
$$8m = 5x$$
$$\frac{8m}{5} = x$$

7. (C) $\dfrac{2}{12} = \dfrac{1}{6} = 16\frac{2}{3}\%$

8. (E) $\quad 140\% = 1.40$

$$1.40 \cdot 70 = 98$$

9. (C) $280\% = \dfrac{280}{100} = \dfrac{28}{10} = \dfrac{14}{5}$

10. (A) $\dfrac{16}{12} = \dfrac{4}{3} = 133\frac{1}{3}\%$

Verbal Problems Involving Percent

6

DIAGNOSTIC TEST

Directions: Work out each problem. Circle the letter that appears before your answer.

Answers are at the end of the chapter.

1. A book dealer bought 100 books for $1250. If she sold 30% of these at $10 each and the rest at $15 each, what was her total profit?

    (A) $350
    (B) $1350
    (C) $300
    (D) $1050
    (E) $100

2. The Fishman family income for one month is $2000. If 25% is spent for lodging, 35% for food, 5% for clothing, and 10% for savings, how many dollars are left for other expenses?

    (A) $1500
    (B) $400
    (C) $500
    (D) $1600
    (E) $600

3. The enrollment of Kennedy High School dropped from 1200 to 1000 over a three-year period. What was the percent of decrease during this time?

    (A) 20
    (B) $16\frac{2}{3}$
    (C) 25
    (D) 200
    (E) 2

4. A baseball team won 50 of the first 92 games played in a season. If the season consists of 152 games, how many more games must the team win to finish the season winning $62\frac{1}{2}\%$ of games played?

    (A) 37
    (B) 45
    (C) 40
    (D) 95
    (E) 19

5. The Strauss Insurance Company laid off 20% of its employees one year and then increased its staff by $12\frac{1}{2}\%$ the following year. If the firm originally employed 120 workers, what was the net change in staff over the two-year period?

    (A) decrease of 12
    (B) increase of 15
    (C) decrease of 9
    (D) decrease of 24
    (E) increase of 12

6. How much money is saved by buying an article priced at $80 with a 40% discount, rather than buying an article marked at $90 with a discount of 35% then 10%?

    (A) $4.65
    (B) $1.50
    (C) $10.50
    (D) $3.15
    (E) $4.25

7. In Central City, a property owner pays school taxes at the rate of 2% of the first $1500 of assessed valuation, 3% of the next $2000, 5% of the next $3000, and 6% of the remainder. How much must Mr. Williams pay in school taxes each year if his home is assessed at $8000?

    (A) $300
    (B) $230
    (C) $600
    (D) $330
    (E) $195

8. Jeffrey delivers newspapers for a salary of $20 per week plus a 4% commission on all sales. One week his sales amounted to $48. What was his income that week?

    (A) $19.20
    (B) $21.92
    (C) $1.92
    (D) $39.20
    (E) $32

9. At Baker High, 3 out of every 4 graduates go on to college. Of these, 2 out of every 3 graduate from college. What percent of students graduating from Baker High will graduate from college?

    (A) $66\frac{2}{3}$
    (B)   75
    (C)   50
    (D) $33\frac{1}{3}$
    (E)   25

10. The basic sticker price on Mr. Feldman's new car was $3200. The options he desired cost an additional $1800. What percent of the total price was made up of options?

    (A) $56\frac{1}{4}$
    (B)   36
    (C)   64
    (D)   18
    (E)   9

Certain types of business situations are excellent applications of percent. Study the following examples carefully as they are problems you will encounter in everyday life as well as on these examinations.

1. PERCENT OF INCREASE OR DECREASE

The percent of increase or decrease is found by putting the amount of increase or decrease over the original amount and changing this fraction to a percent by multiplying by 100.

Example:

   The number of automobiles sold by the Cadcoln Dealership increased from 300 one year to 400 the following year. What was the percent of increase?

Solution:

   There was an increase of 100, which must be compared to the original 300.

$$\frac{100}{300} = \frac{1}{3} = 33\frac{1}{3}\%$$

Example:

The Sunset School dismisses 20% of its staff of 150 due to budgetary problems. By what percent must it now increase its staff to return to the previous level?

Solution:

$$20\% = \frac{1}{5} \qquad \frac{1}{5} \cdot 150 = 30$$

The school now has 150 - 30 or 120 employees. To increase by 30, the percent of increase is

$$\frac{30}{120} = \frac{1}{4} = 25\%.$$

Exercise 1

Work out each problem. Circle the letter that appears before your answer.

1. Mrs. Morris receives a salary raise from $25,000 to $27,500. Find the percent of increase.

   (A) 9
   (B) 10
   (C) 90
   (D) 15
   (E) $3\% = \dfrac{3}{100} \quad \dfrac{3}{100} \cdot 140 = \dfrac{420}{100}$

2. The population of Stormville has increased from 80,000 to 100,000 in the last twenty years. Find the percent of increase.

   (A) 20
   (B) 25
   (C) 80
   (D) 60
   (E) 10

3. The value of Super Company Stock dropped from $25 a share to $21 a share. Find the percent of decrease.

   (A) 4
   (B) 8
   (C) 12
   (D) 16
   (E) 20

4. The Rubins bought their home for $30,000 and sold it for $60,000. What was the percent of increase?

   (A) 100
   (B) 50
   (C) 200
   (D) 300
   (E) 150

5. During the pre-holiday rush, Martin's Department Store increased its sales staff from 150 to 200 persons. By what percent must it now decrease its sales staff to return to the usual number of salespersons?

   (A) 25
   (B) $33\frac{1}{3}$
   (C) 20
   (D) 40
   (E) 75

2. DISCOUNT

A discount is usually expressed as a percent of the marked price, which will be deducted from the marked price to determine the sale price. If an article is sold at a 20% discount, the buyer pays 80% of the marked price. Instead of first finding the amount of discount by finding 20% of the marked price and subtracting to find the sale price, it is shorter and easier to find 80% of the marked price directly.

Example:

A store offers a 25% discount on all appliances for paying cash. How much will a microwave oven marked at $400 cost if payment is made in cash?

Solution:

We can find 25% or $\frac{1}{4}$ of $400, which is $100, then subtract $100 from $400 to get a cash price of $300. The danger in this method is that the amount of discount, $100, is sure to be among the

multiple-choice answers, as students often look for the first answer they get without bothering to

finish the problem. It is safer, and easier, to realize that a 25% discount means 75% must be paid.

75% = $\frac{3}{4}$ and $\frac{3}{4}$ of $400 is $300.

Some problems deal with successive discounts. In such cases, the first discount is figured on the marked price, while the second discount is figured on the intermediate price.

Example:

Johnson's Hardware Store is having a moving sale in which everything in the store is being marked down 20% with an additional 5% discount for paying cash. What will be the net cost of a toaster, paid with cash, marked at $25?

Solution:

The first discount is 20% or $\frac{1}{5}$. We then pay $\frac{4}{5}$ of $25 or $20. An additional 5% is given off this

amount. $\frac{5}{100} = \frac{1}{20}$ off. $\frac{19}{20} \cdot 20 = \$19$. The net price is $19.

Exercise 2

Work out each problem. Circle the letter that appears before your answer.

1. How much is saved by buying a freezer marked at $600 with a discount of 20% rather than one marked at $600 with a discount of 10% then 10%?

    (A) $6
    (B) $8
    (C) $10
    (D) $12
    (E) $20

2. Mr. Kaplan builds a home at a cost of $60,000. After pricing the home for sale by adding 25% of his expenses, he offers a discount of 20% to encourage sales. What did he make on the house?

    (A) $15,000
    (B) $1500
    (C) $0
    (D) $5000
    (E) $1200

3. Christmas cards are sold after Christmas for 90 cents a box instead of $1.20 a box. The rate of discount is

(A) 20%
(B) 25%
(C) 30%
(D) $33\frac{1}{3}\%$.
(E) 40%

4. A television set listed at $160 is offered at a $12\frac{1}{2}\%$ discount during a storewide sale. If an additional 3% is allowed on the net price for payment in cash, how much can Josh save by buying this set during the sale for cash?

(A) $24.36
(B) $24.80
(C) $17.20
(D) $24.20
(E) $23.20

5. Pam pays $6 for a sweater after receiving a discount of 25%. What was the marked price of the sweater?

(A) $9
(B) $12
(C) $7
(D) $7.50
(E) $8

3. COMMISSION

In order to inspire sales, many companies pay their salespeople a percentage of the money the salespeople bring in. This is called a commission.

Example:

Mr. Silver sells shoes at the Emporium, where he is paid $100 per week plus a 5% commission on all his sales. How much does he earn in a week in which his sales amount to $1840?

Solution:

Find 5% of $1840 and add this amount to $100.

$$1840$$
$$\times .05$$
$$\overline{\$92.00} + \$100 = \$192$$

Example:

Audrey sells telephone order merchandise for a cosmetics company. She keeps 12% of all money collected. One month she was able to keep $108. How much did she forward to the cosmetics company?

Solution:

We must first find the total amount of her sales by asking: 108 is 12% of what number?
$108 = .12x$
$10800 = 12x$
$900 = x$
If Audrey collected $900 and kept $108, she sent the company $792.

Exercise 3

Work out each problem. Circle the letter that appears before your answer.

1. Janice receives a 6% commission for selling newspaper advertisements. If she sells 15 ads for $50 each, how much does she earn?

   (A) $30
   (B) $40
   (C) $45
   (D) $18
   (E) $450

2. Michael sells appliances and receives a salary of $125 per week plus a 5% commission on all sales over $750. How much does he earn in a week in which his sales amount to $2130?

   (A) $69
   (B) $294
   (C) $106.50
   (D) $194
   (E) $162.50

3. Mr. Rosen receives a salary of $100 per month plus a commission of 3% of his sales. What was the amount of his sales in a month in which he earned a total salary of $802?

   (A) $23,500
   (B) $23,400
   (C) $7800
   (D) $7900
   (E) $7700

4. Bobby sent $27 to the newspaper dealer for whom he delivers papers, after deducting his 10% commission. How many papers did he deliver if they sell for 20 cents each?

   (A) 150
   (B) 135
   (C) 600
   (D) 160
   (E) 540

5. Mrs. Mitherz wishes to sell her home. She must pay the real estate agent who makes the sale 8% of the selling price. At what price must she sell her home if she wishes to net $73,600?

   (A) $79,488
   (B) $75,000
   (C) $80,000
   (D) $82,400
   (E) $84,322

4. PROFIT AND LOSS

When a merchant purchases an item, he adds a percent of this cost to what he paid to arrive at a selling price. This amount is called his profit.

Example:

A radio sells for $40, giving the dealer a 25% profit. What was his cost?

Solution:

If the dealer gets back all of his cost plus an extra 25%, then the $40 sales price represents 125% of his cost.

$1.25x = 40$

$125x = 4000$

$x = \$32$

Example:

Joan's Boutique usually sells a handbag for $80, which yields a $33\frac{1}{3}\%$ profit. During a special sale, the profit is cut to 10%. What is the sale price of the handbag?

Solution:

$80 represents $133\frac{1}{3}\%$ or $\frac{4}{3}$ of the cost.

$$\frac{4}{3}x = 80$$

$$4x = 240$$

$$x = 60$$

If the cost was $60 and the dealer wishes to add 10% for profit, he must add 10% of $60 or $6, making the sale price $66.

If a merchant sells an article for less than his cost, he takes a loss. A loss is figured as a percent of his cost in the same manner we figured a profit in the previous examples.

Exercise 4

Work out each problem. Circle the letter that appears before your answer.

1. Steve buys a ticket to the opera. At the last moment, he finds he cannot go and sells the ticket to Judy for $10, which was a loss of $16\frac{2}{3}\%$. What was the original price of the ticket?

    (A) $8.33
    (B) $16.66
    (C) $12
    (D) $11.66
    (E) $15

2. Alice bought a bicycle for $120. After using it for only a short time, she sold it to a bike store at a 20% loss. How much money did the bike store give Alice?

    (A) $24
    (B) $96
    (C) $144
    (D) $100
    (E) $108

3. Julie's Dress Shop sold a gown for $150, thereby making a 25% profit. What was the cost of the gown to the dress shop?

    (A) $120
    (B) $112.50
    (C) $117.50
    (D) $187.50
    (E) $125

4. If a music store sells a clarinet at a profit of 20% based on the selling price, what percent is made on the cost?

    (A) 20
    (B) 40
    (C) 25
    (D) 80
    (E) none of these

5. Radio House paid $60 for a tape player. At what price should it be offered for sale if the store offers customers a 10% discount but still wants to make a profit of 20% of the cost?

    (A) $64.80
    (B) $72
    (C) $79.20
    (D) $80
    (E) $84.20

5. TAXES

Taxes are a percent of money spent, money earned, or value.

Example:

Broome County has a 4% sales tax on appliances. How much will Mrs. Steinberg have to pay for a new dryer marked at $240?

Solution:

Find 4% of $240 to figure the tax and add this amount to $240. This can be done in one step by finding 104% of $240.

$$
\begin{array}{r}
240 \\
\times \quad 1.04 \\
\hline
960 \\
24000 \\
\hline
\$249.60
\end{array}
$$

Example:

The Social Security tax is $7\frac{1}{4}\%$. How much must Mrs. Grossman pay in a year if her salary is $2000 per month?

Solution:

Her annual salary is 12(2000) or $24,000. Find $7\frac{1}{4}\%$ of $24,000.

$$7\frac{1}{4}\% = 7.25\% = .0725$$

$$
\begin{array}{r}
24,000 \\
\times .0725 \\
\hline
12\ 0000 \\
48\ 0000 \\
1680\ 0000 \\
\hline
\$1740.0000
\end{array}
$$

Exercise 5

Work out each problem. Circle the letter that appears before your answer.

1. In Manorville, the current rate for school taxes is 7.5% of property value. Find the tax on a house assessed at $20,000.

   (A) $150
   (B) $1500
   (C) $15,000
   (D) $1250
   (E) $105

2. The income tax in a certain state is figured at 2% of the first $1000, 3% of the next $2000, 4% of the next $3000, and 5% thereafter. Find the tax on an income of $25,000.

   (A) $1150
   (B) $1015
   (C) $295
   (D) $280
   (E) $187

3. The sales tax in Nassau County is 7%. If Mrs. Gutman paid a total of $53.50 for new curtains, what was the marked price of the curtains?

   (A) $49.75
   (B) $49
   (C) $57.25
   (D) $50
   (E) $45.86

4. Eric pays r% tax on an article marked at s dollars. How many dollars tax does he pay?

   (A) $\dfrac{s}{100r}$

   (B) rs

   (C) $\dfrac{100s}{r}$

   (D) $100rs$

   (E) $\dfrac{rs}{100}$

5. The sales tax on luxury items is 8%. If Mrs. Behr purchases a mink coat marked at $4000, what will be the total price for the coat, including tax?

   (A) $320
   (B) $4032
   (C) $4320
   (D) $4500
   (E) $500

RETEST

Work out each problem. Circle the letter that appears before your answer.

1. A TV sells for $121. What was the cost if the profit is 10% of the cost?
   (A) $110
   (B) $108.90
   (C) $120
   (D) $116
   (E) $111.11

2. Green's Sport Shop offers its salespeople an annual salary of $10,000 plus a 6% commission on all sales above $20,000. Every employee receives a Christmas bonus of $500. What are Mr. Cahn's total earnings in a year in which his sales amounted to $160,000?
   (A) $18,900
   (B) $18,400
   (C) $19,600
   (D) $20,100
   (E) $8900

3. A car dealer purchased 40 new cars at $6500 each. He sold 40% of them at $8000 each and the rest at $9000 each. What was his total profit?
   (A) $24,000
   (B) $60,000
   (C) $84,000
   (D) $344,000
   (E) $260,000

4. Mr. Adams' income rose from $20,000 one year to $23,000 the following year. What was the percent of increase?
   (A) 3%
   (B) 12%
   (C) 15%
   (D) 13%
   (E) 87%

5. The enrollment at Walden School is 1400. If 20% of the students study French, 25% study Spanish, 10% study Italian, 15% study German, and the rest study no language, how many students do not study a language, assuming each student may study only one language?
   (A) 30
   (B) 42
   (C) 560
   (D) 280
   (E) 420

6. How much money is saved by buying a car priced at $6000 with a single discount of 15% rather than buying the same car with a discount of 10% then 5%?
   (A) $51.30
   (B) $30
   (C) $780
   (D) $87
   (E) $900

7. At the Acme Cement Company, employees contribute to a welfare fund at the rate of 4% of the first $1000 earned, 3% of the next $1000, 2% of the next $1000, and 1% of any additional income. What will Mr. Morris contribute in a year in which he earns $20,000?
   (A) $290
   (B) $200
   (C) $90
   (D) $260
   (E) $240

8. A salesman receives a commission of c% on a sale of D dollars. Find his commission.

   (A) cD

   (B) $\dfrac{cD}{100}$

   (C) $100cD$

   (D) $\dfrac{c}{100D}$

   (E) $\dfrac{100c}{D}$

9. John buys a tape player for $54 after receiving a discount of 10%. What was the marked price?
   (A) $48.60
   (B) $59.40
   (C) $60
   (D) $61.40
   (E) $64

10. What single discount is equivalent to two successive discounts of 15% and 10%?
    (A) 25%
    (B) 24.5%
    (C) 24%
    (D) 23.5%
    (E) 23%

SOLUTIONS TO PRACTICE EXERCISES

Diagnostic Test

1. (E) $30\% = \dfrac{3}{10}$

    $\dfrac{3}{10} \cdot 100 = 30$ books at \$10 each

    $= \$300$ in sales

    $100 - 30 = 70$ books at \$15 each

    $= \$1050$ in sales

    Total sales \$300 + \$1050 = \$1350

    Total profit \$1350 - \$1250 = \$100

2. (C) $25\% + 35\% + 5\% + 10\% = 75\%$

    $100\% - 75\% = 25\%$ for other expenses

    $25\% = \dfrac{1}{4}, \dfrac{1}{4} \cdot \$2000 = \$500$

3. (B) Amount of decrease = 200

    Percent of decrease $= \dfrac{200}{1200} = \dfrac{1}{6} = 16\dfrac{2}{3}\%$

4. (B) $62\dfrac{1}{2}\% = \dfrac{5}{8}$

    $\dfrac{5}{8} \cdot 152 = 95$ total wins needed

    9   5 - 50 = 45 wins still needed

5. (A) $20\% = \dfrac{1}{5}$

    $\dfrac{1}{5} \cdot 120 = 24$ employees laid off

    New number of employees = 96

    $12\dfrac{1}{2}\% = \dfrac{1}{8}$

    $\dfrac{1}{8} \cdot 96 = 12$ employees added to staff

    Therefore final number of employees is 108.
    Net change is 120 - 108 = decrease of 12.

6. (A)

    $40\% = \dfrac{2}{3}$ $\dfrac{2}{5} \cdot 80 = \$32$ off

    \$48 net price

    $35\% = \dfrac{7}{20}$ $\dfrac{7}{20} \cdot 90 = \$31.50$ off

    \$58.50 first net price

    $10\% = \dfrac{1}{10}$ $\dfrac{1}{10} \cdot 58.50 = \$5.85$ off

    \$52.65 net price

    $\$52.65 - \$48 = \$4.65$ was saved.

7. (D) 2% of \$1500 = \$30

    3% of \$2000 = \$60

    5% of \$3000 = \$150

    6% of (\$8000 - \$6500)

    = 6% of \$1500 = \$90

    Total tax = \$330

8. (B) He earns 4% of \$48.

    $\begin{array}{r} 48 \\ \times .04 \\ \hline \$1.92 \end{array}$

    Add this to his base salary of \$20: \$21.92.

9. (C) $\dfrac{2}{3} \cdot \dfrac{3}{4_2} = \dfrac{1}{2} = 50\%$ of the students will graduate from college.

10. (B) Total price is \$5000.

    Percent of total that was options =

    $\dfrac{1800}{5000} = \dfrac{9}{25} = 36\%$

Exercise 1

1. (B) Amount of increase = $2500

   Percent of increase = [amount of increase/original]

   $$\frac{2500}{25000} = \frac{1}{10} = 10\%$$

2. (B) Amount of increase = 20,000

   Percent of increase = $\frac{20,000}{80,000} = \frac{1}{4} = 25\%$

3. (D) Amount of decrease = $4

   Percent of decrease = $\frac{4}{25} = \frac{16}{100} = 16\%$

4. (A) Amount of increase $30,000

   Percent of increase = $\frac{30,000}{30,000} = 1 = 100\%$

5. (A) Amount of decrease = 50

   Percent of decrease = $\frac{50}{200} = \frac{1}{4} = 25\%$

Exercise 2

1. (A) $20\% = \frac{1}{5}$ $\frac{1}{5} \cdot 600 = \$120$ off
   $480 net price
   $10\% = \frac{1}{10}$ $\frac{1}{10} \cdot 600 = \$60$ off
   $540 first net price
   $\frac{1}{10} \cdot 540 = \$54$ off
   $486 net price

   Therefore, $6 is saved.

2. (C) $25\% = \frac{1}{4}$
   $\frac{1}{4} \cdot 60,000 = \$15,000$ added cost
   Original sale price = $75,000

   $20\% = \frac{1}{5}$ $\frac{1}{5} \cdot 75,000 = 15,000$ discount
   Final sale price $60,000

   Therefore he made nothing on the sale.

3. (B) Discount = 30 cents. Rate of discount is figured on the original price.
   $$\frac{30}{120} = \frac{1}{4} = 25\%$$

4. (D) $12\frac{1}{2}\% = \frac{1}{8}$ $\frac{1}{8} \cdot 160 = \$20$ discount
   New sale price = $140
   $3\% = \frac{3}{100}$ $\frac{3}{100} \cdot 140 = \frac{420}{100}$
   = $4.20 second discount

   $135.80 final sale price

   Therefore, $160 - $135.80 or $24.20 was saved.

5. (E) $6 is 75% of the marked price.

   $$6 = \frac{3}{4}x$$
   $$24 = 3x$$
   $$x = \$8$$

Exercise 3

1. (C) She sells 15 ads at $50 each for a total of $750. She earns 6% of this amount.

   $750 \times .06 = \$45.00$

2. (D) He earns 5% of ($2130 - $750).

   $1380 \times .05 = \$69.00$

   Add this to his base salary of $125: $194.

3. (B) If his base salary was $100, his commission amounted to $702. 702 is 3% of what?

   $702 = .03x$

   $70,200 = 3x$

   $\$23,400 = x$

4. (A) $27 is 90% of what he collected.

   $27 = .90x$

   $270 = 9x$

   $x = \$30$

   If each paper sells for 20 cents, he sold $\dfrac{30.00}{.20}$ or 150 papers.

5. (C) $73,600 is 92% of the selling price.

   $73,600 = .92x$

   $7,360,000 = 92x$

   $\$80,000 = x$

Exercise 4

1. (C) $16\dfrac{2}{3}\% = \dfrac{1}{6}$

   $10 is $\dfrac{5}{6}$ of the original price.

   $10 = \dfrac{5}{6}x$

   $60 = 5x$

   $x = 12$

2. (B) The store gave Alice 80% of the price she paid.

   $80\% = \dfrac{4}{5} \qquad \dfrac{4}{5} \cdot 120 = \$96$

3. (A) $150 is 125% of the cost.

   $150 = 1.25x$

   $15,000 = 125x$

   $x = \$120$

4. (C) Work with an easy number such as $100 for the selling price.

   $20\% = \dfrac{1}{5} \quad \dfrac{1}{5} \cdot 100 = \$20$ profit, thereby

   making the cost $80. $\dfrac{20}{80} = \dfrac{1}{4} = 25\%$

5. (D) The dealer wishes to make 20% or $\dfrac{1}{5}$ of

   $60, which is $12 profit. The dealer wishes to

   clear $60 + $12 or $72. $72 will be 90% of the

   marked price.

   $72 = .90x$

   $720 = 9x$

   $x = \$80$

Exercise 5

1. (B)
$$\begin{array}{r} 20{,}000 \\ \times \quad .075 \\ \hline 100\ 000 \\ 1400\ 000 \\ \hline 1500.000 \end{array}$$

2. (A) 2% of $1000   = $20

   3% of $2000 = $60

   4% of $3000 = $120

   5% of ($25,000 - $6,000)

   = 5% of $19,000 = $950

   Total tax = $1150

3. (D) $53.50 is 107% of the marked price

   $53.50 = 1.07x$

   $5350 = 107x$

   $x = \$50$

4. (E) $r\% = \dfrac{r}{100}$ $\dfrac{r}{100} \cdot s = \dfrac{rs}{100}$

5. (C)
$$\begin{array}{r} 4000 \\ \times \quad .08 \\ \hline 320.00 \text{ tax} \end{array}$$ Total price $4320

Retest

1. (A) $121 is 110% of the cost.

   $121 = 1.10x$

   $1210 = 11x$

   $x = \$110$

2. (A) He earns 6% of ($160,000 - $20,000).

$$\begin{array}{r} 140{,}000 \\ \times \quad .06 \\ \hline \$8400.00 \end{array}$$

   Add this to his base salary of $10,000 and his Christmas bonus of $500: $18,900.

3. (C)

   $40\% = \dfrac{2}{3}$ $\dfrac{2}{5} \cdot 40 = 16$ cars at 8000

   each = $128,000 in sales

   $40 - 16 = 24$ cars at $9000 each

   = $216,000 in sales

   Total sales $128,000 + $216,000

   = $344,000

   Total expense $6500 \cdot 40   = $260,000

   Total profit $344,000 - $260,000

   = $84,000

4. (C) Amount of increase = $3000

   Percent of increase $= \dfrac{3000}{20{,}000}$

   $= \dfrac{3}{20} = 15\%$

5. (E) 20% + 25% + 10% + 15% = 70%

   100% - 70% = 30% study no language

   $30\% = \dfrac{3}{10}$ $\dfrac{3}{10} \cdot 1400 = 420$

6. (B) $15\% = \dfrac{3}{20}$ $\dfrac{3}{20} \cdot \$6000 = \$900$ off

$\$5100$ net price

$10\% = \dfrac{1}{10}$ $\dfrac{1}{10} \cdot \$6000 = \$600$ off

$\$5400$ first net price

$5\% = \dfrac{1}{20}$ $\dfrac{1}{20} \cdot 5400 = \$270$ off

$\$5130$ net price

$\$5130 - \$5100 = \$30$ was saved.

7. (D) 4% of $\$1000 = \$40$

3% of $\$1000 = \$30$

2% of $\$1000 = \$20$

1% of $\$17,000 = \$170$

Total contribution $= \$260$

8. (B) $c\% = \dfrac{c}{100}$ $\dfrac{c}{100} \cdot D = \dfrac{cD}{100}$

9. (C) $\$54$ is 90% of the marked price.

$54 = \dfrac{9}{10}x$

$540 = 9x$

$x = \$60$

10. (D) Work with an easy number such as $\$100$.

$15\% = \dfrac{3}{20}$ $\dfrac{3}{20} \cdot \$100 = \$15$ off

$\$85$ first net price

$10\% = \dfrac{1}{10}$ $\dfrac{1}{10} \cdot \$85 = \$8.50$ off

$\$76.50$ net price

$\$100 - \$76.50 = \$23.50$ total discount

$\dfrac{23.50}{100} = 23.5\%$

Averages

DIAGNOSTIC TEST

Directions: Work out each problem. Circle the letter that appears before your answer.

Answers are at the end of the chapter.

1. Find the average of the first ten positive even integers.

   (A) 9
   (B) 10
   (C) 11
   (D) 12
   (E) $5\frac{1}{2}$

2. What is the average of $x - 4$, x, and $x + 4$?

   (A) $3x$
   (B) x
   (C) $x - 1$
   (D) $x + 1$
   (E) $\dfrac{3x - 8}{3}$

3. Find the average of $\sqrt{.09}$, .4, and $\dfrac{1}{2}$.

   (A) .31
   (B) .35
   (C) .04
   (D) .4
   (E) .45

4. Valerie received test grades of 93 and 88 on her first two French tests. What grade must she get on the third test to have an average of 92?

   (A) 95
   (B) 100
   (C) 94
   (D) 96
   (E) 92

5. The average of W and another number is A. Find the other number.

   (A) $A - W$
   (B) $A + W$
   (C) $\dfrac{1}{2}(A - W)$
   (D) $\dfrac{1}{2}(A + W)$
   (E) $2A - W$

6. The weight of three packages are 4 lb. 10 oz., 6 lb. 13 oz, and 3 lb. 6 oz. Find the average weight of these packages.

   (A) 4 lb. 43 oz.
   (B) 4 lb. $7\frac{1}{2}$ oz.
   (C) 4 lb. 15 oz.
   (D) 4 lb. 6 oz.
   (E) 4 lb. 12 oz.

7. If Barbara drove for 4 hours at 50 miles per hour and then for 2 more hours at 60 miles per hour, what was her average rate, in miles per hour, for the entire trip?

(A) 55

(B) $53\frac{1}{3}$

(C) $56\frac{2}{3}$

(D) 53

(E) $54\frac{1}{2}$

8. Mr. Maron employs three secretaries at a salary of $140 per week and five salespeople at a salary of $300 per week. What is the average weekly salary paid to an employee?

(A) $55
(B) $190
(C) $240
(D) $200
(E) $185

9. Which of the following statements are always true?

I.   The average of any three consecutive even integers is the middle integer.
II.   The average of any three consecutive odd integers is the middle integer.
III. The average of any three consecutive multiples of 5 is the middle number.

(A) I only
(B) II only
(C) I and II only
(D) I and III only
(E) I, II, and III

10. Mark has an average of 88 on his first four math tests. What grade must he earn on his fifth test in order to raise his average to 90?

(A) 92
(B) 94
(C) 96
(D) 98
(E) 100

1. SIMPLE AVERAGE

Most students are familiar with the method for finding an average and use this procedure frequently during the school year. To find the average of n numbers, find the sum of all the numbers and divide this sum by n.

Example:

Find the average of 12, 17, and 61.

Solution:

$$
\begin{array}{r}
12 \\
17 \\
+\ \ \underline{61} \\
3)\overline{90} \\
\overline{30}
\end{array}
$$

When the numbers to be averaged form an evenly spaced series, the average is simply the middle number. If we are finding the average of an even number of terms, there will be no middle number. In this case, the average is halfway between the two middle numbers.

Example:

Find the average of the first 40 positive even integers.

Solution:

Since these 40 addends are evenly spaced, the average will be half way between the 20th and 21st even integers. The 20th even integer is 40 (use your fingers to count if needed) and the 21st is 42, so the average of the first 40 positive even integers that range from 2 to 80 is 41.

The above concept must be clearly understood as it would use up much too much time to add the 40 numbers and divide by 40. Using the method described, it is no harder to find the average of 100 evenly spaced terms than it is of 40 terms.

In finding averages, be sure the numbers being added are all of the same form or in terms of the same units. To average fractions and decimals, they must all be written as fractions or all as decimals.

Example:

Find the average of $87\frac{1}{2}\%$, $\frac{1}{4}$, and .6

Solution:

Rewrite each number as a decimal before adding.

$$
\begin{array}{r}
.875 \\
.25 \\
+ .6 \\
\hline
3)\overline{1.725} \\
\hline
.575
\end{array}
$$

Exercise 1

Work out each problem. Circle the letter that appears before your answer.

1. Find the average of $\sqrt{.49}$, $\frac{3}{4}$, and 80%.
    - (A) .72
    - (B) .75
    - (C) .78
    - (D) .075
    - (E) .073

2. Find the average of the first 5 positive integers that end in 3.
    - (A) 3
    - (B) 13
    - (C) 18
    - (D) 23
    - (E) 28

3. The five men on a basketball team weigh 160, 185, 210, 200, and 195 pounds. Find the average weight of these players.
    - (A) 190
    - (B) 192
    - (C) 195
    - (D) 198
    - (E) 180

4. Find the average of a, $2a$, $3a$, $4a$, and $5a$.
    - (A) $3a^5$
    - (B) $3a$
    - (C) $2.8a$
    - (D) $2.8a^5$
    - (E) 3

5. Find the average of $\frac{1}{2}$, $\frac{1}{3}$, and $\frac{1}{4}$.
    - (A) $\frac{1}{9}$
    - (B) $\frac{13}{36}$
    - (C) $\frac{1}{27}$
    - (D) $\frac{13}{12}$
    - (E) $\frac{1}{3}$

2. TO FIND A MISSING NUMBER WHEN AN AVERAGE IS GIVEN

In solving this type of problem, it is easiest to use an algebraic equation that applies the definition of average. That is,

$$\text{average} = \frac{\text{sum of terms}}{\text{number of terms}}$$

Example:

The average of four numbers is 26. If three of the numbers are 50, 12, and 28, find the fourth number.

Solution:

$$\frac{50 + 12 + 28 + x}{4} = 26$$
$$50 + 12 + 28 + x = 104$$
$$90 + x = 104$$
$$x = 14$$

An alternative method of solution is to realize that the number of units below 26 must balance the number of units above 26. 50 is 24 units *above* 26. 12 is 14 units *below* 26. 28 is 2 units *above* 26. Therefore, we presently have 26 units (24 + 2) *above* 26 and only 14 units *below* 26. Therefore the missing number must be 12 units *below* 26, making it 14. When the numbers are easy to work with, this method is usually the fastest. Just watch your arithmetic.

Exercise 2

Work out each problem. Circle the letter that appears before your answer.

1. Dick's average for his freshman year was 88, his sophomore year was 94, and his junior year was 91. What average must he have in his senior year to leave high school with an average of 92?

    (A) 92
    (B) 93
    (C) 94
    (D) 95
    (E) 96

2. The average of *X*, *Y*, and another number is *M*. Find the missing number.

    (A) 3*M* - *X* + *Y*
    (B) 3*M* - *X* - *Y*
    (C) $\dfrac{M + X + Y}{3}$
    (D) *M* - *X* - *Y*
    (E) *M* - *X* + *Y*

3. The average of two numbers is 2*x*. If one of the numbers is *x* + 3, find the other number.

    (A) *x* - 3
    (B) 2*x* - 3
    (C) 3*x* - 3
    (D) -3
    (E) 3*x* + 3

4. On consecutive days, the high temperature in Great Neck was 86°, 82°, 90°, 92°, 80°, and 81°. What was the high temperature on the seventh day if the average high for the week was 84°?

    (A) 79°
    (B) 85°
    (C) 81°
    (D) 77°
    (E) 76°

5. If the average of five consecutive integers is 17, find the largest of these integers.

    (A) 17
    (B) 18
    (C) 19
    (D) 20
    (E) 21

3. WEIGHTED AVERAGE

When some numbers among terms to be averaged occur more than once, they must be given the appropriate weight. For example, if a student received four grades of 80 and one of 90, his average would not be the average of 80 and 90, but rather the average of 80, 80, 80, 80, and 90.

Example:

Mr. Martin drove for 6 hours at an average rate of 50 miles per hour and for 2 hours at an average rate of 60 miles per hour. Find his average rate for the entire trip.

Solution:

$$\frac{6(50) + 2(60)}{8} = \frac{300 + 120}{8} = \frac{420}{8} = 52\frac{1}{2}$$

Since he drove many more hours at 50 miles per hour than at 60 miles per hour, his average rate should be closer to 50 than to 60, which it is. In general, average rate can always be found by dividing the total distance covered by the total time spent traveling.

Exercise 3

Work out each problem. Circle the letter that appears before your answer.

1. In a certain gym class, 6 girls weigh 120 pounds each, 8 girls weigh 125 pounds each, and 10 girls weigh 116 pounds each. What is the average weight of these girls?

   (A) 120
   (B) 118
   (C) 121
   (D) 122
   (E) 119

2. In driving from San Francisco to Los Angeles, Arthur drove for three hours at 60 miles per hour and for 4 hours at 55 miles per hour. What was his average rate, in miles per hour, for the entire trip?

   (A) 57.5
   (B) 56.9
   (C) 57.1
   (D) 58.2
   (E) 57.8

3. In the Linwood School, five teachers earn $15,000 per year, three teachers earn $17,000 per year, and one teacher earns $18,000 per year. Find the average yearly salary of these teachers.

   (A) $16,667
   (B) $16,000
   (C) $17,000
   (D) $16,448
   (E) $16,025

4. During the first four weeks of summer vacation, Danny worked at a camp earning $50 per week. During the remaining six weeks of vacation, he worked as a stock boy earning $100 per week. What was his average weekly wage for the summer?

   (A) $80
   (B) $75
   (C) $87.50
   (D) $83.33
   (E) $82

5. If M students each received a grade of P on a physics test and N students each received a grade of Q, what was the average grade for this group of students?

   (A) $\dfrac{P + Q}{M + N}$

   (B) $\dfrac{PQ}{M + N}$

   (C) $\dfrac{MP + NQ}{M + N}$

   (D) $\dfrac{MP + NQ}{P + Q}$

   (E) $\dfrac{M + N}{P + Q}$

RETEST

Work out each problem. Circle the letter that appears before your answer.

1. Find the average of the first 14 positive odd integers.

    (A) 7.5
    (B) 13
    (C) 14
    (D) 15
    (E) 14.5

2. What is the average of $2x - 3$, $x + 1$, and $3x + 8$?

    (A) $6x + 6$
    (B) $2x - 2$
    (C) $2x + 4$
    (D) $2x + 2$
    (E) $2x - 4$

3. Find the average of $\dfrac{1}{5}$, 25%, and .09.

    (A) $\dfrac{2}{3}$
    (B) .18
    (C) .32
    (D) 20%
    (E) $\dfrac{1}{4}$

4. Andy received test grades of 75, 82, and 70 on three French tests. What grade must he earn on the fourth test to have an average of 80 on these four tests?

    (A) 90
    (B) 93
    (C) 94
    (D) 89
    (E) 96

5. The average of $2P$, $3Q$, and another number is S. Represent the third number in terms of P, Q, and S.

    (A) $S - 2P - 3Q$
    (B) $S - 2P + 3Q$
    (C) $3S - 2P + 3Q$
    (D) $3S - 2P - 3Q$
    (E) $S + 2P - 3Q$

6. The students of South High spent a day on the street collecting money to help cure birth defects. In counting up the collections, they found that 10 cans contained $5.00 each, 14 cans contained $6.50 each, and 6 cans contained $7.80 each. Find the average amount contained in each of these cans.

    (A) $6.14
    (B) $7.20
    (C) $6.26
    (D) $6.43
    (E) $5.82

7. The heights of the five starters on the Princeton basketball team are 6'6", 6'7", 6'9", 6'11", and 7'. Find the average height of these men.

    (A) $6'\ 8\dfrac{1}{5}"$
    (B) 6'9"
    (C) $6'\ 9\dfrac{3}{5}"$
    (D) $6'\ 9\dfrac{1}{5}"$
    (E) $6'\ 9\dfrac{1}{2}"$

8. Which of the following statements is always true?

    I.   The average of the first twenty integers is 10.5
    II. The average of the first ten positive integers is 5.
    III. The average of the first 4 positive integers that end in 2 is 17.

    (A) I only
    (B) II only
    (C) III only
    (D) I and III only
    (E) I, II, and III

9. Karen drove 40 miles into the country at 40 miles per hour and returned home by bus at 20 miles per hour. What was her average rate in miles per hour for the round trip?

    (A) 30
    (B) $25\dfrac{1}{2}$
    (C) $26\dfrac{2}{3}$
    (D) 20
    (E) $27\dfrac{1}{3}$

10. Mindy's average monthly salary for the first four months she worked was $300. What must be her average monthly salary for each of the next 8 months so that her average monthly salary for the year is $350?

    (A) $400
    (B) $380
    (C) $390
    (D) $375
    (E) $370

SOLUTIONS TO PRACTICE EXERCISES

Diagnostic Test

1. (C) The integers are 2, 4, 6, 8, 10, 12, 14, 16, 18, 20. Since these are evenly spaced, the average is the average of the two middle numbers, 10 and 12, or 11.

2. (B) These numbers are evenly spaced, so the average is the middle number x.

3. (D) $\sqrt{.09} = .3$

$$\frac{1}{2} = .5$$

$$.4 = .4$$

$$3\overline{)1.2}$$
$$.4$$

4. (A) 93 is 1 above 92; 88 is 4 below 92. So far, she has 1 point above 92 and 4 points below 92. Therefore, she needs another 3 points above 92, making a required grade of 95.

5. (E) $\dfrac{W + x}{2} = A$

$W + x = 2A$

$x = 2A - W$

6. (C)
    4 lb. 10 oz.
    6 lb. 13 oz.
   +3 lb. 6 oz.
   13 lb. 29 oz.

$$\frac{13\text{lb.}29\text{oz.}}{3} = \frac{12\text{lb.}45\text{oz.}}{3} = 4 \text{ lb. } 15 \text{ oz.}$$

7. (B) $4(50) = 200$

$2(60) = \underline{120}$

$$6\overline{)320}$$

$$53\frac{1}{3}$$

8. (C) $3(140) = 420$

$5(300) = \underline{1500}$

$$8\overline{)1920}$$
$$240$$

9. (E) The average of any three numbers that are evenly spaced is the middle number.

10. (D) Since 88 is 2 below 90, Mark is 8 points below 90 after the first four tests. Thus, he needs a 98 to make the required average of 90.

Exercise 1

1. (B) $\sqrt{.49} = .7$

$$\frac{3}{4} = .75$$

$$80\% = .80$$

$$3\overline{)2.25}$$
$$.75$$

2. (D) The integers are 3, 13, 23, 33, 43. Since these are evenly spaced, the average is the middle integer, 23.

3. (A) $160 + 185 + 210 + 200 + 195 = 950$

$$\frac{950}{5} = 190$$

4. (B) These numbers are evenly spaced, so the average is the middle number, $3a$.

5. (B) $\dfrac{1}{2} + \dfrac{1}{3} + \dfrac{1}{4} = \dfrac{6}{12} + \dfrac{4}{12} + \dfrac{3}{12} = \dfrac{13}{12}$

To divide this sum by 3, multiply by $\dfrac{1}{3}$

$$\frac{13}{12} \cdot \frac{1}{3} = \frac{13}{36}$$

Exercise 2

1. (D) 88 is 4 below 92; 94 is 2 above 92; 91 is 1 below 92. So far, he has 5 points below 92 and only 2 above. Therefore, he needs another 3 points above 92, making the required grade 95.

2. (B) $\dfrac{X + Y + x}{3} = M$

    $X + Y + x = 3M$

    $x = 3M - X - Y$

3. (C) $\dfrac{(x + 3) + n}{2} = 2x$

    $x + 3 + n = 4x$

    $n = 3x - 3$

4. (D) 86° is 2 above the average of 84; 82° is 2 below; 90° is 6 above; 92° is 8 above; 80° is 4 below; and 81° is 3 below. So far, there are 16° above and 9° below. Therefore, the missing term is 7° below the average, or 77°.

5. (C) 17 must be the middle integer, since the five integers are consecutive and the average is, therefore, the middle number. The numbers are 15, 16, 17, 18, and 19.

Exercise 3

1. (A)

    $6(120) = 720$

    $8(125) = 1000$

    $10(116) = \underline{1160}$

    $24)\overline{2880}$

    120

2. (C) $3(60) = 180$

    $4(55) = \underline{220}$

    $7)\overline{400}$

    $57\dfrac{1}{7}$

    which is 57.1 to the nearest tenth.

3. (B) $5(15{,}000) = 75{,}000$

    $3(17{,}000) = 51{,}000$

    $1(18{,}000) = \underline{18{,}000}$

    $9)\overline{144{,}000}$

    $16{,}000$

4. (A) $4(50) = 200$

    $6(100) = \underline{600}$

    $10)\overline{800}$

    80

5. (C) $M(P) = MP$

    $N(Q) = \underline{NQ}$

    $MP + NQ$

    Divide by the number of students, $M + N$.

Retest

1. (C) The integers are 1, 3, 5, 7, 9, 11, 13, 15, 17, 19, 21, 23, 25, 27. Since these are evenly spaced, the average is the average of the two middle numbers 13 and 15, or 14.

2. (D)
$$\begin{array}{r} 2x-3 \\ x+1 \\ +3x+8 \\ \hline 6x+6 \end{array}$$
$$\frac{6x+6}{3} = 2x+2$$

3. (B)
$$\frac{1}{5} = .20$$
$$25\% = .25$$
$$.09 = \underline{.09}$$
$$3)\overline{.54}$$
$$.18$$

4. (B) 75 is 5 below 80; 82 is 2 above 80; 70 is 10 below 80. So far, he is 15 points below and 2 points above 80. Therefore, he needs another 13 points above 80, or 93.

5. (D)
$$\frac{2P+3Q+x}{3} = S$$
$$2P+3Q+x = 3S$$
$$x = 3S - 2P - 3Q$$

6. (C)
$$10(\$5.00) = \$50$$
$$14(\$6.50) = \$91$$
$$6(\$7.80) = \$46.80$$
$$30)\overline{\$187.80}$$
$$\$6.26$$

7. (B) $6'6'' + 6'7'' + 6'11'' + 6'9'' + 7' = 31'33'' = 33'9''$

$$\frac{33'9''}{5} = 6'9''$$

8. (C) I. The average of the first twenty *positive* integers is 10.5.

    II. The average of the first ten positive integers is 5.5.

    III. The first four positive integers that end in 2 are 2, 12, 22, and 32. Their average is 17.

9. (C) Karen drove for 1 hour into the country and returned home by bus in 2 hours. Since the total distance traveled was 80 miles, her average rate for the round trip was $\frac{80}{3}$ or $26\frac{2}{3}$ miles per hour.

10. (D) Since $300 is $50 below $350, Mindy's salary for the first four months is $200 below $350. Therefore, her salary for each of the next 8 months must be $\frac{\$200}{8}$ or $25 above the average of $350, thus making the required salary $375.

Concepts of Algebra—Signed Numbers and Equations

8

DIAGNOSTIC TEST

Directions: Work out each problem. Circle the letter that appears before your answer.

Answers are at the end of the chapter.

1. When +4 is added to -6, the sum is

    (A) -10
    (B) +10
    (C) -24
    (D) -2
    (E) +2

2. The product of $(-3)(+4)\left(-\dfrac{1}{2}\right)\left(-\dfrac{1}{3}\right)$ is

    (A) -1
    (B) -2
    (C) +2
    (D) -6
    (E) +6

3. When the product of (-12) and $\left(+\dfrac{1}{4}\right)$ is divided by the product of (-18) and $\left(-\dfrac{1}{3}\right)$, the quotient is

    (A) +2
    (B) -2
    (C) $+\dfrac{1}{2}$
    (D) $-\dfrac{1}{2}$
    (E) $-\dfrac{2}{3}$

4. Solve for x: $ax + b = cx + d$

    (A) $\dfrac{d-b}{ac}$
    (B) $\dfrac{d-b}{a+c}$
    (C) $\dfrac{d-b}{a-c}$
    (D) $\dfrac{b-d}{ac}$
    (E) $\dfrac{b-d}{a-c}$

5. Solve for y: $\begin{aligned} 7x - 2y &= 2 \\ 3x + 4y &= 30 \end{aligned}$

    (A) 2
    (B) 6
    (C) 1
    (D) 11
    (E) -4

6. Solve for x: $\begin{aligned} x + y &= a \\ x - y &= b \end{aligned}$

    (A) $a + b$
    (B) $a - b$
    (C) $\dfrac{1}{2}(a+b)$
    (D) $\dfrac{1}{2}ab$
    (E) $\dfrac{1}{2}(a-b)$

7. Solve for *x:* $4x^2 - 2x = 0$

    (A) $\frac{1}{2}$ only

    (B) 0 only

    (C) $-\frac{1}{2}$ only

    (D) $\frac{1}{2}$ or 0

    (E) $-\frac{1}{2}$ or 0

8. Solve for *x:* $x^2 - 4x - 21 = 0$

    (A) 7 or 3
    (B) -7 or -3
    (C) -7 or 3
    (D) 7 or -3
    (E) none of these

9. Solve for *x:* $\sqrt{x+1} - 3 = -7$

    (A) 15
    (B) 47
    (C) 51
    (D) 39
    (E) no solution

10. Solve for *x:* $\sqrt{x^2 + 7} - 1 = x$

    (A) 9
    (B) 3
    (c) -3
    (D) 2
    (E) no solution

1. SIGNED NUMBERS

The rules for operations with signed numbers are basic to successful work in algebra. Be sure you know, and can apply, the following rules.

Addition: To add numbers with the same sign, add the magnitudes of the numbers and keep the same sign. To add numbers with different signs, subtract the magnitudes of the numbers and use the sign of the number with the greater magnitude.

Example:

Add the following:

+4	-4	-4	+4
+7	-7	+7	-7
+11	-11	+3	-3

Subtraction: Change the sign of the number to be subtracted and proceed with the rules for addition. Remember that subtracting is really adding the additive inverse.

Example:

Subtract the following:

+4	-4	-4	+4
+7	-7	+7	-7
-3	+3	-11	+11

Multiplication: If there is an odd number of negative factors, the product is negative. An even number of negative factors gives a positive product.

Example:

Find the following products:

$$(+4)(+7) = +28 \quad (-4)(-7) = +28$$
$$(+4)(-7) = -28 \quad (-4)(+7) = -28$$

Division: If the signs are the same, the quotient is positive. If the signs are different, the quotient is negative.

Example:

Divide the following:

$$\frac{+28}{+4} = +7 \qquad \frac{-28}{+4} = -7$$
$$\frac{-28}{-4} = +7 \qquad \frac{+28}{-4} = -7$$

Exercise 1

Work out each problem. Circle the letter that appears before your answer.

1. At 8 A.M. the temperature was -4°. If the temperature rose 7 degrees during the next hour, what was the thermometer reading at 9 A.M.?
    (A) +11°
    (B) -11°
    (C) +7°
    (D) +3°
    (E) -3°

2. In Asia, the highest point is Mount Everest, with an altitude of 29,002 feet, while the lowest point is the Dead Sea, 1286 feet below sea level. What is the difference in their elevations?
    (A) 27,716 feet
    (B) 30,288 feet
    (C) 28,284 feet
    (D) 30,198 feet
    (E) 27,284 feet

3. Find the product of (-6)(-4)(-4) and (-2).
    (A) -16
    (B) +16
    (C) -192
    (D) +192
    (E) -98

4. The temperatures reported at hour intervals on a winter evening were +4°, 0°, -1°, -5°, and -8°. Find the average temperature for these hours.
    (A) -10°
    (B) -2°
    (C) +2°
    (D) $-2\frac{1}{2}$°
    (E) -3°

5. Evaluate the expression $5a - 4x - 3y$ if $a = -2$, $x = -10$, and $y = 5$.
    (A) +15
    (B) +25
    (C) -65
    (D) -35
    (E) +35

2. SOLUTION OF LINEAR EQUATIONS

Equations are the basic tools of algebra. The techniques of solving an equation are not difficult. Whether an equation involves numbers or only letters, the basic steps are the same.

1. If there are fractions or decimals, remove them by multiplication.

2. Remove any parentheses by using the distributive law.

3. Collect all terms containing the unknown for which you are solving on the same side of the equal sign. Remember that whenever a term crosses the equal sign from one side of the equation to the other, it must pay a toll. That is, it must change its sign.

4. Determine the coefficient of the unknown by combining similar terms or factoring when terms cannot be combined.

5. Divide both sides of the equation by the coefficient.

Example:

Solve for x: $5x - 3 = 3x + 5$

Solution:

$2x = 8$

$x = 4$

Example:

Solve for x: $\dfrac{2}{3}x - 10 = \dfrac{1}{4}x + 15$

Solution:

Multiply by 12. $8x - 120 = 3x + 180$

$$5x = 300$$

$$x = 60$$

Example:

Solve for x: $.3x + .15 = 1.65$

Solution:

Multiply by 100. $30x + 15 = 165$

$$30x = 150$$

$$x = 5$$

Example:

Solve for x: $ax - r = bx - s$

Solution:

$$ax - bx = r - s$$

$$x(a - b) = r - s$$

$$x = \frac{r - s}{a - b}$$

Peterson's Math Exercises for the SAT

Example:

Solve for *x:* 6*x* - 2 = 8(*x* - 2)

Solution:

$$6x - 2 = 8x - 16$$
$$14 = 2x$$
$$x = 7$$

Exercise 2

Work out each problem. Circle the letter that appears before your answer.

1. Solve for *x:* 3*x* - 2 = 3 + 2*x*

    (A) 1
    (B) 5
    (C) -1
    (D) 6
    (E) -5

2. Solve for *a:* 8 - 4(*a* - 1) = 2 + 3(4 - *a*)

    (A) $-\dfrac{5}{3}$

    (B) $-\dfrac{7}{3}$

    (C) 1
    (D) -2
    (E) 2

3. Solve for *x:* $\dfrac{1}{8}y + 6 = \dfrac{1}{4}y$

    (A) 48
    (B) 14
    (C) 6
    (D) 1
    (E) 2

4. Solve for *x:* .02(*x* - 2) = 1

    (A) 2.5
    (B) 52
    (C) 1.5
    (D) 51
    (E) 6

5. Solve for *x:* 4(*x* - *r*) = 2*x* + 10*r*

    (A) 7*r*
    (B) 3*r*
    (C) *r*
    (D) 5.5*r*

    (E) $2\dfrac{1}{3}r$

3. SIMULTANEOUS EQUATIONS IN TWO UNKNOWNS

In solving equations with two unknowns, it is necessary to work with two equations simultaneously. The object is to eliminate one of the unknowns, resulting in an equation with one unknown that can be solved by the methods of the previous section. This can be done by multiplying one or both equations by suitable constants in order to make the coefficients of one of the unknowns the same. Remember that multiplying *all* terms in an equation by the same constant does not change its value. The unknown can then be removed by adding or subtracting the two equations. When working with simultaneous equations, always be sure to have the terms containing the unknowns on one side of the equation and the remaining terms on the other side.

Example:

Solve for x: $7x + 5y = 15$
$$5x - 9y = 17$$

Solution:

Since we wish to solve for x, we would like to eliminate the y terms. This can be done by multiplying the top equation by 9 and the bottom equation by 5. In doing this, both y coefficients will have the same magnitude.

Multiplying the first by 9, we have

$63x + 45y = 135$

Multiplying the second by 5, we have

$25x - 45y = 85$

Since the y terms now have opposite signs, we can eliminate y by adding the two equations. If they had the same signs, we would eliminate by subtracting the two equations.

Adding, we have

$$63x + 45y = 135$$
$$\underline{25x - 45y \qquad = 85}$$
$$88x = 220$$
$$x = 2\frac{1}{2}$$

Since we were only asked to solve for x, we stop here. If we were asked to solve for both x and y, we would now substitute $2\frac{1}{2}$ for x in either equation and solve the resulting equation for y.

$$7(2.5) + 5y = 15$$
$$17.5 + 5y = 15$$
$$5y = -2.5$$
$$y = -.5 \text{ or } -\frac{1}{2}$$

Example:

Solve for *x:* $ax + by = r$

$$cx - dy = s$$

Solution:

Multiply the first equation by *d* and the second by *b* to eliminate the *y* terms by addition.

$$adx + bdy = dr$$
$$\underline{bcx - bdy = bs}$$
$$adx + bcx = dr + bs$$

Factor out *x* to determine the coefficient of *x*.

$$x(ad + bc) = dr + bs$$
$$x = \frac{dr + bs}{ad + bc}$$

Exercise 3

Work out each problem. Circle the letter that appears before your answer.

1. Solve for *x:* $x - 3y = 3$
$$2x + 9y = 11$$

   (A) 2
   (B) 3
   (C) 4
   (D) 5
   (E) 6

2. Solve for *x:* $.6x + .2y = 2.2$
$$.5x - .2y = 1.1$$

   (A) 1
   (B) 3
   (C) 30
   (D) 10
   (E) 11

3. Solve for *y:* $2x + 3y = 12b$
$$3x - y = 7b$$

   (A) $7\frac{1}{7}b$
   (B) $2b$
   (C) $3b$

   (D) $1\frac{2}{7}$
   (E) $-b$

4. If $2x = 3y$ and $5x + y = 34$, find *y*.

   (A) 4
   (B) 5
   (C) 6
   (D) 6.5
   (E) 10

5. If $x + y = -1$ and $x - y = 3$, find *y*.

   (A) 1
   (B) -2
   (C) -1
   (D) 2
   (E) 0

4. QUADRATIC EQUATIONS

In solving quadratic equations, there will always be two roots, even though these roots may be equal. A complete quadratic equation is of the form $ax^2 + bx + c = 0$, where a, b, and c are integers. At the level of this examination, $ax^2 + bx + c$ can always be factored. If b and/or c is equal to 0, we have an incomplete quadratic equation, which can still be solved by factoring and will still have two roots.

Example:

$$x^2 + 5x = 0$$

Solution:

Factor out a common factor of x.

$$x(x + 5) = 0$$

If the product of two factors is 0, either factor may be set equal to 0, giving $x = 0$ or $x + 5 = 0$. From these two linear equations, we find the two roots of the given quadratic equation to be $x = 0$ and $x = -5$.

Example:

$$6x^2 - 8x = 0$$

Solution:

Factor out a common factor of $2x$.

$$2x(3x - 4) = 0$$

Set each factor equal to 0 and solve the resulting linear equations for x.

$$2x = 0 \qquad 3x - 4 = 0$$
$$x = 0 \qquad 3x = 4$$
$$x = \frac{4}{3}$$

The roots of the given quadratic are 0 and $\frac{4}{3}$.

Example:

$$x^2 - 9 = 0$$

Solution:

$$x^2 = 9$$
$$x = \pm 3$$

Remember there must be two roots. This equation could also have been solved by factoring $x^2 - 9$ into $(x + 3)(x - 3)$ and setting each factor equal to 0. Remember that the difference of two perfect squares can always be factored, with one factor being the sum of the two square roots and the second being the difference of the two square roots.

Example:

$$x^2 - 8 = 0$$

Solution:

Since 8 is not a perfect square, this cannot be solved by factoring.

$$x^2 = 8$$
$$x = \pm\sqrt{8}$$

Simplifying the radical, we have $\sqrt{4} \cdot \sqrt{2}$, or $x = \pm 2\sqrt{2}$

Example:

$16x^2 - 25 = 0$

Solution:

Factoring, we have
$(4x - 5)(4x + 5) = 0$
Setting each factor equal to 0, we have

$$x = \pm\frac{5}{4}$$

If we had solved without factoring, we would have found $16x^2 = 25$

$$x^2 = \frac{25}{16}$$

$$x = \pm\frac{5}{4}$$

Example:

$x^2 + 6x + 8 = 0$

Solution:

$(x + 2)(x + 4) = 0$
If the last term of the trinomial is positive, both binomial factors must have the same sign, since the last two terms multiply to a positive product. If the middle term is also positive, both factors must be positive since they also add to a positive sum. Setting each factor equal to 0, we have $x = -4$ or $x = -2$

Example:

$x^2 - 2x - 15 = 0$

Solution:

We are now looking for two numbers that multiply to -15; therefore they must have opposite signs. To give -2 as a middle coefficient, the numbers must be -5 and +3.
$(x - 5)(x + 3) = 0$
This equation gives the roots 5 and -3.

Exercise 4

Work out each problem. Circle the letter that appears before your answer.

1. Solve for x: $x^2 - 8x - 20 = 0$
   - (A) 5 and -4
   - (B) 10 and -2
   - (C) -5 and 4
   - (D) -10 and -2
   - (E) -10 and 2

2. Solve for x: $25x^2 - 4 = 0$
   - (A) $\dfrac{4}{25}$ and $-\dfrac{4}{25}$
   - (B) $\dfrac{2}{5}$ and $-\dfrac{2}{5}$
   - (C) $\dfrac{2}{5}$ only
   - (D) $-\dfrac{2}{5}$ only
   - (E) none of these

3. Solve for *x:* $6x^2 - 42x = 0$

   (A) 7 only
   (B) -7 only
   (C) 0 only
   (D) 7 and 0
   (E) -7 and 0

4. Solve for *x:* $x^2 - 19x + 48 = 0$

   (A) 8 and 6
   (B) 24 and 2
   (C) -16 and -3
   (D) 12 and 4
   (E) none of these

5. Solve for *x:* $3x^2 = 81$

   (A) $9\sqrt{3}$
   (B) $\pm 9\sqrt{3}$
   (C) $3\sqrt{3}$
   (D) $\pm 3\sqrt{3}$
   (E) ± 9

5. EQUATIONS CONTAINING RADICALS

In solving equations containing radicals, it is important to get the radical alone on one side of the equation. Then square both sides to eliminate the radical sign. Solve the resulting equation. Remember that all solutions to radical equations must be checked, as squaring both sides may sometimes result in extraneous roots. In squaring each side of an equation, do not make the mistake of simply squaring each term. The entire side of the equation must be multiplied by itself.

Example:

$$\sqrt{x-3} = 4$$

Solution:

$$x - 3 = 16$$
$$x = 19$$

Checking, we have $\sqrt{16} = 4$, which is true.

Example:

$$\sqrt{x-3} = -4$$

Solution:

$$x - 3 = 16$$
$$x = 19$$

Checking, we have $\sqrt{16} = -4$, which is not true, since the radical sign means the principal, or positive, square root only. $\sqrt{16}$ is 4, not -4; therefore, this equation has no solution.

Example:

$$\sqrt{x^2 - 7} + 1 = x$$

Solution:

First get the radical alone on one side, then square.

$$\sqrt{x^2 - 7} = x - 1$$
$$x^2 - 7 = x^2 - 2x + 1$$
$$-7 = -2x + 1$$
$$2x = 8$$
$$x = 4$$

Checking, we have

$$\sqrt{9} + 1 = 4$$
$$3 + 1 = 4,$$

which is true.

Exercise 5

Work out each problem. Circle the letter that appears before your answer.

1. Solve for *y:* $\sqrt{2y} + 11 = 15$
   - (A) 4
   - (B) 2
   - (C) 8
   - (D) 1
   - (E) no solution

2. Solve for *x:* $4\sqrt{2x - 1} = 12$
   - (A) 18.5
   - (B) 4
   - (C) 10
   - (D) 5
   - (E) no solution

3. Solve for *x:* $\sqrt{x^2 - 35} = 5 - x$
   - (A) 6
   - (B) -6
   - (C) 3
   - (D) -3
   - (E) no solution

4. Solve for *y:* $26 = 3\sqrt{2y} + 8$
   - (A) 6
   - (B) 18
   - (C) 3
   - (D) -6
   - (E) no solution

5. Solve for *x:* $\sqrt{\dfrac{2x}{5}} = 4$
   - (A) 10
   - (B) 20
   - (C) 30
   - (D) 40
   - (E) no solution

RETEST

Work out each problem. Circle the letter that appears before your answer.

1. When -5 is subtracted from the sum of -3 and +7, the result is
   (A) +15
   (B) -1
   (C) -9
   (D) +9
   (E) +1

2. The product of $\left(-\dfrac{1}{2}\right)(-4)(+12)\left(-\dfrac{1}{6}\right)$ is
   (A) 2
   (B) -2
   (C) 4
   (D) -4
   (E) -12

3. When the sum of -4 and -5 is divided by the
   product of 9 and $-\dfrac{1}{27}$, the result is
   (A) -3
   (B) +3
   (C) -27
   (D) +27
   (E) $-\dfrac{1}{3}$

4. Solve for x: $7b + 5d = 5x - 3b$
   (A) $2bd$
   (B) $2b + d$
   (C) $5b + d$
   (D) $3bd$
   (E) $2b$

5. Solve for y: $2x + 3y = 7$
   $3x - 2y = 4$
   (A) 6
   (B) $5\dfrac{4}{5}$
   (C) 2
   (D) 1
   (E) $5\dfrac{1}{3}$

6. Solve for x: $3x + 2y = 5a + b$
   $4x - 3y = a + 7b$
   (A) $a + b$
   (B) $a - b$
   (C) $2a + b$
   (D) $17a + 17b$
   (E) $4a - 6b$

7. Solve for x: $8x^2 + 7x = 6x + 4x^2$
   (A) $-\dfrac{1}{4}$
   (B) 0 and $\dfrac{1}{4}$
   (C) 0
   (D) 0 and $-\dfrac{1}{4}$
   (E) none of these

8. Solve for x: $x^2 + 9x - 36 = 0$
   (A) -12 and +3
   (B) +12 and -3
   (C) -12 and -3
   (D) 12 and 3
   (E) none of these

9. Solve for x: $\sqrt{x^2 + 3} = x + 1$
   (A) ±1
   (B) 1
   (C) -1
   (D) 2
   (E) no solution

10. Solve for x: $2\sqrt{x} = -10$
    (A) 25
    (B) -25
    (C) 5
    (D) -5
    (E) no solution

SOLUTIONS TO PRACTICE EXERCISES

Diagnostic Test

1. (D) $(+4) + (-6) = -2$

2. (B) An odd number of negative signs gives a negative product.

$$(-3)(+4^2)\left(-\frac{1}{2}\right)\left(-\frac{1}{3}\right) = -2$$

3. (D) The product of (-12) and $\left(+\frac{1}{4}\right)$ is -3. The product of (-18) and $\left(-\frac{1}{3}\right)$ is 6.

$$-\frac{3}{6} = -\frac{1}{2}$$

4. (C) $ax + b = cx + d$

$ax - cx = d - b$

$(a - c)x = d - b$

$x = \dfrac{d - b}{a - c}$

5. (B) Multiply the first equation by 3, the second by 7, and subtract.

$$21x - 6y = 6$$
$$21x + 28y = 210$$
$$-34y = -204$$
$$y = 6$$

6. (C) Add the two equations.

$x + y = a$

$x - y = b$

$2x = a + b$

$x = \dfrac{1}{2}(a + b)$

7. (D) $2x(2x - 1) = 0$

$2x = 0 \qquad 2x - 1 = 0$

$x = 0$ or $\dfrac{1}{2}$

8. (D) $(x - 7)(x + 3) = 0$

$x - 7 = 0 \qquad x + 3 = 0$

$x = 7$ or -3

9. (E) $\sqrt{x+1} - 3 = -7$

$\sqrt{x+1} = -4$

$x + 1 = 16$

$x = 15$

Checking, $\sqrt{16} - 3 = -7$, which is not true.

10. (B) $\sqrt{x^2 + 7} - 1 = x$

$\sqrt{x^2 + 7} = x + 1$

$x^2 + 7 = x^2 + 2x + 1$

$7 = 2x + 1$

$6 = 2x$

$x = 3$

Checking, $\sqrt{16} - 1 = 3$, which is true.

Exercise 1

1. (D) $(-4) + (+7) = +3$

2. (B) $(29,002) - (-1286) = 30,288$

3. (D) An even number of negative signs gives a positive product.

$6 \times 4 \times 4 \times 2 = 192$

4. (B)
$$\frac{+4 + 0 + (-1) + (-5) + (-8)}{5} = \frac{-10}{5} = -2°$$

5. (A) $5(-2) - 4(-10) - 3(5) = -10 + 40 - 15 = +15$

Exercise 2

1. (B) $3x - 2 = 3 + 2x$

    $x = 5$

2. (D) $8 - 4a + 4 = 2 + 12 - 3a$

    $12 - 4a = 14 - 3a$

    $-2 = a$

3. (A) Multiply by 8 to clear fractions.

    $y + 48 = 2y$

    $48 = y$

4. (B) Multiply by 100 to clear decimals.

    $2(x - 2) = 100$

    $2x - 4 = 100$

    $2x = 104$

    $x = 52$

5. (A) $4x - 4r = 2x + 10r$

    $2x = 14r$

    $x = 7r$

Exercise 3

1. (C) Multiply first equation by 3, then add.

    $3x - 9y = 9$

    $\underline{2x + 9y = 11}$

    $5x = 20$

    $x = 4$

2. (B) Multiply each equation by 10, then add.

    $6x + 2y = 22$

    $\underline{5x - 2y = 11}$

    $11x = 33$

    $x = 3$

3. (B) Multiply first equation by 3, second by 2, then subtract.

    $6x + 9y = 36b$

    $\underline{6x - 2y = 14b}$

    $11y = 22b$

    $y = 2b$

4. (A) $2x - 3y = 0$

    $5x + y = 34$

    Multiply first equation by 5, second by 2, and subtract.

    $10x - 15y = 0$

    $\underline{10x + 2y = 68}$

    $-17y = -68$

    $y = 4$

5. (B) Subtract equations.

    $x + y = -1$

    $\underline{x - y = 3}$

    $2y = -4$

    $y = -2$

Exercise 4

1. (B) $(x - 10)(x + 2) = 0$

   $x - 10 = 0 \quad x + 2 = 0$

   $x = 10$ or -2

2. (B) $(5x - 2)(5x + 2) = 0$

   $5x - 2 = 0 \quad 5x + 2 = 0$

   $x = \dfrac{2}{5}$ or $-\dfrac{2}{5}$

3. (D) $6x(x - 7) = 0$

   $6x = 0 \quad x - 7 = 0$

   $x = 0$ or 7

4. (E) $(x - 16)(x - 3) = 0$

   $x - 16 = 0 \quad x - 3 = 0$

   $x = 16$ or 3

5. (D) $x^2 = 27$

   $x = \pm\sqrt{27}$

   But $\sqrt{27} = \sqrt{9} \cdot \sqrt{3} = 3\sqrt{3}$

   Therefore $x = \pm 3\sqrt{3}$

Exercise 5

1. (C) $\sqrt{2y} = 4$

   $2y = 16$

   $y = 8$

   Checking, $\sqrt{16} = 4$, which is true.

2. (D) $4\sqrt{2x - 1} = 12$

   $\sqrt{2x - 1} = 3$

   $2x - 1 = 9$

   $2x = 10$

   $x = 5$

   Checking, $4\sqrt{9} = 12$, which is true.

3. (E) $x^2 - 35 = 25 - 10x + x^2$

   $-35 = 25 - 10x$

   $10x = 60$

   $x = 6$

   Checking, $\sqrt{1} = 5 - 6$, which is not true.

4. (B) $18 = 3\sqrt{2y}$

   $6 = \sqrt{2y}$

   $36 = 2y$

   $y = 18$

   Checking, $26 = 3\sqrt{36} + 8$

   $26 = 3(6) + 8$, which is true.

5. (D) $\dfrac{2x}{5} = 16$

   $2x = 80$

   $x = 40$

   Checking, $\sqrt{\dfrac{80}{5}} = \sqrt{16} = 4$, which is true.

Retest

1. (D) $(-3) + (+7) - (-5) = (+9)$

2. (D) An odd number of negative signs gives a negative product.

    $$\left(-\frac{1}{2}\right)\left(-4^2\right)\left(+\cancel{12}^2\right)\left(-\frac{1}{6}\right) = -4$$

3. (D) The sum of (-4) and (-5) is (-9). The

    product of 9 and $-\dfrac{1}{27}$ is $-\dfrac{1}{3}$.

    $$\frac{-9}{-\frac{1}{3}} = +27$$

4. (B) $7b + 5d = 5x - 3b$

    $10b + 5d = 5x$

    $x = 2b + d$

5. (D) Multiply first equation by 3, second by 2, then subtract.

    $$6x + 9y \quad\;\; = 21$$
    $$\underline{6x - 4y = 8}$$
    $$13y = 13$$
    $$y = 1$$

6. (A) Multiply first equation by 3, second by 2, then add.

    $$9x + 6y = 15a + 3b$$
    $$\underline{8x - 6y = 2a + 14b}$$
    $$17x = 17a + 17b$$
    $$x = a + b$$

7. (D) $4x^2 + x = 0$

    $$x(4x + 1) = 0$$
    $$x = 0 \qquad 4x + 1 = 0$$
    $$x = 0 \text{ or } -\frac{1}{4}$$

8. (A) $(x + 12)(x - 3) = 0$

    $$x + 12 = 0 \quad x - 3 = 0$$
    $$x = -12 \text{ or } + 3$$

9. (B) $\sqrt{x^2 + 3} = x + 1$

    $$x^2 + 3 = x^2 + 2x + 1$$
    $$3 = 2x + 1$$
    $$2 = 2x$$
    $$x = 1$$

    Checking, $\sqrt{4} = 1 + 1$, which is true.

10. (E) $2\sqrt{x} = -10$

    $$\sqrt{x} = -5$$
    $$x = 25$$

    Checking, $2\sqrt{25} = -10$, which is not true.

Literal Expressions

DIAGNOSTIC TEST

Directions: Work out each problem. Circle the letter that appears before your answer.

Answers are at the end of the chapter.

1. If one book costs c dollars, what is the cost, in dollars, of m books?

   (A) $m + c$

   (B) $\dfrac{m}{c}$

   (C) $\dfrac{c}{m}$

   (D) mc

   (E) $\dfrac{mc}{100}$

2. Represent the cost, in dollars, of k pounds of apples at c cents per pound.

   (A) kc

   (B) $100kc$

   (C) $\dfrac{kc}{100}$

   (D) $100k + c$

   (E) $\dfrac{k}{100} + c$

3. If p pencils cost c cents, what is the cost of one pencil?

   (A) $\dfrac{c}{p}$

   (B) $\dfrac{p}{c}$

   (C) pc

   (D) $p - c$

   (E) $p + c$

4. Express the number of miles covered by a train in one hour if it covers r miles in h hours.

   (A) rh

   (B) $\dfrac{h}{r}$

   (C) $\dfrac{r}{h}$

   (D) $r + h$

   (E) $r - h$

5. Express the number of minutes in h hours and m minutes.

   (A) mh

   (B) $\dfrac{h}{60} + m$

   (C) $60(h + m)$

   (D) $\dfrac{h + m}{60}$

   (E) $60h + m$

6. Express the number of seats in the school auditorium if there are r rows with s seats each and s rows with r seats each.

   (A) $2rs$
   (B) $2r + 2s$
   (C) $rs + 2$
   (D) $2r + s$
   (E) $r + 2s$

7. How many dimes are there in n nickels and q quarters?

    (A) $10nq$

    (B) $\dfrac{n+q}{10}$

    (C) $\dfrac{1}{2}n + \dfrac{5}{2}q$

    (D) $10n + 10q$

    (E) $2n + \dfrac{q}{10}$

8. Roger rents a car at a cost of D dollars per day plus c cents per mile. How many dollars must he pay if he uses the car for 5 days and drives 1000 miles?

    (A) $5D + 1000c$

    (B) $5D + \dfrac{c}{1000}$

    (C) $5D + 100c$

    (D) $5D + 10c$

    (E) $5D + c$

9. The cost of a long-distance telephone call is c cents for the first three minutes and m cents for each additional minute. Represent the price of a call lasting d minutes if d is more than 3.

    (A) $c + md$
    (B) $c + md - 3m$
    (C) $c + md + 3m$
    (D) $c + 3md$
    (E) cmd

10. The sales tax in Morgan County is $m\%$. Represent the total cost of an article priced at \$D.

    (A) $D + mD$

    (B) $D + 100mD$

    (C) $D + \dfrac{mD}{100}$

    (D) $D + \dfrac{m}{100}$

    (E) $D + 100m$

1. COMMUNICATING WITH LETTERS

Many students who have no trouble computing with numbers panic at the sight of letters. If you understand the concepts of a problem in which numbers are given, you simply need to apply the same concepts to letters. The computational processes are exactly the same. Just figure out what you would do if you had numbers and do exactly the same thing with the given letters.

Example:

Express the number of inches in y yards, f feet, and i inches.

Solution:

We must change everything to inches and add. Since a yard contains 36 inches, y yards will contain $36y$ inches. Since a foot contains 12 inches, f feet will contain $12f$ inches. The total number of inches is $36y + 12f + i$.

Example:

Find the number of cents in $2x$ - 1 dimes.

Solution:

To change dimes to cents we must multiply by 10. Think that 7 dimes would be 7 times 10 or 70 cents. Therefore the number of cents in $2x$ - 1 dimes is $10(2x - 1)$ or $20x - 10$.

Example:

Find the total cost of sending a telegram of *w* words if the charge is *c* cents for the first 15 words and *d* cents for each additional word, if *w* is greater than 15.

Solution:

To the basic charge of *c* cents, we must add *d* for each word over 15. Therefore, we add *d* for (*w* - 15) words. The total charge is *c* + *d*(*w* - 15) or *c* + *dw* - 15*d*.

Example:

Kevin bought *d* dozen apples at *c* cents per apple and had 20 cents left. Represent the number of cents he had before this purchase.

Solution:

In *d* dozen, there are 12*d* apples. 12*d* apples at *c* cents each cost 12*dc* cents. Adding this to the 20 cents he has left, we find he started with 12*dc* + 20 cents.

Exercise 1

Work out each problem. Circle the letter that appears before your answer.

1. Express the number of days in *w* weeks and *w* days.
    (A) $7w^2$
    (B) $8w$
    (C) $7w$
    (D) $7 + 2w$
    (E) w^2

2. The charge on the Newport Ferrry is *D* dollars for the car and driver and *m* cents for each additional passenger. Find the charge, in dollars, for a car containing four people.
    (A) $D + .03m$
    (B) $D + 3m$
    (C) $D + 4m$
    (D) $D + 300m$
    (E) $D + 400m$

3. If *g* gallons of gasoline cost *m* dollars, express the cost of *r* gallons.
    (A) $\dfrac{mr}{g}$

    (B) $\dfrac{rg}{m}$

    (C) rmg

    (D) $\dfrac{mg}{r}$

    (E) $\dfrac{m}{rg}$

4. How many quarters are equivalent to *n* nickels and *d* dimes?
    (A) $5n + 10d$
    (B) $25n + 50d$

    (C) $\dfrac{n + d}{25}$

    (D) $25n + 25d$

    (E) $\dfrac{n + 2d}{5}$

5. A salesman earns a base salary of $100 per week plus a 5% commission on all sales over $500. Find his total earnings in a week in which he sells *r* dollars worth of merchandise, with *r* being greater than 500.
    (A) $125 + .05r$
    (B) $75 + .05r$
    (C) $125r$
    (D) $100 + .05r$
    (E) $100 - .05r$

RETEST

Work out each problem. Circle the letter that appears before your answer.

1. If a school consists of b boys, g girls, and t teachers, represent the number of students in each class if each class contains the same number of students. (Assume that there is one teacher per class.)

    (A) $\dfrac{b+g}{t}$

    (B) $t(b+g)$

    (C) $\dfrac{b}{t}+g$

    (D) $bt+g$

    (E) $\dfrac{bg}{t}$

2. Represent the total cost, in cents, of b books at D dollars each and r books at c cents each.

    (A) $\dfrac{bD}{100}+rc$

    (B) $\dfrac{bD+rc}{100}$

    (C) $100bD+rc$

    (D) $bD+100rc$

    (E) $bD+\dfrac{rc}{100}$

3. Represent the number of feet in y yards, f feet, and i inches.

    (A) $\dfrac{y}{3}+f+12i$

    (B) $\dfrac{y}{3}+f+\dfrac{i}{12}$

    (C) $3y+f+i$

    (D) $3y+f+\dfrac{i}{12}$

    (E) $3y+f+12i$

4. In a group of m men, b men earn D dollars per week and the rest earn half that amount each. Represent the total number of dollars paid to these men in a week.

    (A) $bD+b-m$

    (B) $\dfrac{1}{2}D(b+m)$

    (C) $\dfrac{3}{2}bD+mD$

    (D) $\dfrac{3}{2}D(b+m)$

    (E) $bD+\dfrac{1}{2}mD$

5. Ken bought d dozen roses for r dollars. Represent the cost of one rose.

    (A) $\dfrac{r}{d}$

    (B) $\dfrac{d}{r}$

    (C) $\dfrac{12d}{r}$

    (D) $\dfrac{12r}{d}$

    (E) $\dfrac{r}{12d}$

6. The cost of mailing a package is c cents for the first b ounces and d cents for each additional ounce. Find the cost, in cents, for mailing a package weighing f ounces if f is more than b.

    (A) $(c+d)(f-b)$
    (B) $c+d(f-b)$
    (C) $c+bd$
    (D) $c+(d-b)$
    (E) $b+(f-b)$

7. Josh's allowance is m cents per week. Represent the number of dollars he gets in a year.

    (A) $\dfrac{3m}{25}$

    (B) $5200m$

    (C) $1200m$

    (D) $\dfrac{13m}{25}$

    (E) $\dfrac{25m}{13}$

8. If it takes T tablespoons of coffee to make c cups, how many tablespoons of coffee are needed to make d cups?

(A) $\dfrac{Tc}{d}$

(B) $\dfrac{T}{dc}$

(C) $\dfrac{Td}{c}$

(D) $\dfrac{d}{Tc}$

(E) $\dfrac{cd}{T}$

9. The charge for renting a rowboat on Loon Lake is D dollars per hour plus c cents for each minute into the next hour. How many dollars will Mr. Wilson pay if he used a boat from 3:40 P.M. to 6:20 P.M.?

(A) $D + 40c$
(B) $2D + 40c$
(C) $2D + 4c$
(D) $2D + .4c$
(E) $D + 4.c$

10. The cost for developing and printing a roll of film is c cents for processing the roll and d cents for each print. How much will it cost, in cents, to develop and print a roll of film with 20 exposures?

(A) $20c + d$
(B) $20(c + d)$
(C) $c + 20d$

(D) $c + \dfrac{d}{20}$

(E) $\dfrac{c + d}{20}$

SOLUTIONS TO PRACTICE EXERCISES

Diagnostic Test

1. (D) This can be solved by a proportion, comparing books to dollars.

$$\frac{1}{c} = \frac{m}{x}$$

$$x = mc$$

2. (C) The cost in cents of k pounds at c cents per pound is kc. To convert this to dollars, we divide by 100.

3. (A) This can be solved by a proportion, comparing pencils to cents.

$$\frac{p}{c} = \frac{1}{x}$$

$$x = \frac{c}{p}$$

4. (C) This can be solved by a proportion, comparing miles to hours.

$$\frac{r}{h} = \frac{x}{1}$$

$$\frac{r}{h} = x$$

5. (E) There are 60 minutes in an hour. In h hours there are $60h$ minutes. With m additional minutes, the total is $60h + m$.

6. (A) r rows with s seats each have a total of rs seats. s rows with r seats each have a total of sr seats. Therefore, the school auditorium has a total of $rs + sr$ or $2rs$ seats.

7. (C) In n nickels, there are $5n$ cents. In q quarters, there are $25q$ cents. Altogether we have $5n + 25q$ cents. To see how many dimes this is, divide by 10.

$$\frac{5n + 25q}{10} = \frac{n + 5q}{2} = \frac{1}{2}n + \frac{5}{2}q$$

8. (D) The daily charge for 5 days at D dollars per day is $5D$ dollars. The charge, in cents, for 1000 miles at c cents per mile is $1000c$ cents. To change this to dollars, we divide by 100 and get $10c$ dollars. Therefore, the total cost in dollars is $5D + 10c$.

9. (B) The cost for the first 3 minutes is c cents. The number of additional minutes is $(d - 3)$ and the cost at m cents for each additional minute is thus $m(d - 3)$ or $md - 3m$. Therefore, the total cost is $c + md - 3m$.

10. (C) The sales tax is $\frac{m}{100} \cdot D$ or $\frac{mD}{100}$.

Therefore, the total cost is $D + \frac{mD}{100}$.

Exercise 1

1. (B) There are 7 days in a week. *w* weeks contain 7*w* days. With *w* additional days, the total number of days is 8*w*.

2. (A) The charge is *D* dollars for car and driver. The three additional persons pay *m* cents each, for a total of 3*m* cents. To change this to dollars, divide by 100, for a total of $\frac{3m}{100}$ dollars. This can be written in decimal form as .03*m*. The total charge in dollars is then $D + .03m$.

3. (A) This can be solved by a proportion, comparing gallons to dollars.

$$\frac{g}{m} = \frac{r}{x}$$
$$gx = mr$$
$$x = \frac{mr}{g}$$

4. (E) In *n* nickels, there are 5*n* cents. In *d* dimes, there are 10*d* cents. Altogether, we have $5n + 10d$ cents. To see how many quarters this gives, divide by 25.

$$\frac{5n + 10d}{25} = \frac{n + 2d}{5},$$

since a fraction can be simplified when *every* term is divided by the same factor, in this case 5.

5. (B) Commission is paid on (*r* - 500) dollars. His commission is .05(*r* - 500) or .05*r* - 25. When this is added to his base salary of 100, we have 100 + .05*r* - 25, or 75 + .05*r*.

Retest

1. (A) The total number of boys and girls is $b + g$.

   Since there are *t* teachers, and thus *t* classes, the number of students in each class is $\frac{b + g}{t}$.

2. (C) The cost, in dollars, of *b* books at *D* dollars each is *bD* dollars. To change this to cents, we multiply by 100 and get 100*bD* cents. The cost of *r* books at *c* cents each is *rc* cents. Therefore, the total cost, in cents, is $100bD + rc$.

3. (D) In *y* yards there are 3*y* feet. In *i* inches there are $\frac{i}{12}$ feet. Therefore, the total number of feet is $3y + f + \frac{i}{12}$.

4. (B) The money earned by *b* men at *D* dollars per week is *bD* dollars. The number of men remaining is $(m - b)$, and since they earn $\frac{1}{2}D$ dollars per week, the money they earn is

$$\frac{1}{2}D(m - b) = \frac{1}{2}mD - \frac{1}{2}bD.$$ Therefore, the total amount earned is

$$bD + \frac{1}{2}mD - \frac{1}{2}bD = \frac{1}{2}bD + \frac{1}{2}mD = \frac{1}{2}D(b + m)$$

5. (E) This can be solved by a proportion, comparing roses to dollars. Since *d* dozen roses equals 12*d* roses,

$$\frac{12d}{r} = \frac{1}{x}$$
$$12d \cdot x = r$$
$$x = \frac{r}{12d}$$

6.   (B) The cost for the first *b* ounces is *c* cents. The number of additional ounces is (*f* - *b*), and the cost at *d* cents for each additional ounce is (*f* - *b*)*d*. Therefore, the total cost is *c* + *d*(*f* - *b*).

7.   (D) Since there are 52 weeks in a year, his allowance in cents is 52*m*. To change to dollars, we divide by 100 and get $\frac{52m}{100}$ or $\frac{13m}{25}$.

8. (C) This can be solved by a proportion comparing tablespoons to cups.

$$\frac{T}{c} = \frac{x}{d}$$
$$cx = Td$$
$$x = \frac{Td}{c}$$

9.   (D) The amount of time from 3:40 P.M. to 6:20 P.M. is 2 hrs. 40 min. Therefore, the charge at *D* dollars per hour and *c* cents per minute into the next hour is 2*D* dollars + 40*c* cents or 2*D* + .4*c* dollars.

10. (C) The cost for processing the roll is *c* cents. The cost for printing 20 exposures at *d* cents per print is 20*d* cents. Therefore, the total cost is *c* + 20*d*.

Roots and Radicals

DIAGNOSTIC TEST

Directions: Work out each problem. Circle the letter that appears before your answer.

Answers are at the end of the chapter.

1. The sum of $\sqrt{75}$ and $\sqrt{12}$ is

   (A) $\sqrt{87}$
   (B) $7\sqrt{3}$
   (C) $3\sqrt{5} + 3\sqrt{2}$
   (D) $29\sqrt{3}$
   (E) $3\sqrt{3}$

2. The difference between $\sqrt{125}$ and $\sqrt{45}$ is

   (A) $4\sqrt{5}$
   (B) $2\sqrt{5}$
   (C) 2
   (D) $5\sqrt{2}$
   (E) 10

3. The product of $\sqrt{9x}$ and $\sqrt{4x}$ is

   (A) $6\sqrt{x}$
   (B) $36\sqrt{x}$
   (C) $36x$
   (D) $6x$
   (E) $6x^2$

4. If $\dfrac{2}{x} = \sqrt{.16}$, then x equals

   (A) 50
   (B) 5
   (C) $.5$
   (D) $.05$
   (E) $.005$

5. The square root of 17,956 is exactly

   (A) 132
   (B) 133
   (C) 134
   (D) 135
   (E) 137

6. The square root of 139.24 is exactly

   (A) 1.18
   (B) 11.8
   (C) 118
   (D) $.118$
   (E) 1180

7. Find $\sqrt{\dfrac{x^2}{36} + \dfrac{x^2}{25}}$.

   (A) $\dfrac{11x}{30}$
   (B) $\dfrac{9x}{30}$
   (C) $\dfrac{x}{11}$
   (D) $\dfrac{2x}{11}$
   (E) $x\dfrac{\sqrt{61}}{30}$

8. $\sqrt{x^2 + y^2}$ is equal to

   (A) $x + y$
   (B) $x - y$
   (C) $(x + y)(x - y)$
   (D) $\sqrt{x^2} + \sqrt{y^2}$
   (E) none of these

9. Divide $8\sqrt{12}$ by $2\sqrt{3}$.

   (A) 16
   (B) 9
   (C) 8
   (D) 12
   (E) 96

10. $\left(\sqrt{2}\right)^5$ is equal to

    (A) 2
    (B) $2\sqrt{2}$
    (C) 4
    (D) $4\sqrt{2}$
    (E) 8

1. ADDITION AND SUBTRACTION OF RADICALS

The conditions under which radicals can be added or subtracted are much the same as the conditions for letters in an algebraic expression. The radicals act as a label, or unit, and must therefore be exactly the same. In adding or subtracting, we add or subtract the coefficients, or rational parts, and carry the radical along as a label, which does not change.

Example:

$$\sqrt{2} + \sqrt{3} \text{ cannot be added}$$
$$\sqrt{2} + \sqrt[3]{2} \text{ cannot be added}$$
$$4\sqrt{2} + 5\sqrt{2} = 9\sqrt{2}$$

Often, when radicals to be added or subtracted are not the same, simplification of one or more radicals will make them the same. To simplify a radical, we remove any perfect square factors from underneath the radical sign.

Example:

$$\sqrt{12} = \sqrt{4} \cdot \sqrt{3} = 2\sqrt{3}$$
$$\sqrt{27} = \sqrt{9} \cdot \sqrt{3} = 3\sqrt{3}$$

If we wish to add $\sqrt{12} + \sqrt{27}$, we must first simplify each one. Adding the simplified radicals gives a sum of $5\sqrt{3}$.

Example:

$$\sqrt{125} + \sqrt{20} - \sqrt{500}$$

Solution:

$$\sqrt{25} \cdot \sqrt{5} + \sqrt{4} \cdot \sqrt{5} - \sqrt{100} \cdot \sqrt{5}$$
$$5\sqrt{5} + 2\sqrt{5} - 10\sqrt{5}$$
$$-3\sqrt{5}$$

Exercise 1

Work out each problem. Circle the letter that appears before your answer.

1. Combine $4\sqrt{27} - 2\sqrt{48} + \sqrt{147}$
   (A) $27\sqrt{3}$
   (B) $-3\sqrt{3}$
   (C) $9\sqrt{3}$
   (D) $10\sqrt{3}$
   (E) $11\sqrt{3}$

2. Combine $\sqrt{80} + \sqrt{45} - \sqrt{20}$
   (A) $9\sqrt{5}$
   (B) $5\sqrt{5}$
   (C) $-\sqrt{5}$
   (D) $3\sqrt{5}$
   (E) $-2\sqrt{5}$

3. Combine $6\sqrt{5} + 3\sqrt{2} - 4\sqrt{5} + \sqrt{2}$
   (A) 8
   (B) $2\sqrt{5} + 3\sqrt{2}$
   (C) $2\sqrt{5} + 4\sqrt{2}$
   (D) $5\sqrt{7}$
   (E) 5

4. Combine $\dfrac{1}{2} \cdot \sqrt{180} + \dfrac{1}{3} \cdot \sqrt{45} - \dfrac{2}{5} \cdot \sqrt{20}$

   (A) $3\sqrt{10} + \sqrt{15} + 2\sqrt{2}$

   (B) $\dfrac{16}{5}\sqrt{5}$

   (C) $\sqrt{97}$

   (D) $\dfrac{24}{5}\sqrt{5}$

   (E) none of these

5. Combine $5\sqrt{mn} - 3\sqrt{mn} - 2\sqrt{mn}$

   (A) 0

   (B) 1

   (C) $\sqrt{mn}$

   (D) mn

   (E) $-\sqrt{mn}$

2. MULTIPLICATION AND DIVISION OF RADICALS

In multiplication and division, we again treat the radicals as we would treat letters in an algebraic expression. They are factors and must be treated as such.

Example:

$$\sqrt{2} \cdot \sqrt{3} = \sqrt{6}$$

Example:

$$4\sqrt{2} \cdot 5\sqrt{3} = 20 \cdot \sqrt{6}$$

Example:

$$(3\sqrt{2})^2 = 3\sqrt{2} \cdot 3\sqrt{2} = 9 \cdot 2 = 18$$

Example:

$$\dfrac{\sqrt{8}}{\sqrt{2}} = \sqrt{4} = 2$$

Example:

$$\dfrac{10\sqrt{20}}{2\sqrt{4}} = 5\sqrt{5}$$

Example:

$$\sqrt{2}(\sqrt{8} + \sqrt{18}) = \sqrt{16} + \sqrt{36} = 4 + 6 = 10$$

Exercise 2

Work out each problem. Circle the letter that appears before your answer.

1. Multiply and simplify: $2\sqrt{18} \cdot 6\sqrt{2}$

   (A) 72

   (B) 48

   (C) $12\sqrt{6}$

   (D) $8\sqrt{6}$

   (E) 36

2. Find $\left(3\sqrt{3}\right)^3$

   (A) $27\sqrt{3}$

   (B) $81\sqrt{3}$

   (C) 81

   (D) $9\sqrt{3}$

   (E) 243

3. Multiply and simplify: $\frac{1}{2}\sqrt{2}(\sqrt{6}+\frac{1}{2}\sqrt{2})$

(A) $\sqrt{3}+\frac{1}{2}$

(B) $\frac{1}{2}\cdot\sqrt{3}$

(C) $\sqrt{6}+1$

(D) $\sqrt{6}+\frac{1}{.2}$

(E) $\sqrt{6}+2$

4. Divide and simplify: $\frac{\sqrt{32b^3}}{\sqrt{8b}}$

(A) $2\sqrt{b}$

(B) $\sqrt{2b}$

(C) $2b$

(D) $\sqrt{2b^2}$

(E) $b\sqrt{2b}$

5. Divide and simplify: $\frac{15\sqrt{96}}{5\sqrt{2}}$

(A) $7\sqrt{3}$

(B) $7\sqrt{12}$

(C) $11\sqrt{3}$

(D) $12\sqrt{3}$

(E) $40\sqrt{3}$

3. SIMPLIFYING RADICALS CONTAINING A SUM OR DIFFERENCE

In simplifying radicals that contain several terms under the radical sign, we must combine terms before taking the square root.

Example:

$$\sqrt{16+9}=\sqrt{25}=5$$

It is not true that $\sqrt{16+9}=\sqrt{16}+\sqrt{9}$, which would be 4 + 3, or 7.

Example:

$$\sqrt{\frac{x^2}{16}-\frac{x^2}{25}}=\sqrt{\frac{25x^2-16x^2}{400}}=\sqrt{\frac{9x^2}{400}}=\frac{3x}{20}$$

Exercise 3

Work out each problem. Circle the letter that appears before your answer.

1. Simplify $\sqrt{\frac{x^2}{9}+\frac{x^2}{16}}$

(A) $\frac{25x^2}{144}$

(B) $\frac{5x}{12}$

(C) $\frac{5x^2}{12}$

(D) $\frac{x}{7}$

(E) $\frac{7x}{12}$

2. Simplify $\sqrt{36y^2+64x^2}$

(A) $6y+8x$

(B) $10xy$

(C) $6y^2+8x^2$

(D) $10x^2y^2$

(E) cannot be done

3. Simplify $\sqrt{\frac{x^2}{64}-\frac{x^2}{100}}$

(A) $\frac{x}{40}$

(B) $-\frac{x}{2}$

(C) $\frac{x}{2}$

(D) $\frac{3x}{40}$

(E) $\frac{3x}{80}$

4. Simplify $\sqrt{\dfrac{y^2}{2} - \dfrac{y^2}{18}}$

   (A) $\dfrac{2y}{3}$

   (B) $\dfrac{y}{5}$

   (C) $\dfrac{10y}{3}$

   (D) $\dfrac{y\sqrt{3}}{6}$

   (E) cannot be done

5. $\sqrt{a^2 + b^2}$ is equal to

   (A) $a + b$

   (B) $a - b$

   (C) $\sqrt{a^2} + \sqrt{b^2}$

   (D) $(a + b)(a - b)$

   (E) none of these

4. FINDING THE SQUARE ROOT OF A NUMBER

In finding the square root of a number, the first step is to pair off the digits in the square root sign in each direction from the decimal point. If there is an odd number of digits *before* the decimal point, insert a zero at the *beginning* of the number in order to pair digits. If there is an odd number of digits *after* the decimal point, add a zero at the *end*. It should be clearly understood that these zeros are place holders only and in no way change the value of the number. Every *pair* of numbers in the radical sign gives one digit of the square root.

Example:

   Find the number of digits in the square root of 328,329.

Solution:

   Pair the numbers beginning at the decimal point.

   $\sqrt{32\ 83\ 29}\cdot$

   Each pair will give one digit in the square root. Therefore the square root of 328,329 has three digits.

If we were asked to find the square root of 328,329, we would look among the multiple-choice answers for a three-digit number. If there were more than one, we would have to use additional criteria for selection. Since our number ends in 9, its square root must end in a digit that, when multiplied by itself, ends in 9. Going through the digits from 0 to 9, this could be 3 ($3 \cdot 3 = 9$) or 7 ($7 \cdot 7 = 49$). Only one of these would appear among the choices, as this examination will not call for extensive computation, but rather for sound mathematical reasoning.

Example:

   The square root of 4624 is exactly

   (A)   64

   (B)   65

   (C)   66

   (D)   67

   (E)   68

Solution:

   Since all choices contain two digits, we must reason using the last digit. It must be a number that, when multiplied by itself, will end in 4. Among the choices, the only possibility is 68 as 64^2 will end in 6, 65^2 will end in 5, 66^2 in 6, and 67^2 in 9.

Exercise 4

Work out each problem. Circle the letter that appears before your answer.

1. The square root of 17,689 is exactly
    (A)   131
    (B)   132
    (C)   133
    (D)   134
    (E)   136

2. The number of digits in the square root of 64,048,009 is
    (A)   4
    (B)   5
    (C)   6
    (D)   7
    (E)   8

3. The square root of 222.01 is exactly
    (A)   14.3
    (B)   14.4
    (C)   14.6
    (D)   14.8
    (E)   14.9

4. The square root of 25.6036 is exactly
    (A)   5.6
    (B)   5.06
    (C)   5.006
    (D)   5.0006
    (E)   5.00006

5. Which of the following square roots can be found exactly?
    (A) $\sqrt{.4}$
    (B) $\sqrt{.9}$
    (C) $\sqrt{.09}$
    (D) $\sqrt{.02}$
    (E) $\sqrt{.025}$

RETEST

Work out each problem. Circle the letter that appears before your answer.

1. The sum of $2\sqrt{8}$, $4\sqrt{50}$, and $3\sqrt{18}$ is
    - (A) $33\sqrt{6}$
    - (B) $9\sqrt{76}$
    - (C) $33\sqrt{2}$
    - (D) $135\sqrt{6}$
    - (E) $136\sqrt{2}$

2. The difference between $\frac{1}{2}\sqrt{180}$ and $\frac{2}{5}\sqrt{20}$ is
    - (A) $\frac{1}{10}\sqrt{160}$
    - (B) $16\frac{2}{5}\sqrt{5}$
    - (C) $16\frac{2}{5}$
    - (D) $\frac{11}{5}\sqrt{5}$
    - (E) $\frac{2}{5}\sqrt{5}$

3. The product of $a\sqrt{2x}$ and $x\sqrt{6x}$ is
    - (A) $2ax^2\sqrt{3}$
    - (B) $12ax^3$
    - (C) $(2ax)^2\sqrt{3}$
    - (D) $12ax^2$
    - (E) $12ax$

4. Divide $42\sqrt{40r^3t^6}$ by $3\sqrt{5rt^2}$
    - (A) $56rt^2\sqrt{2}$
    - (B) $28rt\sqrt{2rt}$
    - (C) $28rt^2\sqrt{2}$
    - (D) $28rt\sqrt{2t}$
    - (E) $56rt\sqrt{2t}$

5. Solve for x: $\frac{3}{x} = \sqrt{.09}$
    - (A) 10
    - (B) 1
    - (C) .1
    - (D) .01
    - (E) 1.1

6. Find $\sqrt{\dfrac{a^2}{b^2} + \dfrac{a^2}{b^2}}$
    - (A) $\dfrac{a^2}{b^2}$
    - (B) $\dfrac{a}{b}$
    - (C) $\dfrac{2a}{b}$
    - (D) $\dfrac{a\sqrt{2}}{b}$
    - (E) $\dfrac{a\sqrt{2}}{b^2}$

7. The square root of 213.16 is exactly
    - (A) 14.2
    - (B) 14.3
    - (C) 14.8
    - (D) 14.9
    - (E) 14.6

8. The number of digits in the square root of 14,161 is
    - (A) 5
    - (B) 4
    - (C) 3
    - (D) 2
    - (E) 6

9. $(2\sqrt{3})^5$ is equal to
    - (A) $32\sqrt{3}$
    - (B) $288\sqrt{3}$
    - (C) $10\sqrt{3}$
    - (D) $90\sqrt{3}$
    - (E) $16\sqrt{3}$

10. Find $\sqrt{\dfrac{25m^4}{36c^{64}d^{16}}}$
    - (A) $\dfrac{5m^2}{6c^8d^4}$
    - (B) $\dfrac{5m^2}{6c^{32}d^4}$
    - (C) $\dfrac{5m^2}{6c^{32}d^8}$
    - (D) $\dfrac{5m^2}{6c^8d^8}$
    - (E) $\dfrac{5m}{6c^{16}d^4}$

SOLUTIONS TO PRACTICE EXERCISES

Diagnostic Test

1. (B) $\sqrt{75} = \sqrt{25} \cdot \sqrt{3} = 5\sqrt{3}$

   $\sqrt{12} = \sqrt{4} \cdot \sqrt{3} = 2\sqrt{3}$

   $5\sqrt{3} + 2\sqrt{3} = 7\sqrt{3}$

2. (B) $\sqrt{125} = \sqrt{25} \cdot \sqrt{5} = 5\sqrt{5}$

   $\sqrt{45} = \sqrt{9} \cdot \sqrt{5} = 3\sqrt{5}$

   $5\sqrt{5} - 3\sqrt{5} = 2\sqrt{5}$

3. (D) $\sqrt{9x} \cdot \sqrt{4x} = \sqrt{36x^2} = 6x$

4. (B) $\sqrt{.16} = .4$

   $\dfrac{2}{x} = .4$ Multiply by x.

   $2 = .4x$

   $x = 5$

5. (C) Since the last digit is 6, the square root must end in 4 or 6.

6. (B) Since the number has two digits to the right of the decimal point, its square root will have one digit to the right of the decimal point.

7. (E) $\sqrt{\dfrac{25x^2 + 36x^2}{900}} = \sqrt{\dfrac{61x^2}{900}} = x\dfrac{\sqrt{61}}{30}$

8. (E) It is not possible to find the square root of separate terms.

9. (C) $\dfrac{8\sqrt{12}}{2\sqrt{3}} = 4\sqrt{4} = 4 \cdot 2 = 8$

10. (D) $(\sqrt{2})(\sqrt{2}) = 2$. Therefore,

    $(\sqrt{2}) \cdot (\sqrt{2}) \cdot \sqrt{2} \cdot \sqrt{2} \cdot \sqrt{2} = 4\sqrt{2}$

Exercise 1

1. (E) $4\sqrt{27} = 4\sqrt{9} \cdot \sqrt{3} = 12\sqrt{3}$

   $2\sqrt{48} = 2\sqrt{16} \cdot \sqrt{3} = 8\sqrt{3}$

   $\sqrt{147} = \sqrt{49} \cdot \sqrt{3} = 7\sqrt{3}$

   $12\sqrt{3} - 8\sqrt{3} + 7\sqrt{3} = 11\sqrt{3}$

2. (B) $\sqrt{80} = \sqrt{16} \cdot \sqrt{5} = 4\sqrt{5}$

   $\sqrt{45} = \sqrt{9} \cdot \sqrt{5} = 3\sqrt{5}$

   $\sqrt{20} = \sqrt{4} \cdot \sqrt{5} = 2\sqrt{5}$

   $4\sqrt{5} + 3\sqrt{5} - 2\sqrt{5} = 5\sqrt{5}$

3. (C) Only terms with the same radical may be combined.

   $6\sqrt{5} - 4\sqrt{5} = 2\sqrt{5}$

   $3\sqrt{2} + \sqrt{2} = 4\sqrt{2}$

   Therefore we have $2\sqrt{5} + 4\sqrt{2}$

4. (B) $\dfrac{1}{2} \cdot \sqrt{180} = \dfrac{1}{2} \cdot \sqrt{36} \cdot \sqrt{5} = 3\sqrt{5}$

   $\dfrac{1}{3} \cdot \sqrt{45} = \dfrac{1}{3} \cdot \sqrt{9} \cdot \sqrt{5} = \sqrt{5}$

   $\dfrac{2}{5} \cdot \sqrt{20} = \dfrac{2}{5} \cdot \sqrt{4} \cdot \sqrt{5} = \dfrac{4}{5}\sqrt{5}$

   $3\sqrt{5} + \sqrt{5} - \dfrac{4}{5} \cdot \sqrt{5} = 4\sqrt{5} - \dfrac{4}{5}\sqrt{5}$

   $= 3\dfrac{1}{5}\sqrt{5} = \dfrac{16}{5}\sqrt{5}$

5. (A) $5\sqrt{mn} - 5\sqrt{mn} = 0$

Exercise 2

1. (A) $2\sqrt{18}\cdot 6\sqrt{2}=12\sqrt{36}=12\cdot 6=72$

2. (B) $3\sqrt{3}\cdot 3\sqrt{3}\cdot 3\sqrt{3}=27(3\sqrt{3})=81\cdot\sqrt{3}$

3. (A) Using the distributive law, we have

$$\frac{1}{2}\sqrt{12}+\frac{1}{4}\cdot 2=\frac{1}{2}\sqrt{4}\cdot\sqrt{3}+\frac{1}{2}=\sqrt{3}+\frac{1}{2}$$

4. (C) Dividing the numbers in the radical sign, we have $\sqrt{4b^2}=2b$

5. (D) $3\sqrt{48}=3\sqrt{16}\cdot\sqrt{3}=12\sqrt{13}$

Exercise 3

1. (B) $\sqrt{\dfrac{16x^2+9x^2+x^2}{144}}=\sqrt{\dfrac{25x^2}{144}}=\dfrac{5x}{12}$

2. (E) The terms cannot be combined and it is not possible to take the square root of separated terms.

3. (D)

$$\sqrt{\dfrac{100x^2-64x^2}{6400}}=\sqrt{\dfrac{36x^2}{6400}}=\dfrac{6x}{80}=\dfrac{3x}{40}$$

4. (A) $\sqrt{\dfrac{18y^2-2y^2}{36}}=\sqrt{\dfrac{16y^2}{36}}=\dfrac{4y}{6}=\dfrac{2y}{3}$

5. (E) It is not possible to find the square root of separate terms.

Exercise 4

1. (C) Since the last digit is 9, the square root must end in 3 or 7.

2. (A) Every pair of digits in the given number gives one digit of the square root.

3. (E) Since the number ends in 1, its square root must end in 1 or 9.

4. (B) Since the number has four digits to the right of the decimal point, its square root will have two digits to the right of the decimal point.

5. (C) In order to take the square root of a decimal, it must have an even number of decimal places so that its square root will have exactly half as many. In addition to this, the digits must form a perfect square $(\sqrt{.09}=.3)$.

Retest

1. (C) $2\sqrt{8} = 2\sqrt{4} \cdot \sqrt{2} = 4\sqrt{2}$

   $4\sqrt{50} = 4\sqrt{25} \cdot \sqrt{2} = 20\sqrt{2}$

   $3\sqrt{18} = 3\sqrt{9} \cdot \sqrt{2} = 9\sqrt{2}$

   $4\sqrt{2} + 20\sqrt{2} + 9\sqrt{2} = 33\sqrt{2}$

2. (D) $\dfrac{1}{2}\sqrt{180} = \dfrac{1}{2}\sqrt{36} \cdot \sqrt{5} = 3\sqrt{5}$

   $\dfrac{2}{5}\sqrt{20} = \dfrac{2}{5}\sqrt{4} \cdot \sqrt{5} = \dfrac{4}{5}\sqrt{5}$

   $3\sqrt{5} - \dfrac{4}{5}\sqrt{5} = \dfrac{11}{5}\sqrt{5}$

3. (A) $a\sqrt{2x} \cdot x\sqrt{6x} = ax\sqrt{12x^2} = 2ax^2\sqrt{3}$

4. (C) $\dfrac{42\sqrt{40r^3t^6}}{3\sqrt{5rt^2}} = 14\sqrt{8r^2t^4}$

   $14\sqrt{8r^2t^4} = 28rt^2\sqrt{2}$

5. (A) $\sqrt{.09} = .3$

   $\dfrac{3}{x} = .3$ \qquad Multiply by x.

   $3 = .3x$

   $x = 10$

6. (D) $\sqrt{\dfrac{2a^2}{b^2}} = \dfrac{a\sqrt{2}}{b}$

7. (E) Since the last digit is 6, the square root must end in 4 or 6.

8. (C) A five-digit number has a three-digit square root.

9. (B)

   $2\sqrt{3} \cdot 2\sqrt{3} \cdot 2\sqrt{3} \cdot 2\sqrt{3} \cdot 2\sqrt{3} = 32\left(9\sqrt{3}\right) = 288\sqrt{3}$

10. (C) $\sqrt{\dfrac{25m^4}{36c^{64}d^{16}}} = \dfrac{5m^2}{6c^{32}d^8}$

Factoring and Algebraic Fractions

DIAGNOSTIC TEST

Directions: Work out each problem. Circle the letter that appears before your answer.

Answers are at the end of the chapter.

1. Find the sum of $\dfrac{n}{4}$ and $\dfrac{2n}{3}$.

    (A) $\dfrac{2n^2}{7}$

    (B) $\dfrac{3n}{7}$

    (C) $\dfrac{11n}{12}$

    (D) $\dfrac{2n^2}{12}$

    (E) $\dfrac{9n}{12}$

2. Combine into a single fraction: $2 - \dfrac{a}{b}$.

    (A) $\dfrac{2-a}{b}$

    (B) $\dfrac{2-a}{2-b}$

    (C) $\dfrac{a-2b}{b}$

    (D) $\dfrac{2b-a}{b}$

    (E) $\dfrac{2a-b}{b}$

3. Divide $\dfrac{x-5}{x+5}$ by $\dfrac{5-x}{5+x}$.

    (A) 1

    (B) -1

    (C) $\dfrac{(x-5)^2}{(x+5)^2}$

    (D) $-\dfrac{(x-5)^2}{(x+5)^2}$

    (E) 0

4. Find an expression equivalent to $\left(\dfrac{3x^2}{y}\right)^3$.

    (A) $\dfrac{27x^5}{3y}$

    (B) $\dfrac{9x^6}{y^3}$

    (C) $\dfrac{9x^5}{y^3}$

    (D) $\dfrac{27x^5}{y^3}$

    (E) $\dfrac{27x^6}{y^3}$

5. Simplify $\dfrac{1}{2+\dfrac{a}{\dfrac{b}{a}}}$

(A) $\dfrac{2a+1}{b}$

(B) $\dfrac{2a+1}{a}$

(C) $\dfrac{2a+1}{ab}$

(D) $\dfrac{4a^2+1}{xy}$

(E) $\dfrac{2b+1}{b}$

6. Simplify $\dfrac{\dfrac{1}{a}-\dfrac{1}{b}}{2}$

(A) $\dfrac{b-a}{2}$

(B) $\dfrac{a-b}{2}$

(C) $\dfrac{b-a}{2ab}$

(D) $\dfrac{ba}{2}$

(E) $\dfrac{2ab}{b+a}$

7. If $x + y = 16$ and $x^2 - y^2 = 48$, then $x - y$ equals

(A) 3
(B) 32
(C) 4
(D) 36
(E) 6

8. If $(x + y)^2 = 100$ and $xy = 20$, find $x^2 + y^2$.

(A) 100
(B) 20
(C) 40
(D) 60
(E) 80

9. If $\dfrac{1}{x}+\dfrac{1}{y}=\dfrac{1}{2}$ and $\dfrac{1}{x}-\dfrac{1}{y}=\dfrac{1}{4}$, find

$\dfrac{1}{x^2}-\dfrac{1}{y^2}$

(A) $\dfrac{3}{4}$

(B) $\dfrac{1}{4}$

(C) $\dfrac{3}{16}$

(D) $\dfrac{1}{8}$

(E) $\dfrac{7}{8}$

10. The trinomial $x^2 - x - 20$ is exactly divisible by

(A) $x - 4$
(B) $x - 10$
(C) $x + 4$
(D) $x - 2$
(E) $x + 5$

1. SIMPLIFYING FRACTIONS

In simplifying fractions, we must divide the numerator and denominator by the same factor. We can multiply or divide both the numerator and denominator of a fraction by the same number without changing the value of the fraction. However, if we were to add or subtract the same number in the numerator and denominator, the value of the fraction would not remain the same. When we simplify $\frac{9}{12}$ to $\frac{3}{4}$, we are really saying that $\frac{9}{12} = \frac{3 \cdot 3}{3 \cdot 4}$ and then dividing the numerator and denominator by 3. We may not say that $\frac{9}{12} = \frac{5+4}{5+7}$ and then say that $\frac{9}{12} = \frac{4}{7}$. This is a serious error in algebra as well. $\frac{9t}{12t} = \frac{3}{4}$ because we divide numerator and denominator by $3t$. However, $\frac{9+t}{12+t}$ cannot be simplified, as there is no factor that divides into the *entire* numerator as well as the *entire* denominator. *Never cancel terms!* That is, never cancel parts of numerators or denominators containing + or - signs unless they are enclosed in parentheses as parts of factors. This is one of the most frequent student errors. Be very careful to avoid it.

Example:

Simplify $\dfrac{4b^2 + 8b}{3b^3 + 6b^2}$

Solution:

Factoring the numerator and denominator by removing the largest common factor in both cases, we

have $\dfrac{4b(b+2)}{3b^2(b+2)}$

The factors common to both numerator and denominator are b and $(b + 2)$. Dividing these out, we have $\dfrac{4}{3b}$.

Example:

Simplify $\dfrac{x^2 + 6x + 8}{x^2 + x - 12}$ to simplest form.

Solution:

There are no common factors here, but both numerator and denominator may be factored as

trinomials. $\dfrac{(x+4)(x+2)}{(x+4)(x-3)}$ gives $\dfrac{(x+2)}{(x-3)}$ as a final answer. Remember not to cancel the x's as

they are *terms* and not *factors.*

Example:

Simplify $\dfrac{10 - 2x}{x^2 - 4x - 5}$ to simplest form.

Solution:

The numerator contains a common factor, while the denominator must be factored as a trinomial.

$2\left(\dfrac{5 - x}{(x-5)(x+1)}\right)$

When numbers are reversed around a minus sign, they may be turned around by factoring out a $(-1).5 - x = (-1)(x - 5)$. Doing this will enable us to simplify the fraction to $\dfrac{-2}{x+1}$. Remember that if the terms had been reversed around a plus sign, the factors could have been divided without factoring further, as $a + b = b + a$, by the cummulative law of addition. Subtraction, however, is not commulative, necessitating the factoring of -1.

Exercise 1

Work out each problem. Circle the letter that appears before your answer.

1. Simplify to simplest form: $\dfrac{3x^3 - 3x^2 y}{9x^2 - 9xy}$

    (A) $\dfrac{x}{6}$

    (B) $\dfrac{x}{3}$

    (C) $\dfrac{2x}{3}$

    (D) 1

    (E) $\dfrac{x-y}{3}$

2. Simplify to simplest form: $\dfrac{2x - 8}{12 - 3x}$

    (A) $-\dfrac{2}{3}$

    (B) $\dfrac{2}{3}$

    (C) $-\dfrac{4}{3}$

    (D) $\dfrac{4}{3}$

    (E) $-\dfrac{3}{2}$

3. Find the value of $\dfrac{3x - y}{y - 3x}$ when $x = \dfrac{2}{7}$ and $y = \dfrac{3}{10}, y \pi 3x.$

    (A) $\dfrac{24}{70}$

    (B) $\dfrac{11}{70}$

    (C) 0

    (D) 1

    (E) -1

4. Simplify to simplest form: $\dfrac{b^2 + b - 12}{b^2 + 2b - 15}$

    (A) $\dfrac{4}{5}$

    (B) $-\dfrac{4}{3}$

    (C) $\dfrac{b+4}{b+5}$

    (D) $\dfrac{b-4}{b-5}$

    (E) $-\dfrac{b+4}{b+5}$

5. Simplify to simplest form: $\dfrac{2x + 4y}{6x + 12y}$

    (A) $\dfrac{2}{3}$

    (B) $-\dfrac{2}{3}$

    (C) $-\dfrac{1}{3}$

    (D) $\dfrac{1}{3}$

    (E) 3

2. ADDITION OR SUBTRACTION OF FRACTIONS

In adding or subtracting fractions, it is necessary to have the fractions expressed in terms of the same common denominator. When adding or subtracting two fractions, use the same shortcuts used in arithmetic. Remember that $\frac{a}{b} + \frac{c}{d} = \frac{ad + bc}{bd}$, and that $\frac{a}{b} - \frac{c}{d} = \frac{ad - bc}{bd}$. All sums or differences should be simplified to simplest form.

Example:

Add $\frac{3}{a} + \frac{2}{b}$

Solution:

Add the two cross products and put the sum over the denominator product: $\frac{3b + 2a}{ab}$

Example:

Add $\frac{2a}{3} + \frac{4a}{5}$

Solution:

$$\frac{10a + 12a}{15} = \frac{22a}{15}$$

Example:

Add $\frac{5a}{a + b} + \frac{5b}{a + b}$

Solution:

Since both fractions have the same denominator, we must simply add the numerators and put the sum over the same denominator.

$$\frac{5a + 5b}{a + b} = \frac{5(a + b)}{a + b} = 5$$

Example:

Subtract $\frac{4r - s}{6} - \frac{2r - 7s}{6}$

Solution:

Since both fractions have the same denominator, we subtract the numerators and place the difference over the same denominator. Be very careful of the minus sign between the fractions as it will change the sign of each term in the second numerator.

$$\frac{4r - s - (2r - 7s)}{6} = \frac{4r - s - 2r + 7s}{6} = \frac{2r + 6s}{6} = \frac{2(r + 3s)}{6} = \frac{r + 3s}{3}$$

Exercise 2

Work out each problem. Circle the letter that appears before your answer.

1. Subtract $\dfrac{6x+5y}{2x} - \dfrac{4x+y}{2x}$
    - (A) $1+4y$
    - (B) $4y$
    - (C) $1+2y$
    - (D) $\dfrac{x+2y}{x}$
    - (E) $\dfrac{x+3y}{x}$

2. Add $\dfrac{3c}{c+d} + \dfrac{3d}{c+d}$
    - (A) $\dfrac{6cd}{c+d}$
    - (B) $\dfrac{3cd}{c+d}$
    - (C) $\dfrac{3}{2}$
    - (D) 3
    - (E) $\dfrac{9cd}{c+d}$

3. Add $\dfrac{a}{5} + \dfrac{3a}{10}$
    - (A) $\dfrac{4a}{15}$
    - (B) $\dfrac{a}{2}$
    - (C) $\dfrac{3a^2}{50}$
    - (D) $\dfrac{2a}{25}$
    - (E) $\dfrac{3a^2}{15}$

4. Add $\dfrac{x+4}{6} + \dfrac{1}{2}$
    - (A) $\dfrac{x+7}{6}$
    - (B) $\dfrac{x+5}{8}$
    - (C) $\dfrac{x+4}{12}$
    - (D) $\dfrac{x+5}{12}$
    - (E) $\dfrac{x+5}{6}$

5. Subtract $\dfrac{3b}{4} - \dfrac{7b}{10}$
    - (A) $-\dfrac{2b}{3}$
    - (B) $\dfrac{b}{5}$
    - (C) $\dfrac{b}{20}$
    - (D) b
    - (E) $\dfrac{2b}{3}$

3. MULTIPLICATION OR DIVISION OF FRACTIONS

In multiplying or dividing fractions, we must first factor all numerators and denominators and may then divide all factors common to any numerator and any denominator. Remember always to invert the fraction following the division sign. Where exponents are involved, they are added in multiplication and subtracted in division.

Example:

Find the product of $\dfrac{x^3}{y^2}$ and $\dfrac{y^3}{x^2}$.

Solution:

Factors common to both numerator and denominator are x^2 in the first numerator and second denominator and y^2 in the first denominator and second numerator. Dividing by these common factors, we are left with $\dfrac{x}{1} \cdot \dfrac{y}{1}$. Finally, we multiply the resulting fractions, giving an answer of xy.

Example:

Divide $\dfrac{15a^2b}{2}$ by $5a^3$.

Solution:

We invert the divisor and multiply.

$$\dfrac{15a^2b}{2} \cdot \dfrac{1}{5a^3}$$

We can divide the first numerator and second denominator by $5a^2$, giving $\dfrac{3b}{2} \cdot \dfrac{1}{a}$ or $\dfrac{3b}{2a}$.

Exercise 3

Work out each problem. Circle the letter that appears before your answer.

1. Find the product of $\dfrac{x^2}{y^3}$ and $\dfrac{y^4}{x^5}$.

   (A) $\dfrac{y^2}{x^3}$

   (B) $\dfrac{y}{x^3}$

   (C) $\dfrac{x^3}{y}$

   (D) $\dfrac{x^8}{y^7}$

   (E) $\dfrac{x}{y}$

2. Multiply c by $\dfrac{b}{c}$

   (A) $\dfrac{b}{c^2}$

   (B) $\dfrac{c^2}{b}$

   (C) b

   (D) c

   (E) bc^2

3. Divide $\dfrac{ax}{by}$ by $\dfrac{x}{y}$

   (A) $\dfrac{ax^2}{by^2}$

   (B) $\dfrac{b}{a}$

   (C) $\dfrac{a}{b}$

   (D) $\dfrac{by^2}{ax^2}$

   (E) $\dfrac{ay}{bx}$

4. Divide $4abc$ by $\dfrac{2a^2b}{3d^2}$

    (A) $\dfrac{8a^3b^2c}{3d^2}$

    (B) $\dfrac{a}{6cd^2}$

    (C) $\dfrac{2ac}{bd^2}$

    (D) $\dfrac{6cd^2}{a}$

    (E) $\dfrac{5cd^2}{a}$

5. Divide $\dfrac{3a^2c^4}{4b^2}$ by $6ac^2$

    (A) $\dfrac{ac^2}{8b^2}$

    (B) $\dfrac{ac^2}{4b^2}$

    (C) $\dfrac{4b^2}{ac^2}$

    (D) $\dfrac{8b^2}{ac^2}$

    (E) $\dfrac{ac^2}{6b^2}$

4. COMPLEX ALGEBRAIC FRACTIONS

Complex algebraic fractions are simplified by the same methods reviewed earlier for arithmetic fractions. To eliminate the fractions within the fraction, multiply *each term* of the entire complex fraction by the lowest quantity that will eliminate them all.

Example:

    Simplify $\dfrac{\dfrac{3}{x}+\dfrac{2}{y}}{6}$

Solution:

    We must multiply *each term* by xy, giving $\dfrac{3y+2x}{6xy}$.

    No more simplification is possible beyond this. Remember *never* to cancel terms or parts of terms. We may only simplify by dividing factors.

Exercise 4

Work out each problem. Circle the letter that appears before your answer.

1. Simplify $\dfrac{\dfrac{1}{5}-\dfrac{3}{2}}{\dfrac{3}{4}}$

 (A) $\dfrac{15}{26}$

 (B) $-\dfrac{15}{26}$

 (C) 2

 (D) $\dfrac{26}{15}$

 (E) $-\dfrac{26}{15}$

2. Simplify $\dfrac{\dfrac{a}{x^2}}{\dfrac{a^2}{x}}$

 (A) $\dfrac{x}{a}$

 (B) $\dfrac{1}{a^2x}$

 (C) $\dfrac{1}{ax}$

 (D) ax

 (E) $\dfrac{a}{x}$

3. Simplify $\dfrac{\dfrac{1}{x}-\dfrac{1}{y}}{\dfrac{1}{x}+\dfrac{1}{y}}$

 (A) $\dfrac{x-y}{x+y}$

 (B) $\dfrac{x+y}{x-y}$

 (C) $\dfrac{y-x}{x+y}$

 (D) -1

 (E) $-xy$

4. Simplify $1+\dfrac{\dfrac{1}{x}}{\dfrac{1}{y}}$

 (A) $\dfrac{x+y}{x}$

 (B) $2y$

 (C) $x+1$

 (D) $\dfrac{y+1}{x}$

 (E) $\dfrac{xy+1}{y}$

5. Simplify $2+\dfrac{\dfrac{1}{t}}{\dfrac{2}{t^2}}$

 (A) t^2+t

 (B) t^3

 (C) $\dfrac{2t+1}{2}$

 (D) $t+1$

 (E) $\dfrac{4+t}{2}$

5. USING FACTORING TO FIND MISSING VALUES

Certain types of problems may involve the ability to factor in order to evaluate a given expression. In particular, you should be able to factor the difference of two perfect squares. If an expression consists of two terms that are separated by a minus sign, the expression can always be factored into two binomials, with one containing the sum of the square roots and the other their difference. This can be stated by the identity $x^2 - y^2 = (x + y)(x - y)$.

Example:

If $m^2 - n^2 = 48$ and $m + n = 12$, find $m - n$.

Solution:

Since $m^2 - n^2$ is equal to $(m + n)(m - n)$, these two factors must multiply to 48. If one of them is 12, the other must be 4.

Example:

If $(a + b)^2 = 48$ and $ab = 6$, find $a^2 + b^2$.

Solution:

$(a + b)^2$ is equal to $a^2 + 2ab + b^2$. Substituting 6 for ab, we have $a^2 + 2(6) + b^2 = 48$ and $a^2 + b^2 = 36$.

Exercise 5

Work out each problem. Circle the letter that appears before your answer.

1. If $a + b = \dfrac{1}{3}$ and $a - b = \dfrac{1}{4}$, find $a^2 - b^2$.

    (A) $\dfrac{1}{12}$

    (B) $\dfrac{1}{7}$

    (C) $\dfrac{2}{7}$

    (D) $\dfrac{1}{6}$

    (E) none of these

2. If $(a - b)^2 = 40$ and $ab = 8$, find $a^2 + b^2$.

    (A) 5
    (B) 24
    (C) 48
    (D) 56
    (E) 32

3. If $a + b = 8$ and $a^2 - b^2 = 24$, then $a - b =$

    (A) 16
    (B) 4
    (C) 3
    (D) 32
    (E) 6

4. The trinomial $x^2 + 4x - 45$ is exactly divisible by

    (A) $x + 9$
    (B) $x - 9$
    (C) $x + 5$
    (D) $x + 15$
    (E) $x - 3$

5. If $\dfrac{1}{c} - \dfrac{1}{d} = 5$ and $\dfrac{1}{c} + \dfrac{1}{d} = 3$, then

    $\dfrac{1}{c^2} - \dfrac{1}{d^2} =$

    (A) 16
    (B) 34
    (C) 2
    (D) 15
    (E) cannot be determined

RETEST

Work out each problem. Circle the letter that appears before your answer.

1. Find the sum of $\dfrac{2n}{5}$ and $\dfrac{n}{10}$.

   (A) $\dfrac{3n}{50}$

   (B) $\dfrac{1}{2}n$

   (C) $\dfrac{2n^2}{50}$

   (D) $\dfrac{2n^2}{10}$

   (E) $\dfrac{3n}{10}$

2. Combine into a single fraction: $\dfrac{x}{y} - 3$

   (A) $\dfrac{x - 3y}{y}$

   (B) $\dfrac{x - 3}{y}$

   (C) $\dfrac{x - 9}{3y}$

   (D) $\dfrac{x - 3y}{3}$

   (E) $\dfrac{x - 3y}{3y}$

3. Divide $\dfrac{x^2 + 2x - 8}{4 + x}$ by $\dfrac{2 - x}{3}$.

   (A) 3
   (B) -3
   (C) $3(x - 2)$

   (D) $\dfrac{3}{2 - x}$

   (E) none of these

4. Find an expression equivalent to $\left(\dfrac{5a^3}{b}\right)^3$.

   (A) $\dfrac{15a^6}{b^3}$

   (B) $\dfrac{15a^9}{b^3}$

   (C) $\dfrac{125a^6}{b^3}$

   (D) $\dfrac{125a^9}{b^3}$

   (E) $\dfrac{25a^6}{b^3}$

5. Simplify $\dfrac{3 - \dfrac{1}{x}}{\dfrac{y}{x}}$

   (A) $\dfrac{2}{y}$

   (B) $\dfrac{2x}{y}$

   (C) $\dfrac{3 - x}{y}$

   (D) $\dfrac{3x - 1}{x}$

   (E) $\dfrac{3x - 1}{y}$

6. $\dfrac{3 - \dfrac{1}{x}}{\dfrac{3}{x^2}}$ is equal to

   (A) $\dfrac{x^2 - x}{3}$

   (B) $\dfrac{3x^2 - x}{3}$

   (C) $x^2 - x$

   (D) $\dfrac{3x - 1}{3}$

   (E) $\dfrac{3 - x}{3}$

7. If $a^2 - b^2 = 100$ and $a + b = 25$, then $a - b =$
   - (A)   4
   - (B)   75
   - (C)   -4
   - (D)   -75
   - (E)   5

8. The trinomial $x^2 - 8x - 20$ is exactly divisible by
   - (A) $x - 5$
   - (B) $x - 4$
   - (C) $x - 2$
   - (D) $x - 10$
   - (E) $x - 1$

9. If $\dfrac{1}{a} - \dfrac{1}{b} = 6$ and $\dfrac{1}{a} + \dfrac{1}{b} = 5$, find $\dfrac{1}{a^2} - \dfrac{1}{b^2}$.
   - (A)   30
   - (B)   -11
   - (C)   61
   - (D)   11
   - (E)   1

10. If $(x - y)^2 = 30$ and $xy = 17$, find $x^2 + y^2$.
   - (A)   -4
   - (B)   4
   - (C)   13
   - (D)   47
   - (E)   64

SOLUTIONS TO PRACTICE EXERCISES

Diagnostic Test

1. (C) $\dfrac{3n + 8n}{12} = \dfrac{11n}{12}$

2. (D) $\dfrac{2}{1} - \dfrac{a}{b} = \dfrac{2b - a}{b}$

3. (B) $\dfrac{x - 5}{x + 5} \cdot \dfrac{5 + x}{5 - x}$ divide $x + 5$.

   $\dfrac{x - 5}{5 - x} = \dfrac{x - 5}{-1(x - 5)} = -1$

4. (E) $\dfrac{3x^2}{y} \cdot \dfrac{3x^2}{y} \cdot \dfrac{3x^2}{y} = \dfrac{27x^6}{y^3}$

5. (E) Multiply every term by a.

   $\dfrac{2b + 1}{b}$

6. (C) Multiply every term by ab.

   $\dfrac{b - a}{2ab}$

7. (A) $x^2 - y^2 = (x + y)(x - y) = 48$

   Substituting 16 for $x + y$, we have

   $16(x - y) = 48$

   $x - y = 3$

8. (D) $(x + y)^2 = x^2 + 2xy + y^2 = 100$

   Substituting 20 for xy, we have

   $x^2 + 40 + y^2 = 100$

   $x^2 + y^2 = 60$

9. (D) $\left(\dfrac{1}{x} + \dfrac{1}{y}\right)\left(\dfrac{1}{x} - \dfrac{1}{y}\right) = \dfrac{1}{x^2} - \dfrac{1}{y^2}$

   $\left(\dfrac{1}{2}\right)\left(\dfrac{1}{4}\right) = \dfrac{1}{x^2} - \dfrac{1}{y^2}$

   $\dfrac{1}{8} = \dfrac{1}{x^2} - \dfrac{1}{y^2}$

10. (C) $x^2 - x - 20 = (x - 5)(x + 4)$

Exercise 1

1. (B) $\dfrac{3x^2(x-y)}{9x(x-y)} = \dfrac{x}{3}$

2. (A) $\dfrac{2(x-4)}{3(4-x)} = -\dfrac{2}{3}$

3. (E) $\dfrac{3x-y}{y-3x} = -1$ regardless of the values of x

   and y, as long as the denominator is not 0.

4. (C) $\dfrac{(b+4)(b-3)}{(b+5)(b-3)} = \dfrac{(b+4)}{(b+5)}$

5. (D) $\dfrac{2(x+2y)}{6(x+2y)} = \dfrac{2}{6} = \dfrac{1}{3}$

Exercise 2

1. (D) $\dfrac{6x+5y}{2x} - \dfrac{4x+y}{2x}$

   $= \dfrac{6x+5y-4x-y}{2x} = \dfrac{2x+4y}{2x}$

   $= \dfrac{2(x+2y)}{2x} = \dfrac{x+2y}{x}$

2. (D) $\dfrac{3c+3d}{c+d} = \dfrac{3(c+d)}{c+d} = 3$

3. (B) $\dfrac{2a+3a}{10} = \dfrac{5a}{10} = \dfrac{a}{2}$

4. (A) $\dfrac{x+4+3}{6} = \dfrac{x+7}{6}$

5. (C) $\dfrac{3b(10)-4(7b)}{4(10)} = \dfrac{30b-28b}{40}$

   $= \dfrac{2b}{40} = \dfrac{b}{20}$

Exercise 3

1. (B) Divide x^2 and y^3.

   $\dfrac{1}{1} \cdot \dfrac{y}{x^3} = \dfrac{y}{x^3}$

2. (C) $c \cdot \dfrac{b}{c} = b$

3. (C) $\dfrac{ax}{by} \cdot \dfrac{y}{x}$ Divide y and x. $\dfrac{a}{b}$

4. (D) $4abc \cdot \dfrac{3d^2}{2a^2b}$ Divide 2, a, and b.

   $2c \cdot \dfrac{3d^2}{a} = \dfrac{6cd^2}{a}$

5. (A) $\dfrac{3a^2c^4}{4b^2} \cdot \dfrac{1}{6ac^2}$ Divide 3, a, and c^2.

   $\dfrac{ac^2}{4b^2} \cdot \dfrac{1}{2} = \dfrac{ac^2}{8b^2}$

Exercise 4

1. (E) Multiply every term by 20.

   $\dfrac{4-30}{15} = \dfrac{-26}{15}$

2. (C) Multiply every term by x^2.

   $\dfrac{a}{a^2x} = \dfrac{1}{ax}$

3. (C) Multiply every term by xy.

   $\dfrac{y-x}{y+x}$

4. (A) Multiply every term by xy.

   $\dfrac{x+y}{x}$

5. (E) Multiply every term by $\dfrac{t^2}{2}$.

   $\dfrac{4+t}{2}$

Exercise 5

1. (A) $(a + b)(a - b) = a^2 - b^2$

$$\left(\frac{1}{3}\right)\left(\frac{1}{4}\right) = a^2 - b^2$$

$$\frac{1}{12} = a^2 - b^2$$

2. (D) $(a - b)^2 = a^2 - 2ab + b^2 = 40$

Substituting 8 for ab, we have

$$a^2 - 16 + b^2 = 40$$

$$a^2 + b^2 = 56$$

3. (C) $(a + b)(a - b) = a^2 - b^2$

$$8(a - b) = 24$$

$$(a - b) = 3$$

4. (A) $x^2 + 4x - 45 = (x + 9)(x - 5)$

5. (D) $\left(\dfrac{1}{c} - \dfrac{1}{d}\right)\left(\dfrac{1}{c} + \dfrac{1}{d}\right) = \dfrac{1}{c^2} - \dfrac{1}{d^2}$

$$(5)(3) = \frac{1}{c^2} - \frac{1}{d^2}$$

$$15 = \frac{1}{c^2} - \frac{1}{d^2}$$

Retest

1. (B) $\dfrac{4n + n}{10} = \dfrac{5n}{10} = \dfrac{n}{2} = \dfrac{1}{2}n$

2. (A) $\dfrac{x}{y} - \dfrac{3}{1} = \dfrac{x - 3y}{y}$

3. (B) $\dfrac{x^2 + 2x - 8}{4 + x} \cdot \dfrac{3}{2 - x}$

$$= \frac{(x + 4)(x - 2)}{4 + x} \cdot \frac{3}{2 - x}$$

Divide $x + 4$. $\dfrac{3(x - 2)}{2 - x} = \dfrac{3(x - 2)}{-1(x - 2)} = -3$

4. (D) $\dfrac{5a^3}{b} \cdot \dfrac{5a^3}{b} \cdot \dfrac{5a^3}{b} = \dfrac{125a^9}{b^3}$

5. (E) Multiply every term by x.

$$\frac{3x - 1}{y}$$

6. (B) Multiply every term by x^2.

$$\frac{3x^2 - x}{3}$$

7. (A) $a^2 - b^2 = (a + b)(a - b) = 100$

Substituting 25 for $a + b$, we have

$$25(a - b) = 100$$

$$a - b = 4$$

8. (D) $x^2 - 8x - 20 = (x - 10)(x + 2)$

9. (A) $\left(\dfrac{1}{a} - \dfrac{1}{b}\right)\left(\dfrac{1}{a} + \dfrac{1}{b}\right) = \dfrac{1}{a^2} - \dfrac{1}{b^2}$

$$(6)(5) = \frac{1}{a^2} - \frac{1}{b^2}$$

$$30 = \frac{1}{a^2} - \frac{1}{b^2}$$

10. (E) $(x - y)^2 = x^2 - 2xy + y^2 = 30$

Substituting 17 for xy, we have

$$x^2 - 34 + y^2 = 30$$

$$x^2 + y^2 = 64$$

Problem Solving in Algebra

12

DIAGNOSTIC TEST

Directions: Work out each problem. Circle the letter that appears before your answer.

Answers are at the end of the chapter.

1. Find three consecutive odd integers such that the sum of the first two is four times the third.

   (A) 3, 5, 7
   (B) -3, -1, 1
   (C) -11, -9, -7
   (D) -7, -5, -3
   (E) 9, 11, 13

2. Find the shortest side of a triangle whose perimeter is 64, if the ratio of two of its sides is 4 : 3 and the third side is 20 less than the sum of the other two.

   (A) 6
   (B) 18
   (C) 20
   (D) 22
   (E) 24

3. A purse contains 16 coins in dimes and quarters. If the value of the coins is $2.50, how many dimes are there?

   (A) 6
   (B) 8
   (C) 9
   (D) 10
   (E) 12

4. How many quarts of water must be added to 18 quarts of a 32% alcohol solution to dilute it to a solution that is only 12% alcohol?

   (A) 10
   (B) 14
   (C) 20
   (D) 30
   (E) 34

5. Danny drove to Yosemite Park from his home at 60 miles per hour. On his trip home, his rate was 10 miles per hour less and the trip took one hour longer. How far is his home from the park?

   (A) 65 mi.
   (B) 100 mi.
   (C) 200 mi.
   (D) 280 mi.
   (E) 300 mi.

6. Two cars leave a restaurant at the same time and travel along a straight highway in opposite directions. At the end of three hours they are 300 miles apart. Find the rate of the slower car, if one car travels at a rate 20 miles per hour faster than the other.

   (A) 30
   (B) 40
   (C) 50
   (D) 55
   (E) 60

7. The numerator of a fraction is one half the denominator. If the numerator is increased by 2 and the denominator is decreased by 2, the value of the fraction is $\frac{2}{3}$. Find the numerator of the original fraction.

   (A) 4
   (B) 8
   (C) 10
   (D) 12
   (E) 20

8. Darren can mow the lawn in 20 minutes, while Valerie needs 30 minutes to do the same job. How many minutes will it take them to mow the lawn if they work together?

   (A) 10
   (B) 8
   (C) 16
   (D) $6\frac{1}{2}$
   (E) 12

9. Meredith is 3 times as old as Adam. Six years from now, she will be twice as old as Adam will be then. How old is Adam now?

   (A) 6
   (B) 12
   (C) 18
   (D) 20
   (E) 24

10. Mr. Barry invested some money at 5% and an amount half as great at 4%. His total annual income from both investments was $210. Find the amount invested at 4%.

    (A) $1000
    (B) $1500
    (C) $2000
    (D) $2500
    (E) $3000

In the following sections, we will review some of the major types of algebraic problems. Although not every problem you come across will fall into one of these categories, it will help you to be thoroughly familiar with these types of problems. By practicing with the problems that follow, you will learn to translate words into mathematical equations. You should then be able to handle other types of problems confidently.

In solving verbal problems, it is most important that you read carefully and know what it is that you are trying to find. Once this is done, represent your unknown algebraically. Write the equation that translates the words of the problem into the symbols of mathematics. Solve that equation by the techniques previously reviewed.

1. COIN PROBLEMS

In solving coin problems, it is best to change the value of all monies to cents before writing an equation. Thus, the number of nickels must be multiplied by 5 to give the value in cents, dimes by 10, quarters by 25, half dollars by 50, and dollars by 100.

Example:

> Sue has $1.35, consisting of nickels and dimes. If she has 9 more nickels than dimes, how many nickels does she have?

Solution:

$$\text{Let } x = \text{the number of dimes}$$
$$x + 9 = \text{the number of nickels}$$
$$10x = \text{the value of the dimes in cents}$$
$$5x + 45 = \text{the value of the nickels in cents}$$
$$135 = \text{the value of the money she has in cents}$$
$$10x + 5x + 45 = 135$$
$$15x = 90$$
$$x = 60$$

She has 6 dimes and 15 nickles.

In a problem such as this, you can be sure that 6 would be among the multiple choice answers given. You must be sure to read carefully what you are asked to find and then continue until you have found the quantity sought.

Exercise 1

Work out each problem. Circle the letter that appears before your answer.

1. Marie has $2.20 in dimes and quarters. If the number of dimes is $\frac{1}{4}$ the number of quarters, how many dimes does she have?

    (A) 2
    (B) 4
    (C) 6
    (D) 8
    (E) 10

2. Lisa has 45 coins that are worth a total of $3.50. If the coins are all nickels and dimes, how many more dimes than nickels does she have?

    (A) 5
    (B) 10
    (C) 15
    (D) 20
    (E) 25

3. A postal clerk sold 40 stamps for $5.40. Some were 10-cent stamps and some were 15-cent stamps. How many 10-cent stamps were there?

    (A) 10
    (B) 12
    (C) 20
    (D) 24
    (E) 28

4. Each of the 30 students in Homeroom 704 contributed either a nickel or a quarter to the Cancer Fund. If the total amount collected was $4.70, how many students contributed a nickel?

    (A) 10
    (B) 12
    (C) 14
    (D) 16
    (E) 18

5. In a purse containing nickels and dimes, the ratio of nickels to dimes is 3 : 4. If there are 28 coins in all, what is the value of the dimes?

    (A) 60¢
    (B) $1.12
    (C) $1.60
    (D) 12¢
    (E) $1.00

2. CONSECUTIVE INTEGER PROBLEMS

Consecutive integers are one apart and can be represented algebraically as $x, x + 1, x + 2$, and so on. Consecutive even and odd integers are both two apart and can be represented by $x, x + 2, x + 4$, and so on. *Never* try to represent consecutive odd integers by $x, x + 1, x + 3$, etc., for if x is odd, $x + 1$ would be even.

Example:

Find three consecutive odd integers whose sum is 219.

Solution:

Represent the integers as $x, x + 2$, and $x + 4$. Write an equation stating that their sum is 219.

$$3x + 6 = 219$$
$$3x = 213$$
$$x = 71, \text{ making the integers } 71, 73, \text{ and } 75.$$

Exercise 2

Work out each problem. Circle the letter that appears before your answer.

1. If $n + 1$ is the largest of four consecutive integers, represent the sum of the four integers.
    (A) $4n + 10$
    (B) $4n - 2$
    (C) $4n - 4$
    (D) $4n - 5$
    (E) $4n - 8$

2. If n is the first of two consecutive odd integers, which equation could be used to find these integers if the difference of their squares is 120?
    (A) $(n + 1)^2 - n^2 = 120$
    (B) $n^2 - (n + 1)^2 = 120$
    (C) $n^2 - (n + 2)^2 = 120$
    (D) $(n + 2)^2 - n^2 = 120$
    (E) $[(n + 2) - n]^2 = 120$

3. Find the average of four consecutive odd integers whose sum is 112.
    (A) 25
    (B) 29
    (C) 31
    (D) 28
    (E) 30

4. Find the second of three consecutive integers if the sum of the first and third is 26.
    (A) 11
    (B) 12
    (C) 13
    (D) 14
    (E) 15

5. If $2x - 3$ is an odd integer, find the next even integer.
    (A) $2x - 5$
    (B) $2x - 4$
    (C) $2x - 2$
    (D) $2x - 1$
    (E) $2x + 1$

3. AGE PROBLEMS

In solving age problems, you are usually called upon to represent a person's age at the present time, several years from now, or several years ago. A person's age x years from now is found by adding x to his present age. A person's age x years ago is found by subtracting x from his present age.

Example:

Michelle was 15 years old y years ago. Represent her age x years from now.

Solution:

Her present age is $15 + y$. In x years, her age will be her present age plus x, or $15 + y + x$.

Example:

Jody is now 20 years old and her brother, Glenn, is 14. How many years ago was Jody three times as old as Glenn was then?

Solution:

We are comparing their ages x years ago. At that time, Jody's age $(20 - x)$ was three times Glenn's age $(14 - x)$. This can be stated as the equation

$$20 - x = 3(14 - x)$$
$$20 - x = 42 - 3x$$
$$2x = 22$$
$$x = 11$$

To check, find their ages 11 years ago. Jody was 9 while Glenn was 3. Therefore, Jody was three times as old as Glenn was then.

Exercise 3

Work out each problem. Circle the letter that appears before your answer.

1. Mark is now 4 times as old as his brother Stephen. In 1 year Mark will be 3 times as old as Stephen will be then. How old was Mark two years ago?

    (A) 2
    (B) 3
    (C) 6
    (D) 8
    (E) 9

2. Mr. Burke is 24 years older than his son Jack. In 8 years, Mr. Burke will be twice as old as Jack will be then. How old is Mr. Burke now?

    (A) 16
    (B) 24
    (C) 32
    (D) 40
    (E) 48

3. Lili is 23 years old and Melanie is 15 years old. How many years ago was Lili twice as old as Melanie?

    (A) 7
    (B) 16
    (C) 9
    (D) 5
    (E) 8

4. Two years from now, Karen's age will be $2x + 1$. Represent her age two years ago.

    (A) $2x - 4$
    (B) $2x - 1$
    (C) $2x + 3$
    (D) $2x - 3$
    (E) $2x - 2$

5. Alice is now 5 years younger than her brother Robert, whose age is $4x + 3$. Represent her age 3 years from now.

    (A) $4x - 5$
    (B) $4x - 2$
    (C) $4x$
    (D) $4x + 1$
    (E) $4x - 1$

4. INVESTMENT PROBLEMS

All interest referred to is simple interest. The annual amount of interest paid on an investment is found by multiplying the amount invested, called the principal, by the percent of interest, called the rate.

PRINCIPAL · RATE = INTEREST INCOME

Example:

Mrs. Friedman invested some money in a bank paying 4% interest annually and a second amount, $500 less than the first, in a bank paying 6% interest. If her annual income from both investments was $50, how much money did she invest at 6%?

Solution:

Represent the two investments algebraically.
x = amount invested at 4%
x - 500 = amount invested at 6%
.04x = annual interest from 4% investment
.06(x - 500) = annual interest from 6% investment
.04x + .06(x - 500) = 50
Multiply by 100 to remove decimals.

$$4x + 6(x - 500) = 5000$$
$$4x + 6x - 3000 = 5000$$
$$10x = 8000$$
$$x = 800$$
$$x - 500 = 300$$

She invested $300 at 6%.

Exercise 4

Work out each problem. Circle the letter that appears before your answer.

1. Barbara invested x dollars at 3% and $400 more than this amount at 5%. Represent the annual income from the 5% investment.

    (A) .05x
    (B) .05 (x + 400)
    (C) .05x + 400
    (D) 5x + 40000
    (E) none of these

2. Mr. Blum invested $10,000, part at 6% and the rest at 5%. If x represents the amount invested at 6%, represent the annual income from the 5% investment.

    (A) 5(x - 10,000)
    (B) 5(10,000 - x)
    (C) .05(x + 10,000)
    (D) .05(x - 10,000)
    (E) .05(10,000 - x)

3. Dr. Kramer invested $2000 in an account paying 6% interest annually. How many more dollars must she invest at 3% so that her total annual income is 4% of her entire investment?

    (A) $120
    (B) $1000
    (C) $2000
    (D) $4000
    (E) $6000

4. Marion invested $7200, part at 4% and the rest at 5%. If the annual income from both investments was the same, find her total annual income from these investments.

    (A) $160
    (B) $320
    (C) $4000
    (D) $3200
    (E) $1200

5. Mr. Maxwell inherited some money from his father. He invested $\frac{1}{2}$ of this amount at 5%, $\frac{1}{3}$ of this amount at 6%, and the rest at 3%. If the total annual income from these investments was $300, what was the amount he inherited?

    (A) $600
    (B) $60
    (C) $2000
    (D) $3000
    (E) $6000

5. FRACTION PROBLEMS

A fraction is a ratio between two numbers. If the value of a fraction is $\frac{3}{4}$, it does not mean that the numerator is 3 and the denominator 4. The numerator and denominator could be 9 and 12 respectively, or 1.5 and 2, or 45 and 60, or an infinite number of other combinations. All we know is that the ratio of numerator to denominator will be 3 : 4. Therefore, the numerator may be represented by $3x$ and the denominator by $4x$. The fraction is then represented by $\frac{3x}{4x}$.

Example:

The value of a fraction is $\frac{2}{3}$. If one is subtracted from the numerator and added to the denominator, the value of the fraction is $\frac{1}{2}$. Find the original fraction.

Solution:

Represent the original fraction as $\frac{2x}{3x}$. If one is subtracted from the numerator and added to the denominator, the new fraction is $\frac{2x-1}{3x+1}$. The value of this new fraction is $\frac{1}{2}$.

$$\frac{2x-1}{3x+1} = \frac{1}{2}$$

Cross multiply to eliminate fractions.

$$4x - 2 = 3x + 1$$
$$x = 3$$

The original fraction is $\frac{2x}{3x}$, which is $\frac{6}{9}$.

Exercise 5

Work out each problem. Circle the letter that appears before your answer.

1. A fraction is equivalent to $\frac{4}{5}$. If the numerator is increased by 4 and the denominator is increased by 10, the value of the resulting fraction is $\frac{2}{3}$. Find the numerator of the original fraction.

   (A) 4
   (B) 5
   (C) 12
   (D) 16
   (E) 20

2. What number must be added to both the numerator and the denominator of the fraction $\frac{5}{21}$ to give a fraction equal to $\frac{3}{7}$?

   (A) 3
   (B) 4
   (C) 5
   (D) 6
   (E) 7

3. The value of a certain fraction is $\frac{3}{5}$. If both the numerator and denominator are increased by 5, the new fraction is equivalent to $\frac{7}{10}$. Find the original fraction.

   (A) $\frac{3}{5}$
   (B) $\frac{6}{10}$
   (C) $\frac{9}{15}$
   (D) $\frac{12}{20}$
   (E) $\frac{15}{25}$

4. The denominator of a certain fraction is 5 more than the numerator. If 3 is added to both numerator and denominator, the value of the new fraction is $\frac{2}{3}$. Find the original fraction.

   (A) $\frac{3}{8}$
   (B) $\frac{4}{9}$
   (C) $\frac{11}{16}$
   (D) $\frac{12}{17}$
   (E) $\frac{7}{12}$

5. The denominator of a fraction is twice as large as the numerator. If 4 is added to both numerator and denominator, the value of the fraction is $\frac{5}{8}$. Find the denominator of the original fraction.

   (A) 6
   (B) 10
   (C) 12
   (D) 14
   (E) 16

6. MIXTURE PROBLEMS

There are two kinds of mixture problems with which you should be familiar. The first is sometimes referred to as dry mixture, in which we mix dry ingredients of different values, such as nuts or coffee. Also solved by the same method are problems dealing with tickets at different prices, and similar problems. In solving this type of problem it is best to organize the data in a chart with three rows and columns, labeled as illustrated in the following example.

Example:

Mr. Sweet wishes to mix candy worth 36 cents a pound with candy worth 52 cents a pound to make 300 pounds of a mixture worth 40 cents a pound. How many pounds of the more expensive candy should he use?

Solution:

	No. of pounds ·	Price per pound =	Total value
More expensive	x	52	$52x$
Less expensive	$300 - x$	36	$36(300 - x)$
Mixture	300	40	12000

The value of the more expensive candy plus the value of the less expensive candy must be equal to the value of the mixture. Almost all mixture problems derive their equation from adding the final column in the chart.
$52x + 36(300 - x) = 12000$
Notice that all values were computed in cents to avoid decimals.

$$52x + 10800 - 36x = 1200$$

$$16x = 1200$$

$$x = 75$$

He should use 75 pounds of the more expensive candy.

In solving the second type of mixture problem, we are dealing with percents instead of prices and amounts of a certain ingredient instead of values. As we did with prices, we may omit the decimal point from the percents, as long as we do it in every line of the chart.

Example:

How many quarts of pure alcohol must be added to 15 quarts of a solution that is 40% alcohol to strengthen it to a solution that is 50% alcohol?

Solution:

	No. of quarts ·	Percent Alcohol =	Amount of Alcohol
Diluted	15	40	600
Pure	x	100	$100x$
Mixture	$15 + x$	50	$50(15 + x)$

Notice that the percent of alcohol in pure alcohol is 100. If we had added pure water to weaken the solution, the percent of alcohol in pure water would have been 0. Again, the equation comes from adding the final column since the amount of alcohol in the original solution plus the amount of alcohol added must equal the amount of alcohol in the new solution.

$$600 + 100x = 50(15 + x)$$
$$600 + 100x = 750 + 50x$$
$$50x = 150$$
$$x = 3$$

3 quarts of alcohol should be added.

Exercise 6

Work out each problem. Circle the letter that appears before your answer.

1. Express, in terms of x, the value, in cents, of x pounds of 40-cent cookies and $(30 - x)$ pounds of 50-cent cookies.

   (A) $150 + 10x$
   (B) $150 - 50x$
   (C) $1500 - 10x$
   (D) $1500 - 50x$
   (E) $1500 + 10x$

2. How many pounds of nuts selling for 70 cents a pound must be mixed with 30 pounds of nuts selling at 90 cents a pound to make a mixture that will sell for 85 cents a pound?

   (A) 7.5
   (B) 10
   (C) 22.5
   (D) 40
   (E) 12

3. A container holds 10 pints of a solution which is 20% acid. If 3 quarts of pure acid are added to the container, what percent of the resulting mixture is acid?

   (A) 5
   (B) 10
   (C) 20
   (D) 50
   (E) $33\frac{1}{3}$

4. A solution of 60 quarts of sugar and water is 20% sugar. How much water must be added to make a solution that is 5% sugar?

   (A) 180 qts.
   (B) 120 qts.
   (C) 100 qts.
   (D) 80 qts.
   (E) 20 qts.

5. How much water must be evaporated from 240 pounds of a solution that is 3% alcohol to strengthen it to a solution that is 5% alcohol?

   (A) 120 lbs.
   (B) 96 lbs.
   (C) 100 lbs.
   (D) 84 lbs.
   (E) 140 lbs.

7. MOTION PROBLEMS

The fundamental relationship in all motion problems is that rate times time is equal to distance.

$$RATE \cdot TIME = DISTANCE$$

The problems at the level of this examination usually deal with a relationship between distances. Most motion problems fall into one of three categories.

A. Motion in opposite directions

This can occur when objects start at the same point and move apart, or when they start at a given distance apart and move toward each other. In either case, the distance covered by the first object plus the distance covered by the second is equal to the total distance covered. This can be shown in the following diagram.

In either case, $d_1 + d_2$ = total distance covered.

B. Motion in the same direction

This type of problem is sometimes referred to as a "catch up" problem. Usually two objects leave the same place at different times and at different rates, but the one that leaves later "catches up" to the one that leaves earlier. In such cases the two distances must be equal. If one is still ahead of the other, then an equation must be written expressing this fact.

C. Round trip

In this type of problem, the rate going is different from the rate returning. The times are also different. But if we go somewhere and then return to the starting point, the distances must be equal.

To solve any type of motion problem, it is helpful to organize the information in a chart with columns for rate, time, and distance. A separate line should be used for each moving object. Be very careful of units used. If the rate is given in *miles per hour*, the time must be in *hours* and the distance will be in *miles*.

Example:

> A passenger train and a freight train leave at 10:30 A.M. from stations that are 405 miles apart and travel toward each other. The rate of the passenger train is 45 miles per hour faster than that of the freight train. If they pass each other at 1:30 P.M., how fast was the passenger train traveling?

Solution:

> Notice that each train traveled exactly 3 hours.

	Rate	$\cdot$	Time	=	Distance
Passenger	$x + 45$		3		$3x + 135$
Freight	x		3		$3x$

$$3x + 135 + 3x = 405$$
$$6x = 270$$
$$x = 45$$

The rate of the passenger train was 90 m.p.h.

Example:

Susie left her home at 11 A.M., traveling along Route 1 at 30 miles per hour. At 1 P.M., her brother Richard left home and started after her on the same road at 45 miles per hour. At what time did Richard catch up to Susie?

Solution:

	Rate ·	Time =	Distance
Susie	30	x	$30x$
Richard	45	$x - 2$	$45x - 90$

Since Richard left 2 hours later than Susie, he traveled for $x - 2$ hours, while Susie traveled for x hours. Notice that we do not fill in 11 and 1 in the time column, as these are times on the clock and not actual hours traveled. Since Richard caught up to Susie, the distances must be equal.

$$30x = 45x - 90$$
$$90 = 15x$$
$$x = 6$$

Susie traveled for 6 hours, which means it was 6 hours past 11 A.M., or 5 P.M. when Richard caught up to her.

Example:

How far can Scott drive into the country if he drives out at 40 miles per hour and returns over the same road at 30 miles per hour and spends 8 hours away from home including a one-hour stop for lunch?

Solution:

His actual driving time is 7 hours, which must be divided into two parts. If one part is x, the other is what is left, or $7 - x$.

	Rate ·	Time =	Distance
Going	40	x	$40x$
Return	30	$7 - x$	$210x - 30x$

The distances are equal.

$$40x = 210 - 30x$$
$$70x = 210$$
$$x = 3$$

If he traveled 40 miles per hour for 3 hours, he went 120 miles.

Exercise 7

Work out each problem. Circle the letter that appears before your answer.

1. At 10 A.M. two cars started traveling toward each other from towns 287 miles apart. They passed each other at 1:30 P.M. If the rate of the faster car exceeded the rate of the slower car by 6 miles per hour, find the rate, in miles per hour, of the faster car.

   (A) 38
   (B) 40
   (C) 44
   (D) 48
   (E) 50

2. A motorist covers 350 miles in 8 hours. Before noon he averages 50 miles per hour, but after noon he averages only 40 miles per hour. At what time did he leave?

   (A) 7 A.M.
   (B) 8 A.M.
   (C) 9 A.M.
   (D) 10 A.M.
   (E) 11 A.M.

3. At 3 P.M. a plane left Kennedy Airport for Los Angeles traveling at 600 m.p.h. At 3:30 P.M. another plane left the same airport on the same route traveling at 650 m.p.h. At what time did the second plane overtake the first?

   (A) 5:15 P.M.
   (B) 6:45 P.M.
   (C) 6:50 P.M.
   (D) 7:15 P.M.
   (E) 9:30 P.M.

4. Joe left home at 10 A.M. and walked out into the country at 4 miles per hour. He returned on the same road at 2 miles per hour. If he arrived home at 4 P.M., how many miles into the country did he walk?

   (A) 6
   (B) 8
   (C) 10
   (D) 11
   (E) 12

5. Two cars leave a restaurant at the same time and proceed in the same direction along the same route. One car averages 36 miles per hour and the other 31 miles per hour. In how many hours will the faster car be 30 miles ahead of the slower car?

   (A) 3

   (B) $3\dfrac{1}{2}$

   (C) 4

   (D) 6

   (E) $6\dfrac{1}{4}$

8. WORK PROBLEMS

In most work problems, a job is broken up into several parts, each representing a fractional portion of the entire job. For each part represented, the numerator should represent the time actually spent working, while the denominator should represent the total time needed to do the job alone. The sum of all the individual fractions must be 1 if the job is completed.

Example:

John can complete a paper route in 20 minutes. Steve can complete the same route in 30 minutes. How long will it take them to complete the route if they work together?

Solution:

$$\frac{\text{Time actually spent}}{\text{Time needed to do}}\ \underset{\text{John}}{\frac{x}{20}}\ +\ \underset{\text{Steve}}{\frac{x}{30}}\ =\ 1$$

entire job alone

Multiply by 60 to clear fractions.

$$3x + 2x = 60$$
$$5x = 60$$
$$x = 12$$

Example:

Mr. Powell can mow his lawn twice as fast as his son Mike. Together they do the job in 20 minutes. How many minutes would it take Mr. Powell to do the job alone?

Solution:

If it takes Mr. Powell x hours to mow the lawn, Mike will take twice as long, or $2x$ hours, to mow the lawn.

$$\underset{\text{Mr. Powell}}{\frac{20}{x}}\ +\ \underset{\text{Mike}}{\frac{20}{2x}}\ =\ 1$$

Multiply by $2x$ to clear fractions.

$$40 + 20 = 2x$$
$$60 = 2x$$
$$x = 30 \text{ minutes}$$

Exercise 8

Work out each problem. Circle the letter that appears before your answer.

1. Mr. White can paint his barn in 5 days. What part of the barn is still unpainted after he has worked for x days?

   (A) $\dfrac{x}{5}$

   (B) $\dfrac{5}{x}$

   (C) $\dfrac{x-5}{x}$

   (D) $\dfrac{5-x}{x}$

   (E) $\dfrac{5-x}{5}$

2. Mary can clean the house in 6 hours. Her younger sister Ruth can do the same job in 9 hours. In how many hours can they do the job if they work together?

   (A) $3\dfrac{1}{2}$

   (B) $3\dfrac{3}{5}$

   (C) 4

   (D) $4\dfrac{1}{4}$

   (E) $4\dfrac{1}{2}$

3. A swimming pool can be filled by an inlet pipe in 3 hours. It can be drained by a drainpipe in 6 hours. By mistake, both pipes are opened at the same time. If the pool is empty, in how many hours will it be filled?

   (A) 4

   (B) $4\dfrac{1}{2}$

   (C) 5

   (D) $5\dfrac{1}{2}$

   (E) 6

4. Mr. Jones can plow his field with his tractor in 4 hours. If he uses his manual plow, it takes three times as long to plow the same field. After working with the tractor for two hours, he ran out of gas and had to finish with the manual plow. How long did it take to complete the job after the tractor ran out of gas?

   (A) 4 hours
   (B) 6 hours
   (C) 7 hours
   (D) 8 hours

   (E) $8\dfrac{1}{2}$ hours

5. Michael and Barry can complete a job in 2 hours when working together. If Michael requires 6 hours to do the job alone, how many hours does Barry need to do the job alone?

   (A) 2

   (B) $2\dfrac{1}{2}$

   (C) 3

   (D) $3\dfrac{1}{2}$

   (E) 4

RETEST

Work out each problem. Circle the letter that appears before your answer.

1. Three times the first of three consecutive odd integers is 10 more than the third. Find the middle integer.

    (A) 7
    (B) 9
    (C) 11
    (D) 13
    (E) 15

2. The denominator of a fraction is three times the numerator. If 8 is added to the numerator and 6 is subtracted from the denominator, the resulting fraction is equivalent to $\frac{8}{9}$. Find the original fraction.

    (A) $\frac{16}{18}$

    (B) $\frac{1}{3}$

    (C) $\frac{8}{24}$

    (D) $\frac{5}{3}$

    (E) $\frac{8}{16}$

3. How many quarts of water must be added to 40 quarts of a 5% acid solution to dilute it to a 2% solution?

    (A) 80
    (B) 40
    (C) 60
    (D) 20
    (E) 50

4. Miriam is 11 years older than Charles. In three years she will be twice as old as Charles will be then. How old was Miriam 2 years ago?

    (A) 6
    (B) 8
    (C) 9
    (D) 17
    (E) 19

5. One printing press can print the school newspaper in 12 hours, while another press can print it in 18 hours. How long will the job take if both presses work simultaneously?

    (A) 7 hrs. 12 min.
    (B) 6 hrs. 36 min.
    (C) 6 hrs. 50 min.
    (D) 7 hrs. 20 min.
    (E) 7 hrs. 15 min.

6. Janet has $2.05 in dimes and quarters. If she has four fewer dimes than quarters, how much money does she have in dimes?

    (A) 30¢
    (B) 80¢
    (C) $1.20
    (D) 70¢
    (E) 90¢

7. Mr. Cooper invested a sum of money at 6%. He invested a second sum, $150 more than the first, at 3%. If his total annual income was $54, how much did he invest at 3%?

    (A) $700
    (B) $650
    (C) $500
    (D) $550
    (E) $600

8. Two buses are 515 miles apart. At 9:30 A.M. they start traveling toward each other at rates of 48 and 55 miles per hour. At what time will they pass each other?

    (A) 1:30 P.M.
    (B) 2:30 P.M.
    (C) 2 P.M.
    (D) 3 P.M.
    (E) 3:30 P.M.

9. Carol started from home on a trip averaging 30 miles per hour. How fast must her mother drive to catch up to her in 3 hours if she leaves 30 minutes after Carol?

   (A) 35 m.p.h.
   (B) 39 m.p.h.
   (C) 40 m.p.h.
   (D) 55 m.p.h.
   (E) 60 m.p.h.

10. Dan has twice as many pennies as Frank. If Frank wins 12 pennies from Dan, both boys will have the same number of pennies. How many pennies did Dan have originally?

   (A) 24
   (B) 12
   (C) 36
   (D) 48
   (E) 52

SOLUTIONS TO PRACTICE EXERCISES

Diagnostic Test

1. (D) Represent the integers as x, $x + 2$, and $x + 4$.

$$x + x + 2 = 4(x + 4)$$
$$2x + 2 = 4x + 16$$
$$-14 = 2x$$
$$x = -7, x + 2 = -5, x + 4 = -3$$

2. (B) Represent the first two sides as $4x$ and $3x$, then the third side is $7x - 20$.

$$4x + 3x + (7x - 20) = 64$$
$$14x - 20 = 64$$
$$14x = 84$$
$$x = 6$$

The shortest side is $3(6) = 18$.

3. (D)

$$x = \text{the number of dimes}$$
$$16 - x = \text{the number of quarters}$$
$$10x = \text{value of dimes in cents}$$
$$400 - 25x = \text{value of quarters in cents}$$
$$10x + 400 - 25x = 250$$
$$-15x = -150$$
$$x = 10$$

4. (D)

	No of Quarts ·	Percent Alcohol =	Amount of Alcohol
Original	18	32	576
Added	x	0	0
New	$18 + x$	12	$216 + 12x$

$$576 = 216 + 12x$$
$$360 = 12x$$
$$x = 30$$

5. (E)

	R ·	T =	D
Going	60	x	$60x$
Return	50	$x + 1$	$50x + 50$

$$60x = 50x + 50$$
$$10x = 50$$
$$x = 50$$

If he drove for 5 hours at 60 miles per hour, he drove 300 miles.

6. (B)

	R	$\cdot$	T	$=$	D
Slow	x		3		$3x$
Fast	$x + 20$		3		$3x + 60$

$$3x + 3x + 60 = 300$$
$$6x = 240$$
$$x = 40$$

7. (C) Represent the original fraction by $\dfrac{x}{2x}$.

$$\frac{x+2}{2x-2} = \frac{2}{3}$$

Cross multiply.

$$3x + 6 = 4x - 4$$
$$x = 10$$

8. (E)

Darren   Valerie

$$\frac{x}{20} \quad + \quad \frac{x}{30} \quad = 1$$

Multiply by 60.

$$3x + 2x = 60$$
$$5x = 60$$
$$x = 12$$

9. (A) Let $x =$ Adam's age now

$3x =$ Meredith's age now

$x + 6 =$ Adam's age in 6 years

$3x + 6 =$ Meredith's age in 6 years

$$3x + 6 = 2(x + 6)$$
$$3x + 6 = 2x + 12$$
$$x = 6$$

10. (B) Let $x =$ amount invested at 4%

$2x =$ amount invested at 5%

$$.04x + .05(2x) = 210$$

Multiply by 100 to eliminate decimals.

$$4x + 5(2x) = 21{,}000$$
$$14x = 21{,}000$$
$$x = \$1500$$

Exercise 1

1. (A) Let x = number of dimes

$4x$ = number of quarters

$10x$ = value of dimes in cents

$100x$ = value of quarters in cents

$10x + 100x = 220$

$100x = 220$

$x = 2$

2. (A) Let x = number of nickels

$45 - x$ = number of dimes

$5x$ = value of nickels in cents

$450 - 10x$ = value of dimes in cents

$5x + 450 - 10x = 350$

$-5x = -100$

$x = 20$

20 nickels and 25 dimes

3. (B) Let x = number of 10 - cent stamps

$40 - x$ = number of 15 - cent stamps

$10x$ = value of 10 - cent stamps

$600 - 15x$ = value of 15 - cent stamps

$10x + 600 - 15x = 540$

$-5x = -60$

$x = 12$

4. (C) Let x = number of nickels

$30 - x$ = number of quarters

$5x$ = value of nickels in cents

$750 - 25x$ = value of quarters in cents

$5x + 750 - 25x = 470$

$-20x = -280$

$x = 14$

5. (C) Let $3x$ = number of nickels

$4x$ = number of dimes

$3x + 4x = 28$

$7x = 28$

$x = 4$

There are 16 dimes, worth \$1.60.

Exercise 2

1. (B) Consecutive integers are 1 apart. If the fourth is $n + 1$, the third is n, the second is $n - 1$, and the first is $n - 2$. The sum of these is $4n - 2$.

2. (D) The other integer is $n + 2$. If a difference is positive, the larger quantity must come first.

3. (D) To find the average of any 4 numbers, divide their sum by 4.

4. (C) Represent the integers as x, $x + 1$, and $x + 2$.

$x + x + 2 = 26$

$2x = 24$

$x = 12$

$x + 1 = 13$

5. (C) An even integer follows an odd integer, so simply add 1.

Exercise 3

1. (C) Let x = Stephen's age now

$$4x = \text{Mark's age now}$$
$$x+1 = \text{Stephen's age in 1 year}$$
$$4x+1 = \text{Mark's age in 1 year}$$
$$4x+1 = 3(x+1)$$
$$4x+1 = 3x+3$$
$$x = 2$$

Mark is now 8, so 2 years ago he was 6.

2. (D) Let x = Jack's age now

$$x+24 = \text{Mr. Burke's age now}$$
$$x+8 = \text{Jack's age in 8 years}$$
$$x+32 = \text{Mr. Burke's age in 8 years}$$
$$x+32 = 2(x+8)$$
$$x+32 = 2x+16$$
$$16 = x$$

Jack is now 16, Mr. Burke is 40.

3. (A) The fastest reasoning here is from the answers. Subtract each number from both ages, to see which results in Lili being twice as old as Melanie. 7 years ago, Lili was 16 and Melanie was 8.

4. (D) Karen's age now can be found by subtracting 2 from her age 2 years from now. Her present age is $2x - 1$. To find her age 2 years ago, subtract another 2.

5. (D) Alice's present age is $4x - 2$. In 3 years her age will be $4x + 1$.

Exercise 4

1. (B) She invested $x + 400$ dollars at 5%. The income is $.05(x + 400)$.

2. (E) He invested $10{,}000 - x$ dollars at 5%. The income is $.05(10{,}000 - x)$.

3. (D)   Let x = amount invested at 3%

$$2000 + x = \text{her total investment}$$
$$.06(2000) + .03x = .04(2000 + x)$$

Multiply by 100 to eliminate decimals.

$$6(2000) + 3x = 4(2000 + x)$$
$$12{,}000 + 3x = 8000 + 4x$$
$$4000 = x$$

4. (B)   Let x = amount invested at 4%

$$7200 - x = \text{amount invested at 5%}$$
$$.04x = .05(7200 - x)$$

Multiply by 100 to eliminate decimals.

$$4x = 5(7200 - x)$$
$$4x = 36{,}000 - 5x$$
$$9x = 36{,}000$$
$$x = 4000$$

Her income is $.04(4000) + .05(3200)$. This is $160 + $160, or $320.

5. (E) In order to avoid fractions, represent his inheritance as $6x$. Then $\frac{1}{2}$ his inheritance is $3x$ and $\frac{1}{3}$ his inheritance is $2x$.

$$\text{Let } 3x = \text{amount invested at 5%}$$
$$2x = \text{amount invested at 6%}$$
$$x = \text{amount invested at 3%}$$
$$.05(3x) + .06(2x) + .03(x) = 300$$

Multiply by 100 to eliminate decimals.

$$5(3x) + 6(2x) + 3(x) = 30{,}000$$
$$15x + 12x + 3x = 30{,}000$$
$$30x = 30{,}000$$
$$x = 1000$$

His inheritance was $6x$, or $6000.

Exercise 5

1. (D) Represent the original fraction as $\dfrac{4x}{5x}$.

   $$\dfrac{4x+4}{5x+10} = \dfrac{2}{3}$$

   Cross multiply.

   $$12x + 12 = 10x + 20$$
   $$2x = 8$$
   $$x = 4$$

   The original numerator was $4x$, or 16.

2. (E) While this can be solved using the equation

   $\dfrac{5+x}{21+x} = \dfrac{3}{7}$, it is probably easier to work

   from the answers. Try adding each choice to

   the numerator and denominator of $\dfrac{5}{21}$ to see

   which gives a result equal to $\dfrac{3}{7}$.

   $$\dfrac{5+7}{21+7} = \dfrac{12}{28} = \dfrac{3}{7}$$

3. (C) Here again, it is fastest to reason from the answers. Add 5 to each numerator and denominator to see which will result in a new

   fraction equal to $\dfrac{7}{10}$.

   $$\dfrac{9+5}{15+5} = \dfrac{14}{20} = \dfrac{7}{10}$$

4. (E) Here again, add 3 to each numerator and denominator of the given choices to see which

   will result in a new fraction equal to $\dfrac{2}{3}$.

   $$\dfrac{7+3}{12+3} = \dfrac{10}{15} = \dfrac{2}{3}$$

5. (C) Represent the original fraction by $\dfrac{x}{2x}$.

   $$\dfrac{x+4}{2x+4} = \dfrac{5}{8}$$

   Cross multiply.

   $$8x + 32 = 10x + 20$$
   $$12 = 2x$$
   $$x = 6$$

   The original denominator is $2x$, or 12.

Exercise 6

1. (C) Multiply the number of pounds by the price per pound to get the total value.

$$40(x) + 50(30 - x)$$
$$40x + 1500 - 50x$$
$$1500 - 10x$$

2. (B)

No. of Pounds ·	Price per Pound =	Total Value
x	70	70x
30	90	2700
$x + 30$	85	85(x + 30)

$$70x + 2700 = 85(x + 30)$$
$$70x + 2700 = 85x + 2550$$
$$150 = 15x$$
$$x = 10$$

3. (D)

	No. of Pints	% of Acid	Amount of = Acid
Original	10	.20	2
Added	6	1.00	6
New	16		8

Remember that 3 quarts of acid are 6 pints. There are now 8 pints of acid in 16 pints of solution.

Therefore, the new solution is $\dfrac{1}{2}$ or 50% acid.

4. (A)

No. of Quarts	% of · Sugar =	Amount of Sugar
60	20	1200
x	0	0
$60 + x$	5	5(60 + x)

$$1200 = 5(60 + x)$$
$$1200 = 300 + 5x$$
$$900 = 5x$$
$$x = 180$$

5. (B)

No. of Pounds ·	% of Alcohol =	Amount of Sugar
240	3	720
x	0	0
240 - x	5	5(240 - x)

Notice that when x quarts were evaporated, x was *subtracted* from 240 to represent the number of pounds in the mixture.

$$720 = 5(240 - x)$$
$$720 = 1200 - 5x$$
$$5x = 480$$
$$x = 96$$

Exercise 7

1. (C)

	R	·	T	=	D
Slow	x		3.5		3.5x
Fast	$x + 6$		3.5		3.5($x + 6$)

The cars each traveled from 10 A.M. to 1:30 P.M., which is $3\frac{1}{2}$ hours.

$3.5x + 3.5(x + 6) = 287$

Multiply by 10 to eliminate decimals.

$$35x + 35(x + 6) = 2870$$
$$35x + 35x + 210 = 2870$$
$$70x = 2660$$
$$x = 38$$

The rate of the faster car was $x + 6$ or 44 m.p.h.

2. (C)

	R	·	T	=	D
Before noon	50		x		50x
After noon	40		8 - x		40(8 - x)

The 8 hours must be divided into 2 parts.

$$50x + 40(8 - x) = 350$$
$$50x + 320 - 40x = 350$$
$$10x = 30$$
$$x = 3$$

If he traveled 3 hours before noon, he left at 9 A.M.

3. (E)

R	·	T	=	D
600		x		600x
650		$x - \dfrac{1}{2}$		$650\left(x - \dfrac{1}{2}\right)$

The later plane traveled $\dfrac{1}{2}$ hour less.

$$600x = 650\left(x - \frac{1}{2}\right)$$
$$600x = 650x - 325$$
$$325 = 50x$$
$$6\tfrac{1}{2} = x$$

The plane that left at 3 P.M. traveled for $6\dfrac{1}{2}$ hours. The time is then 9:30 P.M.

4. (B)

	R	·	T	=	D
Going	4		x		4x
Return	2		6 - x		2(6 - x)

He was gone for 6 hours.

$$4x = 2(6 - x)$$
$$4x = 12 - 2x$$
$$6x = 12$$
$$x = 2$$

If he walked for 2 hours at 4 miles per hour, he walked for 8 miles.

5. (D)

R	·	T	=	D
36		x		36x
31		x		31x

They travel the same number of hours.

$$36x - 31x = 30$$
$$5x = 30$$
$$x = 6$$

This problem may be reasoned without an equation. If the faster car gains 5 miles per hour on the slower car, it will gain 30 miles in 6 hours.

Exercise 8

1. (E) In x days, he has painted $\dfrac{x}{5}$ of the barn. To find what part is still unpainted, subtract the part completed from 1. Think of 1 as $\dfrac{5}{5}$.

$$\frac{5}{5} - \frac{x}{5} = \frac{5-x}{5}$$

2. (B)

Mary		Ruth	
$\dfrac{x}{6}$	$+$	$\dfrac{x}{9}$	$=1$

Multiply by 18.

$$3x + 2x = 18$$
$$5x = 18$$
$$x = 3\frac{3}{5}$$

3. (E)

Inlet		Drain	
$\dfrac{x}{3}$	$-$	$\dfrac{x}{6}$	$=1$

Multiply by 6.

$$2x - x = 6$$
$$x = 6$$

Notice the two fractions are subtracted, as the drainpipe does not help the inlet pipe but works against it.

4. (B)

Tractor		Plow	
$\dfrac{2}{4}$	$+$	$\dfrac{x}{12}$	$=1$

This can be done without algebra, as half the job was completed by the tractor; therefore, the second fraction must also be equal to $\dfrac{1}{2}$. x is therefore 6.

5. (C)

Michael		Barry	
$\dfrac{2}{6}$	$+$	$\dfrac{2}{x}$	$=1$

Multiply by $6x$.

$$2x + 12 = 6x$$
$$12 = 4x$$
$$x = 3$$

Retest

1. (B) Represent the integers as x, $x + 2$, and $x + 4$.

$$3x = (x + 4) + 10$$
$$2x = 14$$
$$x = 7$$
$$x + 2 = 9$$

2. (C) Represent the original fraction by $\dfrac{x}{3x}$.

$$\frac{x + 8}{3x - 6} = \frac{8}{9}$$

Cross multiply.

$$9x + 72 = 24x - 48$$
$$120 = 15x$$
$$x = 8$$
$$3x = 24$$

The original fraction is $\dfrac{8}{24}$.

3. (C)

	No. of Quarts	· Percent Alcohol	= Amount of Alcohol
Original	40	5	200
Added	x	0	0
New	$40 + x$	2	$80 + 2x$

$$200 = 80 + 2x$$
$$120 = 2x$$
$$x = 60$$

4. (D) Let x = Charles' age now

$x + 11$ = Miriam's age now

$x + 3$ = Charles' age in 3 years

$x + 14$ = Miriam's age in 3 years

$$x + 14 = 2(x + 3)$$
$$x + 14 = 2x + 6$$
$$x = 8$$

Therefore Miriam is 19 now and 2 years ago was 17.

5. (A)   Fast Press   Slow Press

$$\frac{x}{12} \quad + \quad \frac{x}{18} = 1$$

Multiply by 36.

$$3x + 2x = 36$$
$$5x = 36$$
$$x = 7\frac{1}{5} \text{ hours}$$
$$= 7 \text{ hours } 12 \text{ minutes}$$

6. (A)   Let x = the number of dimes

$x + 4$ = the number of quarters

$10x$ = the value of dimes in cents

$25x + 100$ = the value of quarters in cents

$$10x + 25x + 100 = 205$$
$$35x = 105$$
$$x = 3$$

She has 30¢ in dimes.

7. (A) Let x = amount invested at 6%

$x + 150$ = amount invested at 3%

$$.06x + .03(x + 150) = 54$$

Multiply by 100 to eliminate decimals

$$6x + 3(x + 150) = 5400$$
$$6x + 3x + 450 = 5400$$
$$9x = 4950$$
$$x = \$550$$
$$x + 150 = \$700$$

8. (B)

	R ·	T =	D
Slow	48	x	$48x$
Fast	55	x	$55x$

$$48x + 55x = 515$$
$$103x = 515$$
$$x = 5 \text{ hours}$$

Therefore, they will pass each other 5 hours after 9:30 A.M., 2:30 P.M.

9. (A)

	R ·	T =	D
Carol	30	3.5	105
Mother	x	3	$3x$

$$3x = 105$$
$$x = 35 \text{ m.p.h.}$$

10. (D)

Let x = number of pennies Frank has

$2x$ = number of pennies Dan has

$$x + 12 = 2x - 12$$
$$x = 24$$

Therefore, Dan originally had 48 pennies.

Geometry

13

DIAGNOSTIC TEST

Directions: Work out each problem. Circle the letter that appears before your answer.

Answers are at the end of the chapter.

1. If the angles of a triangle are in the ratio 5 : 6 : 7, the triangle is
   - (A) acute
   - (B) isosceles
   - (C) obtuse
   - (D) right
   - (E) equilateral

2. If the area of a circle whose radius is x is 4, find the area of a circle whose radius is $3x$.
   - (A) 12
   - (B) 36
   - (C) $4\sqrt{3}$
   - (D) 48
   - (E) 144

3. A spotlight is attached to the ceiling 2 feet from one wall of a room and 3 feet from the wall adjacent. How many feet is it from the intersection of the two walls?
   - (A) 4
   - (B) 5
   - (C) $3\sqrt{2}$
   - (D) $\sqrt{13}$
   - (E) $2\sqrt{3}$

4. In parallelogram $ABCD$, angle B is 5 times as large as angle C. What is the measure in degrees of angle B?
   - (A) 30
   - (B) 60
   - (C) 100
   - (D) 120
   - (E) 150

5. A rectangular box with a square base contains 24 cubic feet. If the height of the box is 18 inches, how many feet are there in each side of the base?
   - (A) 4
   - (B) 2
   - (C) $\dfrac{2\sqrt{3}}{3}$
   - (D) $\dfrac{\sqrt{3}}{2}$
   - (E) $\sqrt{3}$

6. In triangle ABC, $AB = BC$. If angle B contains x degrees, find the number of degrees in angle A.
   - (A) x
   - (B) $180 - x$
   - (C) $180 - \dfrac{x}{2}$
   - (D) $90 - \dfrac{x}{2}$
   - (E) $90 - x$

7. In the diagram below, *AB* is perpendicular to *BC*. If angle *XBY* is a straight angle and angle *XBC* contains 37°, find the number of degrees in angle *ABY*.

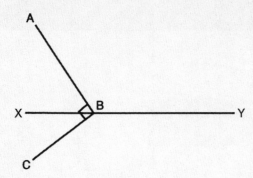

(A) 37
(B) 53
(C) 63
(D) 127
(E) 143

8. If $\overline{AB}$ is parallel to $\overline{CD}$, angle 1 contains 40°, and angle 2 contains 30°, find the number of degrees in angle *FEG*.

(A) 110
(B) 140
(C) 70
(D) 40
(E) 30

9. In a circle whose center is *O*, arc *AB* contains 100°. Find the number of degrees in angle *ABO*.

(A) 50
(B) 100
(C) 40
(D) 65
(E) 60

10. Find the length of the line segment joining the points whose coordinates are (-3, 1) and (5, -5).

(A) 10

(B) $2\sqrt{5}$

(C) $2\sqrt{10}$

(D) 100

(E) $\sqrt{10}$

The questions in this area will expect you to recall some of the numerical relationships learned in geometry. If you are thoroughly familiar with these relationships, you should not find these questions difficult. As mentioned earlier, be particularly careful with units. For example, you cannot multiply a dimension given in feet by another given in inches when you are finding area. Read each question very carefully for the units given. In the following sections, all the needed formulas with illustrations and practice exercises are to help you prepare for the geometry questions on your test.

1. AREAS

A. Rectangle = base · altitude = bh

Area = 40

B. Parallelogram = base · altitude = bh

Area = 40

Notice that the altitude is different from the side. It is always shorter than the second side of the parallelogram, as a perpendicular is the shortest distance from a point to a line.

C. Rhombus = $\frac{1}{2}$ · product of the diagonals = $\frac{1}{2}d_1d_2$

If $AC = 20$ and $BD = 30$, the area of $ABCD = \frac{1}{2}(20)(30) = 300$

D. Square = side · side = s^2

Area = 25

Remember that every square is a rhombus, so that the rhombus formula may be used for a square if the diagonal is given. The diagonals of a square are equal.

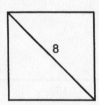

Area = $\dfrac{1}{2}(8)(8) = 32$

Remember also that a rhombus is *not* a square. Therefore do not use the s^2 formula for a rhombus. A rhombus, however, is a parallelogram, so you may use bh if you do not know the diagonals.

E. Triangle = $\dfrac{1}{2}$ · base · altitude = $\dfrac{1}{2}bh$

$A = \dfrac{1}{2}(8)(3) = 12$

F. Equilateral Triangle = $\dfrac{1}{4}$ · side squared · $\sqrt{3} = \dfrac{s^2}{4}\sqrt{3}$

$A = \dfrac{36}{4}\sqrt{3} = 9\sqrt{3}$

G. Trapezoid $= \frac{1}{2} \cdot$ **altitude $\cdot$ sum of bases** $= \frac{1}{2}h(b_1 + b_2)$

$$A = \frac{1}{2}(3)(14) = 21$$

H. Circle $= \pi \cdot$ **radius squared** $= \pi \cdot r^2$

$$A = \pi \cdot (5)^2 = 25\pi$$

Remember that π is the ratio of the circumference of any circle and its diameter. $\pi = \frac{c}{d}$. The approximations you have used for π in the past (3.14 or $\frac{22}{7}$) are just that—approximations. π is an irrational number and cannot be expressed as a fraction or terminating decimal. Therefore all answers involving π should be left in terms of π unless you are given a specific value to substitute for π.

A word about units—Area is measured in square units. That is, we wish to compute how many squares one inch on each side (a square inch) or one foot on each side (a square foot), etc., can be used to cover a given surface. To change from square inches to square feet or square yards, remember that

144 square inches = 1 square foot

9 square feet = 1 square yard

1 square foot   1 square yard

12" = 1'   3' = 1 yd.
12 one inch squares in a row   3 one foot squares in a row
12 rows   3 rows
144 square inches in 1 sq. ft.   9 square feet in 1 sq. yd.

Exercise 1

Work out each problem. Circle the letter that appears before your answer.

1. The dimensions of a rectangular living room are 18 feet by 20 feet. How many square yards of carpeting are needed to cover the floor?

   (A) 360
   (B) 42
   (C) 40
   (D) 240
   (E) 90

2. In a parallelogram whose area is 15, the base is represented by $x + 7$ and the altitude is $x - 7$. Find the base of the parallelogram.

   (A) 8
   (B) 15
   (C) 1
   (D) 34
   (E) 5

3. The sides of a right triangle are 6, 8, and 10. Find the altitude drawn to the hypotenuse.

   (A) 2.4
   (B) 4.8
   (C) 3.4
   (D) 3.5
   (E) 4.2

4. If the diagonals of a rhombus are represented by $4x$ and $6x$, the area may be represented by

   (A) $6x$
   (B) $24x$
   (C) $12x$
   (D) $6x^2$
   (E) $12x^2$

5. A circle is inscribed in a square whose side is 6. Express the area of the circle in terms of π.

   (A) 6π
   (B) 3π
   (C) 9π
   (D) 36π
   (E) 12π

2. PERIMETER

The perimeter of a figure is the distance around the outside. If you were fencing in an area, the number of feet of fencing you would need is the perimeter. Perimeter is measured in linear units, that is, centimeters, inches, feet, meters, yards, etc.

A. Any polygon = sum of all sides

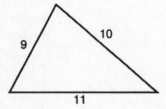

$P = 9 + 10 + 11 = 30$

B. Circle = $\pi \cdot$ diameter = πd

or

$2 \cdot \pi \cdot$ radius = $2\pi r$

Since $2r = d$, these formulas are the same. The perimeter of a circle is called its circumference.

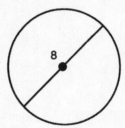

$C = \pi \cdot 8 = 8\pi$

or

$C = 2 \cdot \pi \cdot 4 = 8\pi$

The distance covered by a wheel in one revolution is equal to the circumference of the wheel. In making one revolution, every point on the rim comes in contact with the ground. The distance covered is then the same as stretching the rim out into a straight line.

The distance covered by this wheel in one revolution is $2 \cdot \pi \cdot \dfrac{7}{\pi} = 14$ feet.

Exercise 2

Work out each problem. Circle the letter that appear before your answer.

1. The area of an equilateral triangle is $16\sqrt{3}$. Find its perimeter.
    (A) 24
    (B) 16
    (C) 48
    (D) $24\sqrt{3}$
    (E) $48\sqrt{3}$

2. The hour hand of a clock is 3 feet long. How many feet does the tip of this hand move between 9:30 P.M. and 1:30 A.M. the following day?
    (A) π
    (B) 2π
    (C) 3π
    (D) 4π
    (E) 24π

3. If the radius of a circle is increased by 3, the circumference is increased by
    (A) 3
    (B) 3π
    (C) 6
    (D) 6π
    (E) 4.5

4. The radius of a wheel is 18 inches. Find the number of feet covered by this wheel in 20 revolutions.
    (A) 360π
    (B) 360
    (C) 720π
    (D) 720
    (E) 60π

5. A square is equal in area to a rectangle whose base is 9 and whose altitude is 4. Find the perimeter of the square.
    (A) 36
    (B) 26
    (C) 13
    (D) 24
    (E) none of these

3. RIGHT TRIANGLES

A. Pythagorean theorem

$(\text{leg})^2 + (\text{leg})^2 = (\text{hypotenuse})^2$

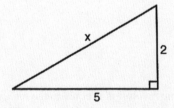

$$(5)^2 + (2)^2 = x^2$$
$$25 + 4 = x^2$$
$$29 = x^2$$
$$x = \sqrt{29}$$

B. Pythagorean triples

These are sets of numbers that satisfy the Pythagorean Theorem. When a given set of numbers such as 3, 4, 5 forms a Pythagorean triple ($3^2 + 4^2 = 5^2$), any multiples of this set such as 6, 8, 10 or 30, 40, 50 also form a Pythagorean triple. Memorizing the sets of Pythagorean triples that follow will save you valuable time in solving problems, for, if you recognize given numbers as multiples of Pythagorean triples, you do not have to do any arithmetic at all. The most common Pythagorean triples that should be memorized are

   3, 4, 5

   5, 12, 13

   8, 15, 17

   7, 24, 25

Squaring 34 and 16 to apply the Pythagorean theorem would take too much time. Instead, recognize the hypotenuse as 2(17). Suspect an 8, 15, 17 triangle. Since the given leg is 2(8), the missing leg will be 2(15) or 30, without any computation at all.

C. 30°-60°-90° triangle

   a)   The leg opposite the 30° angle is one-half the hypotenuse.

   b)   The leg opposite the 60° angle is one-half the hypotenuse · $\sqrt{3}$.

   c)   An altitude in an equilateral triangle forms a 30°-60°-90° triangle and is therefore equal to one-half the side · $\sqrt{3}$.

$$x = 6\sqrt{3}$$

$$y = 4\sqrt{3}$$

$$z = 6$$

$$h = 4\sqrt{3}$$

D. 45°-45°-90° triangle (isosceles right triangle)

a)   Each leg is one-half the hypotenuse times $\sqrt{2}$.

b)   Hypotenuse is leg times $\sqrt{2}$.

c)   The diagonal of a square forms a 45°-45°-90° triangle and is therefore equal to a side times $\sqrt{2}$.

$x = 8$

$y = 3\sqrt{2}$

$z = 6\sqrt{2}$

$d = 4\sqrt{2}$

Exercise 3

Work out each problem. Circle the letter that appears before your answer.

1. A farmer uses 140 feet of fencing to enclose a rectangular field. If the ratio of length to width is 3 : 4, find the diagonal, in feet, of the field.

    (A) 50
    (B) 100
    (C) 20
    (D) 10
    (E) cannot be determined

2. Find the altitude of an equilateral triangle whose side is 20.

    (A) 10
    (B) $20\sqrt{3}$
    (C) $10\sqrt{3}$
    (D) $20\sqrt{2}$
    (E) $10\sqrt{2}$

3. Two boats leave the same dock at the same time, one traveling due west at 8 miles per hour and the other due north at 15 miles per hour. How many miles apart are the boats after three hours?

   (A) 17
   (B) 69
   (C) 75
   (D) 51
   (E) 39

4. Find the perimeter of a square whose diagonal is $6\sqrt{2}$.

   (A) 24
   (B) $12\sqrt{2}$
   (C) 12
   (D) 20
   (E) $24\sqrt{2}$

5. Find the length of *DB*.

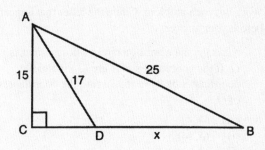

   (A) 8
   (B) 10
   (C) 12
   (D) 15
   (E) 20

4. COORDINATE GEOMETRY

A. Distance between two points =

$$\sqrt{(x_2 - x_1)^2 + (y_2 - y_1)^2}$$

The distance between (-3, 2) and (5, -1) is

$$\sqrt{[-3 - 5]^2 + [2 - (-1)]^2} = \sqrt{(-8)^2 + (3)^2} = \sqrt{64 + 9} = \sqrt{73}$$

B. The midpoint of a line segment =

$$\left(\frac{x_1 + x_2}{2}, \frac{y_1 + y_2}{2} \right)$$

Since a midpoint is in the middle, its coordinates are found by averaging the *x* coordinates and averaging the *y* coordinates. Remember that to find the average of two numbers, you add them and divide by two. Be very careful of signs in adding signed numbers. Review the rules given earlier if necessary.

The midpoint of the segment joining (-4, 1) to (-2, -9) is

$$\left(\frac{-4 + (-2)}{2}, \frac{1 + (-9)}{2} \right) = \left(\frac{-6}{2}, \frac{-8}{2} \right) = (-3, -4)$$

Exercise 4

Work out each problem. Circle the letter that appears before your answer.

1. *AB* is the diameter of a circle whose center is *O*. If the coordinates of *A* are (2, 6) and the coordinates of *B* are (6, 2), find the coordinates of *O*.

   (A) (4, 4)
   (B) (4, -4)
   (C) (2, -2)
   (D) (0, 0)
   (E) (2, 2)

2. *AB* is the diameter of a circle whose center is *O*. If the coordinates of *O* are (2, 1) and the coordinates of *B* are (4, 6), find the coordinates of *A*.

   (A) $\left(3, 3\frac{1}{2}\right)$

   (B) $\left(1, 2\frac{1}{2}\right)$

   (C) (0, -4)

   (D) $\left(2\frac{1}{2}, 1\right)$

   (E) $\left(-1, -2\frac{1}{2}\right)$

3. Find the distance from the point whose coordinates are (4, 3) to the point whose coordinates are (8, 6).

   (A) 5
   (B) 25
   (C) $\sqrt{7}$
   (D) $\sqrt{67}$
   (E) 15

4. The vertices of a triangle are (2, 1), (2, 5), and (5, 1). The area of the triangle is

   (A) 12
   (B) 10
   (C) 8
   (D) 6
   (E) 5

5. The area of a circle whose center is at (0,0) is 16π. The circle passes through each of the following points *except*

   (A) (4, 4)
   (B) (0, 4)
   (C) (4, 0)
   (D) (-4, 0)
   (E) (0, -4)

5. PARALLEL LINES

A. If two lines are parallel and cut by a transversal, the alternate interior angles are congruent.

If $\overline{AB}$ is parallel to $\overline{CD}$, then   angle 1 ≅ angle 3 and

angle 2 ≅ angle 4.

B. If two parallel lines are cut by a transversal, the corresponding angles are congruent.

If $\overline{AB}$ is parallel to $\overline{CD}$, then   angle 1 ≅ angle 5

angle 2 ≅ angle 6

angle 3 ≅ angle 7

angle 4 ≅ angle 8

C. If two parallel lines are cut by a transversal, interior angles on the same side of the transversal are supplementary.

If $\overline{AB}$ is parallel to $\overline{CD}$,   angle 1 + angle 4 = 180°

angle 2 + angle 3 = 180°

Exercise 5

Work out each problem. Circle the letter that appears before your answer.

1. If $\overline{AB}$ is parallel to $\overline{CD}$, $\overline{BC}$ is parallel to $\overline{ED}$, and angle $B = 30°$, find the number of degrees in angle D.

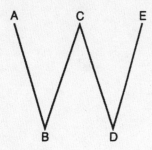

  (A) 30
  (B) 60
  (C) 150
  (D) 120
  (E) none of these

2. If $\overline{AB}$ is parallel to $\overline{CD}$, angle $A = 35°$, and angle $C = 45°$, find the number of degrees in angle AEC.

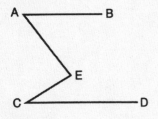

  (A) 35
  (B) 45
  (C) 70
  (D) 80
  (E) 100

3. If $\overline{AB}$ is parallel to $\overline{CD}$ and angle $1 = 130°$, find angle 2.

  (A) 130°
  (B) 100°
  (C) 40°
  (D) 60°
  (E) 50°

4. If $\overline{AB}$ is parallel to $\overline{CD}$, $\overline{EF}$ bisects angle BEG, and $\overline{GF}$ bisects angle EGD, find the number of degrees in angle EFG.

  (A) 40
  (B) 60
  (C) 90
  (D) 120
  (E) cannot be determined

5. If $\overline{AB}$ is parallel to $\overline{CD}$ and angle $1 = x°$, then the sum of angle 1 and angle 2 is

  (A) $2x°$
  (B) $(180 - x)°$
  (C) $180°$
  (D) $(180 + x)°$
  (E) none of these

6. TRIANGLES

A. If two sides of a triangle are congruent, the angles opposite these sides are congruent.

If $\overline{AB} \cong \overline{AC}$, then angle $B \cong$ angle C.

B. If two angles of a triangle are congruent, the sides opposite these angles are congruent.

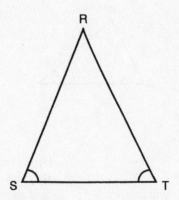

If angle $S \cong$ angle T, then $\overline{RS} \cong \overline{RT}$.

C. The sum of the measures of the angles of a triangle is 180°.

D. The measure of an exterior angle of a triangle is equal to the sum of the measures of the two remote interior angles.

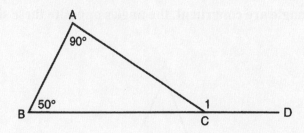

angle 1 = 140°

E. If two angles of one triangle are congruent to two angles of a second triangle, the third angles are congruent.

angle *A* will be congruent to angle *R*

Exercise 6

Work out each problem. Circle the letter that appears before your answer.

1. The angles of a triangle are in the ratio 1 : 5 : 6. This triangle is

   (A) acute
   (B) obtuse
   (C) isosceles
   (D) right
   (E) equilateral

2. If the vertex angle of an isosceles triangle is 50°, find the number of degrees in one of the base angles.

   (A) 50
   (B) 130
   (C) 60
   (D) 65
   (E) 55

3. In triangle *ABC*, angle *A* is three times as large as angle *B*. The exterior angle at *C* is 100°. Find the number of degrees in angle *A*.

   (A) 60
   (B) 80
   (C) 20
   (D) 25
   (E) 75

4. If a base angle of an isosceles triangle is represented by $x°$, represent the number of degrees in the vertex angle.

(A) $180 - x$
(B) $x - 180$
(C) $2x - 180$
(D) $180 - 2x$
(E) $90 - 2x$

5. In triangle ABC, $\overline{AB} = \overline{BC}$. If angle $A = (4x - 30)°$ and angle $C = (2x + 10)°$, find the number of degrees in angle B.

(A) 20
(B) 40
(C) 50
(D) 100
(E) 80

7. POLYGONS

A. The sum of the measures of the angles of a polygon of n sides is $(n - 2)180°$.

Since $ABCDE$ has 5 sides, angle A + angle B + angle C + angle D + angle E = $(5 - 2)180° = 3(180)° = 540°$

B. Properties of a parallelogram

a)   Opposite sides are parallel

b)   Opposite sides are congruent

c)   Opposite angles are congruent

d)   Consecutive angles are supplementary

e)   Diagonals bisect each other

C. Properties of a rectangle

a)   All 5 properties of a parallelogram

b)   All angles are right angles

c)   Diagonals are congruent

D. Properties of a rhombus

a)   All 5 properties of a parallelogram

b)   All sides are congruent

c)   Diagonals are perpendicular to each other

d)   Diagonals bisect the angles

E. Properties of a square

a)   All 5 parallelogram properties

b)   Two additional rectangle properties

c)   Three additional rhombus properties

Exercise 7

Work out each problem. Circle the letter that appears before your answer.

1. Find the number of degrees in the sum of the interior angles of a hexagon.

    (A) 360
    (B) 540
    (C) 720
    (D) 900
    (E) 1080

2. In parallelogram $ABCD$, $AB = x + 4$, $BC = x - 6$, and $CD = 2x - 16$. Find AD.

    (A) 20
    (B) 24
    (C) 28
    (D) 14
    (E) 10

3. In parallelogram $ABCD$, $AB = x + 8$, $BC = 3x$, and $CD = 4x - 4$. $ABCD$ must be a

    (A) rectangle
    (B) rhombus
    (C) trapezoid
    (D) square
    (E) pentagon

4. The sum of the angles in a rhombus is

    (A) 180°
    (B) 360°
    (C) 540°
    (D) 720°
    (E) 450°

5. Which of the following statements is *false?*

    (A) A square is a rhombus.
    (B) A rhombus is a parallelogram.
    (C) A rectangle is a rhombus.
    (D) A rectangle is a parallelogram.
    (E) A square is a rectangle.

8. CIRCLES

A. A central angle is equal in degrees to its intercepted arc.

If arc $AB = 50°$, then angle $AOB = 50°$.

B. An inscribed angle is equal in degrees to one-half its intercepted arc.

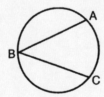

If arc $AC = 100°$, then angle $ABC = 50°$.

C. An angle formed by two chords intersecting in a circle is equal in degrees to one-half the sum of its intercepted arcs.

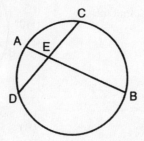

If arc $AD = 30°$ and arc $CB = 120°$, then angle $AED = 75°$.

D. An angle outside the circle formed by two secants, a secant and a tangent, or two tangents is equal in degrees to one-half the difference of its intercepted arcs.

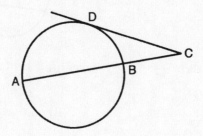

If arc $AD = 120°$ and arc $BD = 30°$, then angle $C = 45°$.

E. Two tangent segments drawn to a circle from the same external point are congruent.

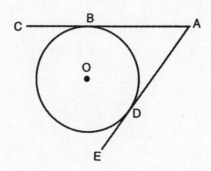

If $\overline{AC}$ and $\overline{AE}$ are tangent to circle O at B and D, then $AB \cong AD$.

Exercise 8

Work out each problem. Circle the letter that appears before your answer.

1. If circle O is inscribed in triangle ABC, find the length of side AB.

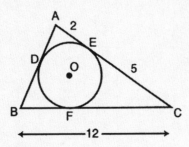

(A)   12
(B)   14
(C)   9
(D)   10
(E)   7

2. Find angle x.

(A)   40°
(B)   20°
(C)   50°
(D)   70°
(E)   80°

3. Find angle x

(A)   120°
(B)   50°
(C)   70°
(D)   40°
(E)   60°

4. Find the number of degrees in arc AC.

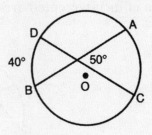

(A)   60
(B)   50
(C)   25
(D)   100
(E)   20

5. The number of degrees in angle ABC is

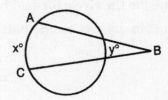

(A) $\dfrac{1}{2}y$

(B) y

(C) $\dfrac{1}{2}x$

(D) $\dfrac{1}{2}(x-y)$

(E) $\dfrac{1}{2}(x+y)$

9. VOLUMES

A. The volume of a rectangular solid is equal to the product of its length, width, and height.

$V = (10)(6)(5) = 300$

B. The volume of a cube is equal to the cube of an edge, since the length, width, and height are all equal.

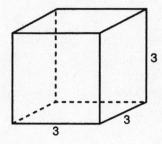

$V = (3)^3 = 27$

C. The volume of a cylinder is equal to π times the square of the radius of the base times the height.

$V = \pi (4)^2 (5) = 80\pi$

Exercise 9

Work out each problem. Circle the letter that appears before your answer.

1. The surface area of a cube is 96 square feet. How many cubic feet are there in the volume of the cube?

   (A) 16
   (B) 4
   (C) 12
   (D) 64
   (E) 32

2. A cylindrical pail has a radius of 7 inches and a height of 10 inches. Approximately how many gallons will the pail hold if there are 231 cubic inches to a gallon? $\left(\text{Use } \pi = \dfrac{22}{7}. \right)$

   (A) .9
   (B) 4.2
   (C) 6.7
   (D) 5.1
   (E) 4.8

3. Water is poured into a cylindrical tank at the rate of 9 cubic inches a minute. How many minutes will it take to fill the tank if its radius is 3 inches and its height is 14 inches?

   $\left(\text{Use } \pi = \dfrac{22}{7}. \right)$

   (A) $14\dfrac{2}{3}$

   (B) 44

   (C) 30

   (D) $27\dfrac{2}{9}$

   (E) 35

4. A rectangular tank 10 inches by 8 inches by 4 inches is filled with water. If the water is to be transferred to smaller tanks in the form of cubes 4 inches on a side, how many of these tanks are needed?

   (A) 4
   (B) 5
   (C) 6
   (D) 7
   (E) 8

5. The base of a tank is 6 feet by 5 feet and its height is 16 inches. Find the number of cubic feet of water in the tank when it is $\dfrac{5}{8}$ full.

   (A) 25
   (B) 40
   (C) 480
   (D) 768
   (E) 300

10. SIMILAR POLYGONS

A. Corresponding angles of similar polygons are congruent.

B. Corresponding sides of similar polygons are in proportion.

If triangle *ABC* is similar to triangle *DEF* and the sides and angles are given as marked, then *EF* must be equal to 12 as the ratio of corresponding sides is 2 : 6 or 1 : 3.

C. When figures are similar, all ratios between corresponding lines are equal. This includes the ratios of corresponding sides, medians, altitudes, angle bisectors, radii, diameters, perimeters, and circumferences. The ratio is referred to as the linear ratio or ratio of similitude.

If triangle *ABC* is similar to triangle *DEF* and the segments are given as marked, then *EH* is equal to 2.5 because the linear ratio is 6 : 3 or 2 : 1.

D. When figures are similar, the ratio of their areas is equal to the square of the linear ratio.

If triangle *ABC* is similar to triangle *DEF*, the area of triangle *ABC* will be 9 times as great as the area of triangle *DEF*. The linear ratio is 12 : 4 or 3 : 1. The area ratio will be the square of this or 9 : 1. If the area of triangle *ABC* had been given as 27, the area of triangle *DEF* would be 3.

E. When figures are similar, the ratio of their volumes is equal to the cube of their linear ratio.

The volume of the larger cube is 8 times the volume of the smaller cube. The ratio of sides is 4 : 2 or 2 : 1. The ratio of areas would be 4 : 1. The ratio of volumes would be 8 : 1.

Exercise 10

Work out each problem. Circle the letter that appears before your answer.

1. If the area of a circle of radius *x* is 5π, find the area of a circle of radius $3x$.

    (A) 10π
    (B) 15π
    (C) 20π
    (D) 30π
    (E) 45π

2. If the length and width of a rectangle are each doubled, the area is increased by

    (A) 50%
    (B) 100%
    (C) 200%
    (D) 300%
    (E) 400%

3. The area of one circle is 9 times as great as the area of another. If the radius of the smaller circle is 3, find the radius of the larger circle.

    (A) 9
    (B) 12
    (C) 18
    (D) 24
    (E) 27

4. If the radius of a circle is doubled, then

   (A) the circumference and area are both doubled
   (B) the circumference is doubled and the area is multiplied by 4
   (C) the circumference is multiplied by 4 and the area is doubled
   (D) the circumference and area are each multiplied by 4
   (E) the circumference stays the same and the area is doubled

5. The volumes of two similar solids are 250 and 128. If a dimension of the larger solid is 25, find the corresponding side of the smaller solid.

   (A) 12.8
   (B) 15
   (C) 20
   (D) 40
   (E) cannot be determined

RETEST

Work out each problem. Circle the letter that appears before your answer.

1. The area of a trapezoid whose bases are 10 and 12 and whose altitude is 3 is

   (A) 66
   (B) 11
   (C) 33
   (D) 25
   (E) $16\frac{1}{2}$

2. The circumference of a circle whose area is 16π is

   (A) 8π
   (B) 4π
   (C) 16π
   (D) 8
   (E) 16

3. Find the perimeter of a square whose diagonal is 8.

   (A) 32
   (B) 16
   (C) $32\sqrt{2}$
   (D) $16\sqrt{2}$
   (E) $32\sqrt{3}$

4. The length of the line segment joining the point $A(4, -3)$ to $B(7, -7)$ is

   (A) $\sqrt{221}$
   (B) $\sqrt{185}$
   (C) 7
   (D) $6\frac{1}{2}$
   (E) 5

5. Find angle x if $\overline{AB}$ is parallel to $\overline{CD}$.

   (A) 35°
   (B) 80°
   (C) 245°
   (D) 65°
   (E) 55°

6. In triangle ABC, the angles are in a ratio of $1 : 1 : 2$. The largest angle of the triangle is

   (A) 45°
   (B) 60°
   (C) 90°
   (D) 120°
   (E) 100°

7. Find the number of degrees in each angle of a regular pentagon.

   (A) 72
   (B) 108
   (C) 60
   (D) 180
   (E) 120

8. Find the number of degrees in arc *AB*.

   (A) 80
   (B) 20
   (C) 60
   (D) 100
   (E) 90

9. Find the edge, in inches, of a cube whose volume is equal to the volume of a rectangular solid 2 in. by 6 in. by 18 in.

   (A) 4
   (B) 8
   (C) 5
   (D) 6
   (E) 7

10. If the volume of one cube is 8 times as great as another, then the ratio of the area of a face of the larger cube to the area of a face of the smaller cube is

   (A) $2:1$

   (B) $4:1$

   (C) $\sqrt{2}:1$

   (D) $8:1$

   (E) $2\sqrt{2}:1$

SOLUTIONS TO PRACTICE EXERCISES

Diagnostic Test

1. (A) Represent the angles as $5x$, $6x$, and $7x$.
   They must add up to 180°.

   $$18x = 180$$
   $$x = 10$$

   The angles are 50°, 60°, and 70°, an acute triangle.

2. (B) The area of a circle is πr^2. The area of a circle with radius x is πx^2, which equals 4. The area of a circle with radius $3x$ is $\pi (3x)^2 = 9\pi x^2 = 9 \cdot 4 = 36$.

3. (D)

   $$2^2 + 3^2 = x^2$$
   $$4 + 9 = x^2$$
   $$13 = x^2$$
   $$\sqrt{13} = x$$

4. (E)

   The sum of the angles in a parallelogram is 360°.

   $$12x = 360°$$
   $$x = 30°$$

   Angle $B = 5x = 5 \cdot 30° = 150°$

5. (A) The volume of a rectangular box is the product of its length, width, and height. Since the height is 18 inches, or $1\frac{1}{2}$ feet, and the length and width of the square base are the same, we have

   $$x \cdot x \cdot 1\frac{1}{2} = 24$$
   $$x^2 = 16$$
   $$x = 4$$

6. (D) The remaining degrees of the triangle are $180 - x$. Since the triangle is isosceles, the remaining angles are equal, each

   $$\frac{180 - x}{2} = 90 - \frac{x}{2}.$$

7. (D)

   Angle $ABX = 90° - 37° = 53°$

   Angle $ABY = 180° - 53° = 127°$

8. (C)

Extend $\overline{FE}$ to H. $\angle EHG = \angle AFE = 40°$.
$\angle HEG$ must equal $110°$ because there are $180°$
in a triangle. Since $\angle FEG$ is the supplement of
$\angle HEG$, $\angle FEG = 70°$.

9. (C)

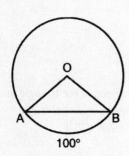

Angle O is a central angle equal to its arc, $100°$.
This leaves $80°$ for the other two angles. Since the
triangle is isosceles (because the legs are both
radii and therefore equal), angle ABO is $40°$.

10. (A) $d = \sqrt{(5 - (3))^2 + (-5 - 1)^2}$

$= \sqrt{(8)^2 + (-6)^2} = \sqrt{64 + 36}$

$= \sqrt{100} = 10$

Exercise 1

1. (C) Find the area in square feet and then convert
    to square yards by dividing by 9. Remember
    there are 9 square feet in one square yard.

    $(18 \cdot 20) \div 9 = 360 \div 9 = 40$ square yards

2. (B) Area of parallelogram $= b \cdot h$

$$(x + 7)(x - 7) = 15$$
$$x^2 - 49 = 15$$
$$x^2 = 64$$
$$x = 8$$
$$\text{Base} = x + 7 = 15$$

3. (B) Area of triangle $= \dfrac{1}{2} \cdot b \cdot h$

    Using one leg as base and the other as altitude,
    the area is $\dfrac{1}{2} \cdot 6 \cdot 8 = 24$. Using the hypotenuse
    as base and the altitude to the hypotenuse will
    give the same area.

$$\frac{1}{2} \cdot 10 \cdot h = 24$$
$$5h = 24$$
$$h = 4.8 \therefore \frac{1}{2} \cdot 10 \cdot 4.8 = 24$$

4. (E) Area of rhombus $= \dfrac{1}{2} \cdot$ product of
    diagonals

$$\text{Area} = \frac{1}{2}(4x)(6x) = \frac{1}{2}(24x^2) = 12x^2$$

5. (C)

radius of circle $= 3$

Area $= \pi r^2 = 9\pi$

Exercise 2

1. (A) Area of equilateral triangle = $\dfrac{s^2}{4}\sqrt{3}$

   Therefore $\dfrac{s^2}{4}$ must equal 16.

   $$s^2 = 64$$
   $$s = 8$$

   Perimeter is $8 + 8 + 8 = 24$

2. (B) In 4 hours the hour hand moves through one-third of the circumference of the clock.

   $$C = 2\pi r = 2\pi(3) \qquad = 6\pi$$
   $$\frac{1}{3} \cdot 6\pi \qquad = 2\pi$$

3. (D) Compare $2\pi r$ with $2\pi(r + 3)$.

   $$2\pi(r + 3) = 2\pi r + 6\pi$$

   Circumference was increased by 6π. Trying this with a numerical value for r will give the same result.

4. (E) In one revolution, the distance covered is equal to the circumference.

   $$C = 2\pi r = 2\pi(18) = 36\pi \text{ inches}$$

   To change this to feet, divide by 12.

   $$\frac{36\pi}{12} = 3\pi \text{ feet}$$

   In 20 revolutions, the wheel will cover $20(3\pi)$ or 60π feet.

5. (D)

   $$\text{Area of rectangle} = b \cdot h = 36$$
   $$\text{Area of square} = s^2 = 36$$
   Therefore $s = 6$ and perimeter $= 24$

Exercise 3

1. (A)

   $$14x = 140$$
   $$x = 10$$

   The rectangle is 30′ by 40′. This is a 3, 4, 5 right triangle, so the diagonal is 50′.

2. (C) The altitude in an equilateral triangle is

   always $\dfrac{1}{2}$ side $\cdot \sqrt{3}$.

3. (D) This is an 8, 15, 17 triangle, making the missing side (3)17, or 51.

4. (A) The diagonal in a square is equal to the side times $\sqrt{2}$. Therefore, the side is 6 and the perimeter is 24.

5. (C)

   Triangle ABC is a 3, 4, 5 triangle with all sides multiplied by 5. Therefore $CB = 20$. Triangle ACD is an 8, 15, 17 triangle. Therefore $CD = 8$. $CB - CD = DB = 12$.

Exercise 4

1. (A) Find the midpoint of AB by averaging the x coordinates and averaging the y coordinates.

    $$\left(\frac{6+2}{2}, \frac{2+6}{2}\right) = (4,4)$$

2. (C) O is the midpoint of AB.

    $$\frac{x+4}{2} = 2 \qquad x+4 = 4,\ x = 0$$

    $$\frac{x+6}{2} = 1 \qquad y+6 = 2,\ y = -4$$

    A is the point $(0, -4)$.

3. (A) $d = \sqrt{(8-4)^2 + (6-3)^2} = \sqrt{4^2 + 3^2}$

    $$= \sqrt{16+9} = \sqrt{25} = 5$$

4. (D) Sketch the triangle and you will see it is a right triangle with legs of 4 and 3.

    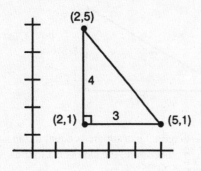

    $$\text{Area} = \frac{1}{2} \cdot b \cdot h = \frac{1}{2} \cdot 4 \cdot 3 = 6$$

5. (A) Area of a circle $= \pi r^2$

    $$\pi r^2 = 16\pi \qquad r = 4$$

Exercise 5

1. (A) Angle B = Angle C because of alternate interior angles. Then Angle C = Angle D for the same reason. Therefore, Angle $D = 30°$.

2. (D)

    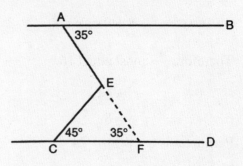

    Extend $\overline{AE}$ to F. $\angle A = \angle EFC$

    $\angle CEF$ must equal $100°$ because there are $180°$ in a triangle. $\angle AEC$ is supplementary to $\angle CEF$. $\angle AEC = 80°$

3. (E)

    $$\angle 1 = \angle 3$$
    $$\angle 2 + \angle 3 = 180°$$
    $$\angle 2 = 50°$$

4. (C) Since $\angle BEG$ and $\angle EGD$ add to $180°$, halves of these angles must add to $90°$. Triangle EFG contains $180°$, leaving $90°$ for $\angle EFG$.

5.

    $$\angle 1 = \angle 3$$
    $$\angle 2 = \angle 4$$
    $$\angle 1 + \angle 2 = \angle 3 + \angle 4$$

    But $\angle 3 + \angle 4 = 180°$. Therefore, $\angle 1 + \angle 2 = 180°$

Exercise 6

1. (D) Represent the angles as x, $5x$, and $6x$. They must add to 180°.

$$12x = 180$$
$$x = 15$$

The angles are 15°, 75°, and 90°.

2. (D) There are 130° left to be split evenly between the base angles (the base angles must be equal). Each one must be 65°.

3. (E)

The exterior angle is equal to the sum of the two remote interior angles.

$$4x = 100$$
$$x = 25$$
$$\text{Angle } A = 3x = 75°$$

4. (D) The other base angle is also x. These two base angles add to $2x$. The remaining degrees of the triangle, or 180 - $2x$, are in the vertex angle.

5. (E)

$$\angle A = \angle C$$
$$4x - 30 = 2x + 10$$
$$2x = 40$$
$$x = 20$$

$\angle A$ and $\angle C$ are each 50°, leaving 80° for $\angle B$.

Exercise 7

1. (C) A hexagon has 6 sides. Sum = $(n - 2)\,180 = 4(180) = 720$

2. (D) Opposite sides of a parallelogram are congruent, so $AB = CD$.

$$x + 4 = 2x - 16$$
$$20 = x$$
$$AD = BC = x - 6 \qquad = 14$$

3. (B) $AB = CD$
$$x + 8 = 4x - 4$$
$$12 = 3x$$
$$x = 4$$
$$AB = 12 \quad BC = 12 \quad CD = 12$$

If all sides are congruent, it must be a rhombus. Additional properties would be needed to make it a square.

4. (B) A rhombus has 4 sides. Sum = $(n - 2)\,180 = 2(180) = 360$

5. (C) Rectangles and rhombuses are both types of parallelograms but do not share the same special properties. A square is both a rectangle and a rhombus with *added* properties.

Exercise 8

1. (C) Tangent segments drawn to a circle from the same external point are congruent. If $CE = 5$, then $CF = 5$, leaving 7 for BF. Therefore BD is also 7. If $AE = 2$, then $AD = 2$.

   $$BD + DA = BA = 9$$

2. (D) Angle O is a central angle equal to its arc, 40°. This leaves 140° for the other two angles. Since the triangle is isosceles, because the legs are equal radii, each angle is 70°.

3. (E) The remaining arc is 120°. The inscribed angle x is $\dfrac{1}{2}$ its intercepted arc.

4. (A) $$50° = \frac{1}{2}\left(40° + AC\right)$$
   $$100° = 40° + AC$$
   $$60° = AC$$

5. (D) An angle outside the circle is $\dfrac{1}{2}$ the difference of its intercepted arcs.

Exercise 9

1. (D) There are 6 equal squares in the surface area of a cube. Each square will have an area of $\dfrac{96}{6}$ or 16. Each edge is 4.
   $$V = e^3 = 4^3 = 64$$

2. (C) $V = \pi r^2 h = \dfrac{22}{7} \cdot 49 \cdot 10 = 1540$ cubic inches

   Divide by 231 to find gallons.

3. (B) $V = \pi r^2 h = \dfrac{22}{7} \cdot 9 \cdot 14 = 396$ cubic inches

   Divide by 9 to find minutes.

4. (B) $V = l \cdot w \cdot h = 10 \cdot 8 \cdot 4 = 320$ cubic inches

   Each small cube $= 4^3 = 64$ cubic inches. Therefore it will require 5 cubes.

5. (A) Change 16 inches to $1\dfrac{1}{3}$ feet.
   $$V = 6 \cdot 5 \cdot 1\frac{1}{3} = 40 \text{ cubic feet when full.}$$
   $$\frac{5}{8} \cdot 40 = 25$$

Exercise 10

1. (E) If the radius is multiplied by 3, the area is multiplied by 3^2 or 9.

2. (D) If the dimensions are all doubled, the area is multiplied by 2^2 or 4. If the new area is 4 times as great as the original area, is has been *increased* by 300%.

3. (A) If the area ratio is 9 : 1, the linear ratio is 3 : 1. Therefore, the larger radius is 3 times the smaller radius.

4. (B) Ratio of circumferences is the same as ratio of radii, but the area ratio is the square of this.

5. (C) We must take the cube root of the volume ratio to find the linear ratio. This becomes much easier if you simplify the ratio first.

$$\frac{250}{128} = \frac{125}{64}$$

The linear ratio is then 5 : 4.

$$\frac{5}{4} = \frac{25}{x}$$
$$5x = 100$$
$$x = 20$$

Retest

1. (C) Area of trapezoid $= \frac{1}{2}h\left(b_1 + b_2\right)$

$$\text{Area} = \frac{1}{2} \cdot 3(10 + 12) = 33$$

2. (A) Area of circle $= \pi r^2 = 16\pi$

Therefore, $r^2 = 16$ or $r = 4$

Circumference of circle $= 2\pi r = 2\pi\,(4) = 8\pi$

3. (D) The side of a square is equal to the diagonal times $\frac{\sqrt{2}}{2}$. Therefore, the side is $4\sqrt{2}$ and the perimeter is $16\sqrt{2}$.

4. (E) $d = \sqrt{\left(7 - 4\right)^2 + \left(-7 - (-3)\right)^2}$

$$= \sqrt{\left(3\right)^2 + \left(-4\right)^2} = \sqrt{9 + 16}$$
$$= \sqrt{25} = 5$$

5. (D)

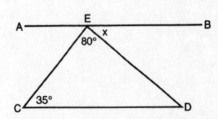

$\angle CDE$ must equal 65° because there are 180° in a triangle. Since $\overline{AB}$ is parallel to $\overline{CD}$, $\angle x = \angle CDE = 65°$.

6. (C) Represent the angles as x, x, and $2x$. They must add to 180°.

$$4x = 180$$
$$x = 45$$

Therefore, the largest angle is $2x = 2(45°) = 90°$.

7. (B) A pentagon has 5 sides. Sum $(n - 2)180 = 3(180) = 540°$

    In a regular pentagon, all the angles are equal.

    Therefore, each angle $= \dfrac{540}{5} = 108°.$

8. (D)

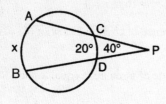

    An angle outside the circle is $\dfrac{1}{2}$ the difference of its intercepted arcs.

    $$40 = \frac{1}{2}(x - 20)$$
    $$80 = x - 20$$
    $$100 = x$$

9. (D) $V = 1 \cdot w \cdot h = 2 \cdot 6 \cdot 18 = 216$

    The volume of a cube is equal to the cube of an edge.

    $$V = e^3$$
    $$216 = e^3$$
    $$6 = e$$

10. (B) If the volume ratio is 8 : 1, the linear ratio is 2 : 1, and the area ratio is the square of this, or 4:1.

Inequalities

14

DIAGNOSTIC TEST

Directions: Work out each problem. Circle the letter that appears before your answer.

Answers are at the end of the chapter.

1. If $4x < 6$, then

    (A) $x = 1.5$

    (B) $x < \dfrac{2}{3}$

    (C) $x > \dfrac{2}{3}$

    (D) $x < \dfrac{3}{2}$

    (E) $x > \dfrac{3}{2}$

2. If $a = b$ and $c > d$, then
    (A) $a + c < b + d$
    (B) $a + c > b + d$
    (C) $a - c > b - d$
    (D) $ac < bd$
    (E) $a + c < b - d$

3. Which value of x will make the following expression true?

    $$\dfrac{3}{5} < \dfrac{x}{10} < \dfrac{4}{5}$$

    (A) 5
    (B) 6
    (C) 7
    (D) 8
    (E) 9

4. In triangle ABC, $AB = AC$ and $EC < DB$. Then

    (A) $DB < AE$
    (B) $DB < AD$
    (C) $AD > AE$
    (D) $AD < AE$
    (E) $AD > EC$

5. In triangle ABC, $-1 > -2$ and $-2 > -3$. Then

    (A) $AC < AB$
    (B) $AC > BC$
    (C) $BC > AC$
    (D) $BC < AB$
    (E) $-3 > -1$

6. If point C lies between A and B on line segment AB, which of the following is always true?
    (A) $AC = CB$
    (B) $AC > CB$
    (C) $CB > AC$
    (D) $AB < AC + CB$
    (E) $AB = CB + AC$

7. If *AC* is perpendicular to *BD*, which of the following is always true?

   I. $AC = BC$
   II. $AC < AB$
   III. $AB > AD$

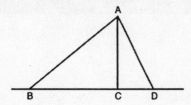

   (A) I only
   (B) II and III only
   (C) II only
   (D) III only
   (E) I and II only

8. If $x < 0$ and $y > 0$, which of the following is always true?

   (A) $x + y > 0$
   (B) $x + y < 0$
   (C) $y - x < 0$
   (D) $x - y < 0$
   (E) $2x > y$

9. In triangle *ABC*, *BC* is extended to *D*. If $-A = 50°$ and $-ACD = 120°$, then

   (A) $BC > AB$
   (B) $AC > AB$
   (C) $BC > AC$
   (D) $AB > AC$
   (E) $-B < -A$

10. In right triangle *ABC*, $-A < -B$ and $-B < -C$. Then

   (A) $-A > 45°$
   (B) $-B = 90°$
   (C) $-B > 90°$
   (D) $-C = 90°$
   (E) $-C > 90°$

1. ALGEBRAIC INEQUALITIES

Algebraic inequality statements are solved in the same manner as equations. However, do not forget that whenever you multiply or divide by a negative number, the order of the inequality, that is, the inequality symbol must be reversed. In reading the inequality symbol, remember that it points to the smaller quantity. $a < b$ is read *a* is less than *b*. $a > b$ is read *a* is greater than *b*.

Example:

Solve for *x*: $12 - 4x < 8$

Solution:

Add -12 to each side.
$-4x < -4$
Divide by -4, remembering to reverse the inequality sign.
$x > 1$

Example:

$6x + 5 > 7x + 10$

Solution:

Collect all the terms containing *x* on the left side of the equation and all numerical terms on the right. As with equations, remember that if a term comes from one side of the inequality to the other, that term changes sign.
$-x > 5$
Divide (or multiply) by -1.
$x < -5$

Exercise 1

Work out each problem. Circle the letter that appears before your answer.

1. Solve for x: $8x < 5(2x + 4)$
   (A) $x > -10$
   (B) $x < -10$
   (C) $x > 10$
   (D) $x < 10$
   (E) $x < 18$

2. Solve for x: $6x + 2 - 8x < 14$
   (A) $x = 6$
   (B) $x = -6$
   (C) $x > -6$
   (D) $x < -6$
   (E) $x > 6$

3. A number increased by 10 is greater than 50. What numbers satisfy this condition?
   (A) $x > 60$
   (B) $x < 60$
   (C) $x > -40$
   (D) $x < 40$
   (E) $x > 40$

4. Solve for x: $-.4x < 4$
   (A) $x > -10$
   (B) $x > 10$
   (C) $x < 8$
   (D) $x < -10$
   (E) $x < 36$

5. Solve for x: $.03n > -.18$
   (A) $n < -.6$
   (B) $n > .6$
   (C) $n > 6$
   (D) $n > -6$
   (E) $n < -6$

6. Solve for b: $15b < 10$
   (A) $b < \dfrac{3}{2}$
   (B) $b > \dfrac{3}{2}$
   (C) $b < -\dfrac{3}{2}$
   (D) $b < \dfrac{2}{3}$
   (E) $b > \dfrac{2}{3}$

7. If $x^2 < 4$, then
   (A) $x > 2$
   (B) $x < 2$
   (C) $x > -2$
   (D) $-2 < x < 2$
   (E) $-2 \leq x \leq 2$

8. Solve for n: $n + 4.3 < 2.7$
   (A) $n > 1.6$
   (B) $n > -1.6$
   (C) $n < 1.6$
   (D) $n < -1.6$
   (E) $n = 1.6$

9. If $x < 0$ and $y < 0$, which of the following is always true?
   (A) $x + y > 0$
   (B) $xy < 0$
   (C) $x - y > 0$
   (D) $x + y < 0$
   (E) $x = y$

10. If $x < 0$ and $y > 0$, which of the following will always be greater than 0?
    (A) $x + y$
    (B) $x - y$
    (C) $\dfrac{x}{y}$
    (D) xy
    (E) $-2x$

2. GEOMETRIC INEQUALITIES

In working with geometric inequalities, certain postulates and theorems should be reviewed.

A. If unequal quantities are added to unequal quantities of the same order, the sums are unequal in the same order.

If $AB > AE$ and
(+) $BC = ED$ then
$AC > AD$

B. If equal quantities are added to unequal quantities, the sums are unequal in the same order.

$AB > AE$ and
(+) $BC = ED$ then
$AC > AD$

C. If equal quantities are subtracted from unequal quantities, the differences are unequal in the same order.

If $AC > AD$ and
(−) $BC = ED$ then
$AB > AE$

D. If unequal quantities are subtracted from equal quantities, the results are unequal in the *opposite* order.

$AB = AC$
(−)$AD < AE$
$DB > EC$

E. Doubles of unequals are unequal in the same order.

M is the midpoint of *AB*

N is the midpoint of *CD*

AM > CN

Therefore *AB > CD*

F. Halves of unequals are unequal in the same order.

$\angle ABC > \angle DEF$

$\overline{BG}$ bisects $\angle ABC$

$\overline{EH}$ bisects $\angle DEF$

Therefore, $\angle 1 > \angle 2$

G. If the first of three quantities is greater than the second, and the second is greater than the third, then the first is greater than the third.

If $\angle A > \angle B$ and $\angle B > \angle C$, then $\angle A > \angle C$.

H. The sum of two sides of a triangle must be greater than the third side.

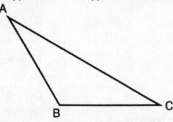

$AB + BC > AC$

I. If two sides of a triangle are unequal, the angles opposite are unequal, with the larger angle opposite the larger side.

If $AB > AC$, then $\angle C > \angle B$.

J. If two angles of a triangle are unequal, the sides opposite these angles are unequal, with the larger side opposite the larger angle.

If $\angle C > \angle B$, then $AB > AC$.

K. An exterior angle of a triangle is greater than either remote interior angle.

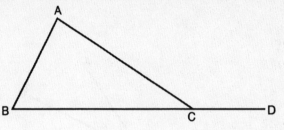

$\angle ACD > \angle B$ and $\angle ACD > \angle A$

Exercise 2

Work out each problem. Circle the letter that appears before your answer.

1. Which of the following statements is true regarding triangle *ABC?*

    (A) $AC > AB$
    (B) $AB > BC$
    (C) $AC > BC$
    (D) $BC > AB$
    (E) $BC > AB + AC$

2. In triangle *RST, RS = ST*. If *P* is any point on *RS,* which of the following statements is always true?

    (A) $PT < PR$
    (B) $PT > PR$
    (C) $PT = PR$
    (D) $PT \geq PR$
    (E) $PT \leq PR$

3. If $\angle A > \angle C$ and $\angle ABD = 120°$, then

    (A) $AC < AB$
    (B) $BC < AB$
    (C) $\angle C > \angle ABC$
    (D) $BC > AC$
    (E) $\angle ABC > \angle A$

4. If $AB \perp CD$ and $\angle 1 > \angle 4$, then

    (A) $\angle 1 > \angle 2$
    (B) $\angle 4 > \angle 3$
    (C) $\angle 2 > \angle 3$
    (D) $\angle 2 < \angle 3$
    (E) $\angle 2 < \angle 4$

5. Which of the following sets of numbers could be the sides of a triangle?

    (A)   1, 2, 3
    (B)   2, 2, 4
    (C)   3, 3, 6
    (D)   1, 1.5, 2
    (E)   5, 6, 12

RETEST

Work out each problem. Circle the letter that appears before your answer.

1. If $2x > -5$, then

(A) $x > \dfrac{5}{2}$

(B) $x > -\dfrac{5}{2}$

(C) $x > -\dfrac{2}{5}$

(D) $x < \dfrac{5}{2}$

(E) $x < -\dfrac{5}{2}$

2. If $m = n$ and $p < q$, then

(A) $m - p < n - q$
(B) $p - m > q - n$
(C) $m - p > n - q$
(D) $mp > nq$
(E) $m + q < n + p$

3. If $\angle 3 > \angle 2$ and $\angle 1 = \angle 2$, then

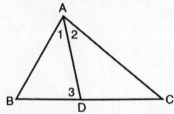

(A) $AB > BD$
(B) $AB < BD$
(C) $DC = BD$
(D) $AD > BD$
(E) $AB < AC$

4. If $\angle 1 > \angle 2$ and $\angle 2 > \angle 3$, then

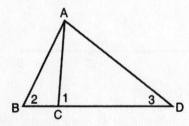

(A) $AB > AD$
(B) $AC > AD$
(C) $AC < CD$
(D) $AD > AC$
(E) $AB > BC$

5. If $\dfrac{x}{2} > 6$, then

(A) $x > 3$
(B) $x < 3$
(C) $x > 12$
(D) $x < 12$
(E) $x > -12$

6. If $AB = AC$ and $\angle 1 > \angle B$, then

(A) $\angle B > \angle C$
(B) $\angle 1 > \angle C$
(C) $BD > AD$
(D) $AB > AD$
(E) $\angle ADC > \angle ADB$

7. Which of the following sets of numbers may be used as the sides of a triangle?

(A) 7, 8, 9
(B) 3, 5, 8
(C) 8, 5, 2
(D) 3, 10, 6
(E) 4, 5, 10

8. In isosceles triangle RST, $RS = ST$. If A is the midpoint of RS and B is the midpoint of ST, then

(A) $SA > ST$
(B) $BT > BS$
(C) $BT = SA$
(D) $SR > RT$
(E) $RT > ST$

9. If $x > 0$ and $y < 0$, which of the following is always true?

(A) $x - y > y - x$
(B) $x + y > 0$
(C) $xy > 0$
(D) $y > x$
(E) $x - y < 0$

10. In triangle ABC, AD is the altitude to BC. Then

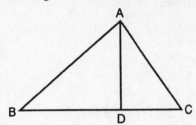

(A) $AD > DC$
(B) $AD < BD$
(C) $AD > AC$
(D) $BD > DC$
(E) $AB > BD$

SOLUTIONS TO PRACTICE EXERCISES

Diagnostic Test

1. (D)
$$4x < 6$$
$$x < \frac{6}{4}$$
Simplify to $x < \dfrac{3}{2}$

2. (B) If equal quantities are added to unequal quantities, the sums are unequal in the same order.

$$c > d$$
$$\underline{(+)a = b}$$
$$a + c \;\; > b + d$$

3. (C) $\dfrac{3}{5} < \dfrac{x}{10} < \dfrac{4}{5}$

Multiply through by 10.

$6 < x < 8$ or x must be between 6 and 8.

4. (D)

If unequal quantities are subtracted from equal quantities, the results are unequal in the opposite order.

$$AC = AB$$
$$\underline{(-)EC < DB}$$
$$AE > AD \text{ or } AD < AE$$

5. (C) If two angles of a triangle are unequal, the sides opposite these angles are unequal, with the larger side opposite the larger angle.

Since $-1 > -2$, $BC > AC$.

6. (E)

$AB = CB + AC$

7. (C) In right triangle ACB, the longest side is the hypotenuse AB. Therefore, side AC is less than AB.

8. (D) A positive subtracted from a negative is always negative.

9. (B)

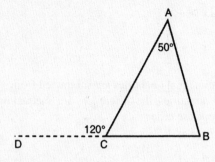

$AB = CB + AC$

$\angle ACB$ is the supplement of $\angle ACD$. Therefore, $\angle ACB = 60°$. $-ABC$ must equal $70°$ because there are $180°$ in a triangle. Since $\angle ABC$ is the largest angle in the triangle, AC must be the longest side. Therefore, $AC > AB$.

10. (D) In a right triangle, the largest angle is the right angle. Since $\angle C$ is the largest angle, $\angle C = 90°$.

Exercise 1

1. (A) $8x < 10x + 20$

    $-2x < 20$

    $x > -10$

2. (C) $-2x < 12$

    $x > -6$

3. (E) $x + 10 > 50$

    $x > 40$

4. (A) $-.4x < 4$

    Multiply by 10 to remove decimals.

    $-4x < 40$

    $x > -10$

5. (D) $.03n > -.18$

    Multiply by 100

    $3n > -18$

    $n > -6$

6. (D) Divide by 15

    $$b < \frac{10}{15}$$

    Simplify to $b < \dfrac{2}{3}$

7. (D) x must be less than 2, but can go no lower than -2, as $(-3)^2$ would be greater than 4.

8. (D) $n + 4.3 < 2.7$

    Subtract 4.3 from each side.

    $n < -1.6$

9. (D) When two negative numbers are added, their sum will be negative.

10. (E) The product of two negative numbers is positive.

Exercise 2

1. (D) Angle A will contain 90°, which is the largest angle of the triangle. The sides from largest to smallest will be *BC, AB, AC*.

2. (B) Since $\angle SRT = \angle STR$, $\angle SRT$ will have to be greater than $\angle PTR$. Therefore, $PT > PR$ in triangle *PRT*.

3. (D) Angle $ABC = 60°$. Since there are 120° left for $\angle A$ and $\angle C$ together and, also $\angle A > \angle C$, then $\angle A$ must contain more than half of 120° and $\angle C$ must contain less than half of 120°. This makes $\angle A$ the largest angle of the triangle. The sides in order from largest to smallest are *BC, AC, AB*.

4. (D) $\angle ABC = \angle ABD$ as they are both right angles. If $\angle 1 > \angle 4$, then $\angle 2$ will be less than $\angle 3$ because we are subtracting unequal quantities ($\angle 1$ and $\angle 4$) from equal quantities ($\angle ABC$ and $\angle ABD$).

5. (D) The sum of any two sides (always try the shortest two) must be greater than the third side.

Retest

1. (B) $2x > -5$

$$x > -\frac{5}{2}$$

2. (C) If unequal quantities are subtracted from equal quantities, the differences are unequal in the opposite order.

$$m = n$$
$$(-)p < q$$
$$m - p > n - q$$

3. (A) Since $\angle 3 > \angle 2$ and $\angle 1 = \angle 2$, $\angle 3 > \angle 1$. If two angles of a triangle are unequal, the sides opposite these angles are unequal, with the larger side opposite the larger angle. Therefore, $AB > BD$.

4. (D) Since $\angle 1 > \angle 2$ and $\angle 2 > \angle 3$, $\angle 1 > \angle 3$. In triangle *ACD* side *AD* is larger than side *AC*, since *AD* is opposite the larger angle.

5. (C) $\dfrac{x}{2} > 6$

$$x > 12$$

6. (B) If two sides of a triangle are equal, the angles opposite them are equal. Therefore $\angle C = \angle B$. Since $\angle 1 > \angle B$, $\angle 1 > \angle C$.

7. (A) The sum of any two sides (always try the shortest two) must be greater than the third side.

8. (C)

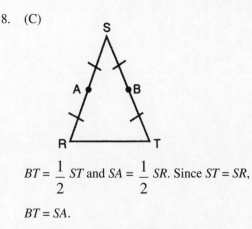

$BT = \dfrac{1}{2} ST$ and $SA = \dfrac{1}{2} SR$. Since $ST = SR$,

$BT = SA$.

9. (A) A positive minus a negative is always greater than a negative minus a positive.

10. (E) In right triangle *ADB*, the longest side is the hypotenuse *AB*. Therefore, $AB > BD$.

On a typical SAT, the non-experimental sections will contain 60 math questions, of which 15 are in a special format called quantitative comparisons.

WHAT IS A QUANTITATIVE COMPARISON?

The format for all quantitative comparison questions is the same: two quantities that are to be compared are placed next to each other in columns labeled A and B. Additional information concerning one or both of the quantities may be centered above the two columns. Your job is to compare the two quantities and to decide which, if either, is greater. Based on your decision, you then choose one of the answers as given in the directions below. These are the same directions that appear on the SAT. They should be memorized to save time on the actual test.

> **Directions: Each of the following questions consists of two quantities, one in Column A and one in Column B. You are to compare the two quantities and choose**

A if the quantity in Column A is greater;

B if the quantity in Column B is greater;

C if the two quantities are equal;

D if the relationship cannot be determined from the information given.

Numbers: All numbers used are real numbers

Figures: Position of points, angles, regions, etc. can be assumed to be in the order shown; and angle measures can be assumed to be positive.

Lines shown as straight can be assumed to be straight.

Figures can be assumed to lie in a plane unless otherwise indicated.

Figures that accompany questions are intended to provide information useful in answering the questions. However, unless a note states that a figure is drawn to scale, you should solve these problems NOT by estimating sizes by sight or by measurement, but by using your knowledge of mathematics.

Note: Since there are only four choices, NEVER MARK (E).

Common Information: In a question, information concerning one or both of the quantities to be compared may be centered above the two columns. A symbol that appears in both columns represents the same thing in Column A as it does in Column B.

The following examples illustrate the four answer choices:

	Column A	**Column B**
Q	5	$\sqrt{\sqrt{100}}$

A   Column A: Given as 5.

Column B: $\sqrt{\sqrt{100}} = \sqrt{10}$, which is slightly larger than 3.

Answer A: Column A is greater than Column B.

	Column A	**Column B**
		$x + 4 = 10$
Q	$\dfrac{x}{2}$	$x - 2$

A   Column A: Since $x + 4 = 10$, $x = 6$. Thus, $\dfrac{x}{2} = \dfrac{6}{2} = 3$.

Column B: $x - 2 = 6 - 2 = 4$.

Answer B: Column B is greater than Column A.

Column A   **Column B**

	Column A	**Column B**
Q	$x + y + z$	$p + q + r$

A   Column A: The sum of the angles in a triangle is 180°.

Column B: Same as above.

Answer C: Column A is equal to Column B.

	Column A	**Column B**
Q	$x^2 + y^2$	$(x + y)^2$

A   The expression in Column B is $(x + y)^2 = x^2 + 2xy + y^2$. This is the same as the expression in Column A with the addition of the middle term $2xy$. Since no information is given about the values of x and y (they can be positive, negative, or zero), the relative size of the expressions in the two columns cannot be determined.

Answer D: The relationship cannot be determined.

STRATEGIES FOR ANSWERING QUANTITATIVE COMPARISONS

Understand the directions

Make sure you understand that the answer to a quantitative comparison question is (A) only if the quantity in Column A is *always* (not just sometimes) greater than that in Column B. Similarly, an answer of (B) means that the quantity in Column B is *always* greater, and an answer of (C) means that the quantities are *always* equal. Choice (D) can be thought of as signifying that under certain circumstances, the size relationship between the entries in Column A and Column B can change.

Watch out for tricks

At first glance, many of the quantitative comparison questions on the SAT appear easy because they are based on topics that you have already studied (arithmetic, algebra, and geometry) and seem not to require much work to determine a solution. On the contrary, a lot of these questions are actually quite tricky. Answers that initially appear to be correct will often be incorrect. Doing well on quantitative comparison questions involves not only knowing the math topics, but also knowing a variety of alternate problem-solving approaches.

Pay attention to the question number

The 15 quantitative comparison questions on the SAT are roughly arranged in increasing order of difficulty. Thus, you should view the first 5 questions as "easy," the next 5 as of "medium" difficulty, and the last 5 as "hard." On a typical SAT, each quantitative comparison question in the first third of the section is answered correctly by approximately 86% of test-takers, while each question in the middle and final thirds is answered correctly by only about 65% and 48% of test-takers, respectively.

Be particularly careful when working in the "hard" third. With these questions, be suspicious of any answer that seems "obviously" correct. If an obvious answer were correct, more than 48% of the people taking the SAT would have answered it correctly. On the other hand, any answer that seems to be obviously correct in the easy third is likely to be correct.

Purely Numerical Questions

In about one-third of the quantitative comparison questions on the SAT, the quantities in both columns will be purely numerical (no variables, just numbers). These questions have only three possible answers.

For purely numerical questions, never choose (D)

Since the relative sizes of two purely numerical quantities can always be determined, the answer to such a question is never (D).

The following strategies will be useful in solving purely numerical questions:

If the math is simple, do it.

Whenever the given computations can be easily performed, simply do them and then compare the results.

	Column A	**Column B**
Q	$\dfrac{5}{6}+1$	$\dfrac{10}{3}-1$

A   Column A: $\dfrac{5}{6}+1=1\dfrac{5}{6}$.

Column B: $\dfrac{10}{3}-1=\dfrac{10}{3}-\dfrac{3}{3}=\dfrac{7}{3}=2\dfrac{1}{3}$.

Answer B: Column B is greater than Column A.

Whenever possible, simplify or factor

Operations that appear to be too time-consuming can often can be simplified by first simplifying fractions or by factoring the given expressions. In general, if you find yourself doing a lengthy computation, you may have missed a shortcut.

	Column A	Column B
Q	$\dfrac{3\cdot3\cdot3\cdot3}{6\cdot6\cdot6\cdot6}$	$\left(\dfrac{1}{2}\right)^4$

A   Column A: $\dfrac{3\cdot3\cdot3\cdot3}{6\cdot6\cdot6\cdot6}=\dfrac{1\cdot1\cdot1\cdot1}{2\cdot2\cdot2\cdot2}=\dfrac{1}{16}$

Column B: $\left(\dfrac{1}{2}\right)^4=\dfrac{1^4}{2^4}=\dfrac{1}{16}$

Answer C: Column A is equal to Column B.

	Column A	Column B
Q	$(403)^2 - (402)^2$	$2(402)$

A   Column A: $(403)^2 - (402)^2$ can be simplified using the formula $x^2 - y^2 = (x + y)(x - y)$.

$(403)^2 - (402)^2 = (403 + 402)(403 - 402)$

$= (805)(1) = 805$.

Column B: $2(402) = 804$.

Answer A: Column A is greater than Column B.

	Column A	Column B
Q	$8^{24} - 8^{23}$	$8^{23}(7)$

A   Column A: $8^{24} - 8^{23} = 8^{23}(8 - 1) = 8^{23}(7)$

Column B: Given as $8^{23}(7)$

Answer C: Column A is equal to Columm B.

Compare terms and factors

Only do as much work as is necessary to determine which quantity is larger. Sums and products can often be compared term-by-term or factor-by-factor.

Column A	Column B
$\dfrac{2}{3} + \dfrac{3}{4} + \dfrac{5}{6}$	$\dfrac{2}{4} + \dfrac{3}{5} + \dfrac{5}{7}$

Q

A   Simply note that each one of the three terms in Column A is larger than the corresponding term in Column B.

That is $\dfrac{2}{3} > \dfrac{2}{4}$, $\dfrac{3}{4} > \dfrac{3}{5}$, and $\dfrac{5}{6} > \dfrac{5}{7}$.

Answer A: Column A is greater than Column B.

Column A	Column B
The number of seconds in a day.	The number of minutes in 50 days.

Q

A   Column A: The number of seconds in a day is $60 \cdot 60 \cdot 24$.

Column B: The number of minutes in 50 days is $60 \cdot 24 \cdot 50$.

Note that the expressions in Column A and Column B have two factors in common, 60 and 24. Since the third factor in Column A is 60 and the third factor in Column B is 50, Column A is greater than Column B.

Answer A: Column A is greater than Column B.

Estimate if you can

Whenever possible, estimate the sizes of the quantities.

Column A	Column B
$\dfrac{334}{999}$	$\dfrac{110}{333}$

Q

A   Note that the quantity in Column A is slightly greater than $\dfrac{1}{3}$, while the quantity in Column B is slightly less than $\dfrac{1}{3}$.

Answer A: Column A is greater than Column B.

Column A	Column B
$\sqrt{10} + \sqrt{17}$	$\sqrt{27}$

Q

A   Column A: $\sqrt{10}$ is slightly larger than 3, and $\sqrt{17}$ is slightly larger than 4. Thus, $\sqrt{10} + \sqrt{17}$ is slightly larger than 7.

Column B: $\sqrt{27}$ is slightly larger than 5.

Answer A: Column A is greater than Column B.

Treat each question as an algebraic inequality

Each quantitative comparison question can be treated as an algebraic inequality. Thus, any operation that can be performed on both sides of an inequality can also be performed on both columns of a quantitative comparison question: (1) You can add the same number to or subtract the same number from both columns; (2) you can multiply or divide both columns by the same *positive* number; (3) you can square both columns (if the entries are positive).

These principles can be used to transform the operations of subtraction and division to the relatively easier operations of addition and multiplication, respectively.

	Column A	Column B
Q	$4.1 + \dfrac{1}{3}$	$5.1 - \dfrac{2}{3}$

A To eliminate the subtraction in Column B, add $\dfrac{2}{3}$ to both columns.

$$4.1 + \frac{1}{3} + \frac{2}{3} \qquad\qquad 5.1 - \frac{2}{3} + \frac{2}{3}$$

$$4.1 + 1 \qquad\qquad\qquad\qquad 5.1$$

$$5.1 \qquad\qquad\qquad\qquad\qquad 5.1$$

Answer C: Column A is equal to Column B.

	Column A	Column B
Q	$\dfrac{1}{5}$	$\dfrac{1}{5} - \dfrac{1}{6} + \dfrac{1}{7} - \dfrac{1}{8} + \dfrac{1}{9}$

A Begin by subtracting the term $\dfrac{1}{5}$ from both columns.

$$0 \qquad\qquad\qquad -\frac{1}{6} + \frac{1}{7} - \frac{1}{8} + \frac{1}{9}$$

Then, to eliminate the subtraction in Column B, add $\dfrac{1}{6}$ and $\dfrac{1}{8}$ to both columns.

$$\frac{1}{6} + \frac{1}{8} \qquad\qquad\qquad \frac{1}{7} + \frac{1}{9}$$

Now simply note that each of the two terms in Column A is larger than the corresponding two terms in Column B.

Answer A: Column A is greater than Column B.

Column A	Column B

Q
$$\dfrac{4}{\sqrt{2}}$$
$$\sqrt{2}$$

A   To eliminate the division in Column A, multiply both columns by $\sqrt{2}$.

$$4 \qquad\qquad\qquad \sqrt{2}\cdot\sqrt{2}$$

Since $\sqrt{2}\cdot\sqrt{2}=2$, Column A is greater than Column B.

Answer A: Column A is greater than Column B.

Column A	Column B

Q
$$\sqrt{89{,}900}$$
$$300$$

A   To eliminate the square root in Column A, square both columns. Column A then becomes 89,900, while Column B becomes 90,000.

Answer B: Column B is greater than Column A.

Use the properties of proper fractions

Remember that when you raise a proper fraction (a fraction less than 1) to a power, the result is *smaller* than the original fraction. Also, when you take the square root of a proper fraction, the result is *larger* than the original fraction (but still, of course, less than 1).

Column A	Column B

Q
$$(0.63)^2$$
$$\sqrt{0.63}$$

A   Simply note that when 0.63 is squared, the result is a number smaller than 0.63, but that when one square root of 0.63 is taken, the result is larger than 0.63.

Answer B: Column B is larger than Column A.

Column A	Column B

Q
$$(1-0.8)^4$$
$$(0.2)^6$$

A   Since $(1-0.8)^4$ is equal to $(0.2)^4$, we are actually comparing $(0.2)^4$ to $(0.2)^6$. Then, recall that the higher the power to which a proper fraction is raised, the smaller the result.

Answer A: Column A is greater than Column B.

QUESTIONS INVOLVING VARIABLES

The remaining two-thirds of the quantitative comparison questions on SAT I involve expressions containing both *numbers* and *variables*. Since the relative size of the two quantities depends on the particular values of the variables, additional strategies can be used. These are illustrated in the problems below.

Use the strategies for purely numerical questions whenever you can

Many of the principles that have already been discussed for purely numerical questions will also apply to questions involving variables. In particular, make use of the concept of treating the two columns as if they were the two sides of an inequality.

$$x < 0$$

<u>Column A</u>	<u>Column B</u>
$x - 3$	$3 - x$

Q

A   To eliminate the subtraction, add both 3 and x to both columns.

$$2x \qquad\qquad\qquad 6$$

Since x is negative, $2x$ is also negative and thus less than 6.

Answer B: Column B is greater than Column A.

$$x \neq 0$$

<u>Column A</u>	<u>Column B</u>
$\dfrac{x^2 + 4x}{2}$	$2x$

Q

A   To eliminate the division in Column A, multiply both columns by 2.

$$x^2 + 4x \qquad\qquad\qquad 4x$$

Now subtract $4x$ from both columns.

$$x^2 \qquad\qquad\qquad 0$$

Since $x \neq 0$, x^2 is positive and thus greater than 0.

Answer A: Column A is greater than Column B.

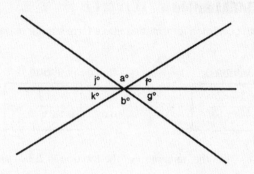

	Column A	**Column B**
Q	$a - (f + g)$	$b - (j + k)$

A To eliminate the subtractions, add both $(f + g)$ and $(j + k)$ to both columns.

$$a + (j + k) \qquad\qquad b + (f + g)$$

Since each column represents three angles that form a straight angle, the sum in each column is 180.

Answer C: Column A is equal to Column B.

Solve the equations in the common information

Whenever possible, solve the equations in the common information to determine the numerical values of the variables in the columns.

$$k + n = 13$$
$$n + 3 = 8$$

	Column A	**Column B**
Q	k	n

A Solving the equation $n + 3 = 8$, we find $n = 5$. Substituting $n = 5$ into the equation $k + n = 13$, we get $k + 5 = 13$, or $k = 8$.

Answer A: Column A is greater than Column B.

Perform the algebraic operations

If algebraic operations are involved in an expression, it is often helpful to begin by performing these operations.

$$y > 0$$

	Column A	**Column B**
Q	$(2 + x)(3 + y)$	$6 + 3x + xy$

A Multiply the expressions in Column A.

$$6 + 3x + 2y + xy \qquad\qquad 6 + 3x + xy$$

Column A is the same as Column B with the addition of the term $2y$. Since y is positive, so is $2y$.

Answer A: Column A is greater than Column B.

Manipulate the common information

Whenever possible, manipulate the common information into a form similar to one of the entries in the columns.

$$3x - y = 10$$

Column A	Column B
$\dfrac{6x - 2y}{3}$	$\dfrac{19}{3}$

Q

A   Notice that in Column A, $6x - 2y$ in the numerator of the fraction is $2(3x - y)$.

Since $3x - y$ is given as 10, $2(3x - y) = 2(10) = 20$. Thus, Column A is equal to $\dfrac{20}{3}$.

Answer A: Column A is greater than Column B.

Substitute numbers for the variables

One of the most useful techniques for solving questions involving variables is to choose sample numerical values for the variables. A single substitution will always eliminate two of the four answer choices. For example, suppose that for a particular numerical value the expression in Column A is larger than the expression in Column B. Then the answer to the question must either be (A) (Column A is *always* larger) or (D) (Column A is *sometimes* larger and *sometimes* not larger).

To determine which of the two remaining possible answer choices is correct, choose a few other values. Be sure to try numbers of different types (negative numbers, fractions, 0, etc.). If, for any of these values, Column A is not larger than Column B, then the answer must be (D). If, on the other hand, Column A is larger for each value you try, then you can reasonably assume that (A) is the correct answer.

$$x \text{ is an integer}$$
$$x > 0$$

Column A	Column B
x^2	$2x$

Q

A   Try some sample values for x. For example, if $x = 1$, $x^2 = 1^2 = 1$ and $2x = 2^1 = 2$. In this case, Column B is larger than Column A. If, on the other hand, $x = 3$, $x^2 = 3^2 = 9$ and $2x = 2^3 = 8$. In this case, Column A is larger than Column B. Therefore, the relative size of the two columns depends on the value of x.

Answer D: The relationship cannot be determined.

Consider whether a variable might be a fraction or a negative number

Remember that powers of, roots of, and divisions by numbers between 0 and 1 (proper fractions) behave the opposite of those greater than 1. Also, negative numbers raised to even powers behave differently than negative numbers raised to odd powers.

Thus, when solving a quantitative comparison question involving variables, carefully note which types of numbers are involved, that is, whether the numbers are greater than 1, between 0 and 1, or negative.

Raising Variables to a Power

$$x > 1$$

Column A	Column B
x^2	x^3

Q

A   When a number greater than 1 is squared, it becomes larger. When the same number is cubed, it becomes even larger.

Answer B: Column B is greater than Column A.

$$0 < x < 1$$

Column A	Column B
x^2	x^3

Q

A   When proper fractions (numbers between 0 and 1) are raised to powers, they behave the opposite of numbers greater than 1. That is, squaring a proper fraction results in a smaller number. When the same proper fraction is cubed, it becomes even smaller.

Answer A: Column A is greater than Column B.

$$x < 0$$

Column A	Column B
x^2	x^3

Q

A   When a negative number is squared, the result is always positive. When a negative number is cubed, the result is always negative.

Answer A: Column A is greater than Column B.

Column A	Column B
x^2	x^3

Q

A   Since no information is given about x, x could be a negative number, zero, a proper fraction, one, or a number greater than one. Therefore, it is impossible to determine the relative sizes of x^2 and x^3.

Answer D: The relationship cannot be determined.

$$x^2 = y^2$$

Column A	Column B
x	y

Q

A   Since both x and y are raised to the same *even* power, they must have the same numerical value, but not necessarily the same sign. For example, x could be + 3 and y could be - 3, in which case $x^2 = y^2$, but x is greater than y. Of course, just the opposite could be the case. That is, x could be - 3 and y could be + 3.

Answer D: The relationship cannot be determined.

Finding the square root of a variable

$$x > 1$$

Column A	**Column B**
x	$\sqrt{x}$

Q

A When the square root of a number greater than 1 is taken, the result is smaller than the original number.

Answer A: Column A is greater than Column B.

$$0 < x < 1$$

Column A	**Column B**
x	$\sqrt{x}$

Q

A When the square root of a proper fraction is taken, the result is larger than the original number.

Answer B: Column B is greater than Column A.

Column A	**Column B**
x	$\sqrt{x}$

Q

A Since no information is given about the value of x, it is impossible to determine the relationship between x and $\sqrt{x}$.

Answer D: The relationship cannot be determined.

Dividing by a variable

$$x > 1$$

Column A	**Column B**
$\dfrac{8}{x}$	$8x$

Q

A When a positive whole number is divided by a number larger than 1, the result is smaller than the original number. When a positive number is multiplied by a number larger than 1, the result is larger than the original number.

Answer B: Column B is greater than Column A.

$$0 < x < 1$$

Column A	**Column B**
$\dfrac{8}{x}$	$8x$

Q

A When a positive whole number is divided by a proper fraction, the result is larger than the original number (e.g., $8 \div \dfrac{1}{2} = 8 \times 2 = 16$). When a positive whole number is multiplied by a proper fraction, the result is smaller than the original number.

Answer A: Column A is greater than Column B.

	Column A	**Column B**
Q	$\dfrac{8}{x}$	$8x$

A   Since no information is given about the value of x, it is impossible to determine the relative values of $\dfrac{8}{x}$ and $8x$.

Answer D: The relationship cannot be determined.

$$\frac{x}{y} = \frac{7}{9}$$

$$x > 0,\ y > 0$$

	Column A	**Column B**
Q	x	y

A   First, remember that 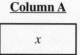 does not mean that $x = 7$ and $y = 9$, but that the ratio of x to y is 7 to 9. For example, x could be 14 and y could be 18. In any case, since x and y are both positive, x must be less than y.

Answer B: Colum B is greater than Column A.

$$\frac{x}{y} = \frac{7}{9}$$

	Column A	**Column B**
Q	x	y

A   If x and y are both positive, then x is less than y. However, if x and y are both negative, then y is less than x. For example, if $x = -7$ and $y = -9$, y is less than x.

Answer D: The relationship cannot be determined.

$$x^3 = y^3$$

	Column A	**Column B**
Q	x	y

A   Since both x and y are raised to the same *odd* power, they must have both the same numerical value and the same sign. That is, they must be the same number.

Answer C: Column A is equal to Column B.

PRACTICE TEST A
Answer Sheet

Section 1

1. Ⓐ Ⓑ Ⓒ Ⓓ Ⓔ   8. Ⓐ Ⓑ Ⓒ Ⓓ Ⓔ   15. Ⓐ Ⓑ Ⓒ Ⓓ Ⓔ   22. Ⓐ Ⓑ Ⓒ Ⓓ Ⓔ
2. Ⓐ Ⓑ Ⓒ Ⓓ Ⓔ   9. Ⓐ Ⓑ Ⓒ Ⓓ Ⓔ   16. Ⓐ Ⓑ Ⓒ Ⓓ Ⓔ   23. Ⓐ Ⓑ Ⓒ Ⓓ Ⓔ
3. Ⓐ Ⓑ Ⓒ Ⓓ Ⓔ   10. Ⓐ Ⓑ Ⓒ Ⓓ Ⓔ   17. Ⓐ Ⓑ Ⓒ Ⓓ Ⓔ   24. Ⓐ Ⓑ Ⓒ Ⓓ Ⓔ
4. Ⓐ Ⓑ Ⓒ Ⓓ Ⓔ   11. Ⓐ Ⓑ Ⓒ Ⓓ Ⓔ   18. Ⓐ Ⓑ Ⓒ Ⓓ Ⓔ   25. Ⓐ Ⓑ Ⓒ Ⓓ Ⓔ
5. Ⓐ Ⓑ Ⓒ Ⓓ Ⓔ   12. Ⓐ Ⓑ Ⓒ Ⓓ Ⓔ   19. Ⓐ Ⓑ Ⓒ Ⓓ Ⓔ
6. Ⓐ Ⓑ Ⓒ Ⓓ Ⓔ   13. Ⓐ Ⓑ Ⓒ Ⓓ Ⓔ   20. Ⓐ Ⓑ Ⓒ Ⓓ Ⓔ
7. Ⓐ Ⓑ Ⓒ Ⓓ Ⓔ   14. Ⓐ Ⓑ Ⓒ Ⓓ Ⓔ   21. Ⓐ Ⓑ Ⓒ Ⓓ Ⓔ

Section 2

1. Ⓐ Ⓑ Ⓒ Ⓓ Ⓔ   6. Ⓐ Ⓑ Ⓒ Ⓓ Ⓔ   11. Ⓐ Ⓑ Ⓒ Ⓓ Ⓔ
2. Ⓐ Ⓑ Ⓒ Ⓓ Ⓔ   7. Ⓐ Ⓑ Ⓒ Ⓓ Ⓔ   12. Ⓐ Ⓑ Ⓒ Ⓓ Ⓔ
3. Ⓐ Ⓑ Ⓒ Ⓓ Ⓔ   8. Ⓐ Ⓑ Ⓒ Ⓓ Ⓔ   13. Ⓐ Ⓑ Ⓒ Ⓓ Ⓔ
4. Ⓐ Ⓑ Ⓒ Ⓓ Ⓔ   9. Ⓐ Ⓑ Ⓒ Ⓓ Ⓔ   14. Ⓐ Ⓑ Ⓒ Ⓓ Ⓔ
5. Ⓐ Ⓑ Ⓒ Ⓓ Ⓔ   10. Ⓐ Ⓑ Ⓒ Ⓓ Ⓔ   15. Ⓐ Ⓑ Ⓒ Ⓓ Ⓔ

Note: Only the answers entered on the grid are scored. Handwritten answers at the top of the column are *not* scored.

PRACTICE TEST A

SECTION 1

25 QUESTIONS

Time: 30 minutes

Circle: Rectangle: Rectangular Solid: Cylinder: Triangle:

$C = 2\pi r$ $A = lw$ $V = lwh$ $V = \pi r^2 h$ $A = \frac{1}{2}bh$ $a^2 + b^2 = c^2$
$A = \pi r^2$

The number of degrees of arc in a circle is 360.
The measure in degrees of a straight angle is 180.
The sum of the measures in degrees of the angles of a triangle is 180.

1. If 20% of a number is 8, what is 25% of the number?

    (A) 2   (B) 10   (C) 12   (D) 11   (E) 15

2. If $x + 3$ is a multiple of 3, which of the following is not a multiple of 3?

    (A) x (B) $x + 6$ (C) $6x + 18$ (D) $2x + 6$ (E) $3x + 5$

3.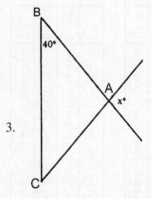

    In the figure above, $AB = AC$. Then $x =$

    (A) 40°   (B) 80°   (C) 100°   (D) 60°   (E) 90°

4. $\left(\dfrac{2}{5} \div \dfrac{2}{3}\right) + \left(\dfrac{1}{2} - \dfrac{1}{10}\right) =$

    (A) $\dfrac{1}{7}$ (B) $-\dfrac{1}{7}$ (C) $\dfrac{19}{15}$ (D) $\dfrac{1}{5}$ (E) 1

5. The toll on the Islands Bridge is $1.00 for car and driver and $.75 for each additional passenger. How many people were riding in a car for which the toll was $3.25?

    (A) 2   (B) 3   (C) 4   (D) 5   (E) none of these

6. If $y^3 = 2y^2$ and $y \neq 0$, then y must be equal to

    (A) 1   (B) $\dfrac{1}{2}$ (C) 2   (D) 3   (E) -1

7. If x and y are negative integers and $x - y = 1$, what is the least possible value for xy?

    (A) 0   (B) 1   (C) 2   (D) 3   (E) 4

8.

    A park is in the shape of a square, a triangle, and a semicircle, attached as in the diagram above. If the area of the square is 144 and the perimeter of the triangle is 28, find the perimeter of the park.

    (A) $52 + 12p$ (B) $52 + 6p$ (C) $40 + 6p$ (D) $34 + 12p$ (E) $32 + 6p$

9. An oil tank has a capacity of 45 gallons. At the beginning of October it is 80% full. At the end of October it is $\dfrac{1}{3}$ full. How many gallons of oil were used in October?

    (A) 21   (B) 25   (C) 41   (D) 27   (E) 30

10.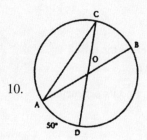

    $\overline{AB}$ and $\overline{CD}$ are diameters of circle O. The number of degrees in angle CAB is

    (A) 50   (B) 100   (C) 130   (D) $12\dfrac{1}{2}$ (E) 25

11. If $\dfrac{a}{b} \cdot \dfrac{b}{c} \cdot \dfrac{c}{d} \cdot \dfrac{d}{e} \cdot x = 1$, then x must equal

    (A) $\dfrac{a}{e}$ (B) $\dfrac{e}{a}$ (C) e (D) $\dfrac{1}{a}$ (E) none of these

12. If the sum of x and y is z and the average of m, n, and p is q, find the value of $x + y + m + n + p$ in terms of z and q.

    (A) $2z + 3q$ (B) $z + 3q$ (C) $z + z + \dfrac{q}{3}$ (D) $\dfrac{z}{2} + \dfrac{q}{3}$ (E) none of these

13. Isosceles triangle *ABC* is inscribed in square *BCDE* as shown. If the area of square *BCDE* is 4, the perimeter of triangle *ABC* is

   (A) 8   (B) $2+\sqrt{5}$ (C) $2+2\sqrt{5}$ (D) $2+\sqrt{10}$ (E) 12

14. If *a* is not 0 or 1, a fraction equivalent to $\dfrac{\dfrac{1}{a}}{2-\dfrac{2}{a}}$ is

   (A) $\dfrac{1}{2a-2}$ (B) $\dfrac{2}{a-2}$ (C) $\dfrac{1}{a-2}$ (D) $\dfrac{1}{a}$ (E) $\dfrac{2}{2a-1}$

15. At 3:30 P.M. the angle between the hands of a clock is

   (A) 90°   (B) 80°   (C) 75°   (D) 72°   (E) 65°

16. A clerk's weekly salary is $320 after a 25% raise. What was his weekly salary before the raise?

   (A) $256   (B) $260   (C) $300   (D) $304   (E) $316

17. The figure below is composed of 5 equal squares. If the area of the figure is 125, find its perimeter.

   (A) 60   (B) 100   (C) 80   (D) 75   (E) 20

18. Which of the following is equal to $\dfrac{1}{2}$ of $\dfrac{3}{5}$?

   (A) 3%   (B) $33\dfrac{1}{3}\%$ (C) 30%   (D) $83\dfrac{1}{3}\%$ (E) 120%

19. The length of an arc of a circle is equal to $\dfrac{1}{5}$ of the circumference of the circle. If the length of the arc is 2π, the radius of the circle is

    (A) 2   (B) 1   (C) 10   (D) 5   (E) $\sqrt{10}$

20. If two sides of a triangle are 3 and 4 and the third side is x, then
    (A) $x = 5$ (B) $x > 7$ (C) $x < 7$ (D) $1 < x < 7$ (E) 1 is % x % 7

21. The smallest integer that, when squared, is less than 5 is
    (A) 0   (B) 1   (C) 2   (D) 3   (E) none of these

22. Mr. Prince takes his wife and two children to the circus. If the price of a child's ticket is $\dfrac{1}{2}$ the price of an adult ticket and Mr. Prince pays a total of $12.60, find the price of a child's ticket.

    (A) $4.20   (B) $3.20   (C) $1.60   (D) $2.10   (E) $3.30

23. If $\begin{pmatrix} a \\ b & c \end{pmatrix}$ is defined as being equal to $ab - c$, then $\begin{pmatrix} 3 \\ 4 & 5 \end{pmatrix} + \begin{pmatrix} 5 \\ 6 & 7 \end{pmatrix}$ is equal to

    (A) 30   (B) 40   (C) 11   (D) 6   (E) 15

24. The diameter of a circle is increased by 50%. The area is increased by
    (A) 50%   (B) 100%   (C) 125%   (D)200%   (E) 250%

25. Of the students at South High, $\dfrac{1}{3}$ are seniors. Of the seniors, $\dfrac{3}{4}$ will go to college next year. What percent of the students at South High will go to college next year?

    (A) 75   (B) 25   (C) $33\dfrac{1}{3}$ (D) 50   (E) 45

SECTION 2

25 QUESTIONS

Time: 30 minutes

PART I

> *Directions:* **For each of the following questions, two quantities are given—one in Column A, the other in Column B. Compare the two quantities and mark your answer sheet as follows: (A) if the quantity in Column A is greater (B) if the quantity in Column B is greater (C) if the quantities are equal (D) if the relationship cannot be determined from the information**

EXAMPLES

	Column A	Column B
	$a > 0$	
	$x > 0$	
E1.	$a - x$	$a + x$

Ⓐ ● Ⓒ Ⓓ

| E2. | The average of 17, 19, 21, 23 | The average of 16, 18, 20, 22 |

● Ⓑ Ⓒ Ⓓ

Notes: (1) Information concerning one or both of the compared quantities will be centered above the two columns for some items.

(2) Symbols that appear in both columns represent the same thing in Column A as in Column B.

(3) Letters such as x, n, and k are symbols for real numbers.

DO NOT MARK CHOICE (E) FOR THESE QUESTIONS. THERE ARE ONLY FOUR ANSWER CHOICES.

Column A	Column B		Column A	Column B

0 is the center of the circle

| 1. Number of degrees in angle 1 | Number of degrees in angle 2 |

$$2x + 3 = 5$$
$$3y + 7 = 10$$

| 2. | x | y |

$x > 0$
$y > 0$

| 3. | $x - y$ | $y - x$ |

$x > 0$
$y < 0$

| 4. | $x - y$ | $x + y$ |

	Column A	**Column B**

$$\frac{x}{36} = \frac{1}{3}$$

5.	$\dfrac{4}{x}$	$\dfrac{1}{3}$

x is an integer

6.	x	$\dfrac{x}{-1}$

7.	Number of seconds in one day	Number of minutes in April

$9 < x < 10$

$9 < y < 11$

8.	x	y

9.	Area of a triangle with base 5 and height 7	Twice the area of a rectangle with bases and height 7

10.	Length of the hypotenuse of a right triangle with legs 9 and 10	Length of the sides of a square with area 180

11.	The total surface area of a cube with edge 6	6 times the total surface area of a cube with edge 2

Questions 12-15 refer to the diagram below.

ABCD is a parallelogram

12.	*AB*	*DC*

13.	*AB*	*BC*

14.	Angle *D*	Angle *BCE*

15.	Angle *D*	Angle *B*

Part II

> *Directions:* **Solve each of the following problems. Write the answer in the corresponding grid on the answer sheet and fill in the ovals beneath each answer you write. Here are some examples.**

Answer: 3/4 (-.75; show answer either way)   *Answer :* 325

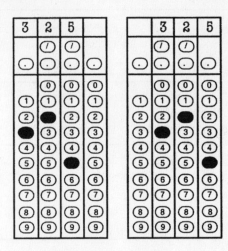

Note: A mixed number such as 3 1/2 must be gridded as 7/2 or as 3.5. If gridded as "3 1/2," it will be read as "thirty-one halves."

Note: Either position is correct.

16. If $a = 4$, what is the value of $\sqrt{a^2 + 9}$?

17. When a certain number is divided by 2, there is no remainder. If there is a remainder when the number is divided by 4, what must the remainder be?

18. If $x = a = x^2$ and $x = \sqrt{8}$, what is the value of a?

19. If $\dfrac{2}{5}x = \dfrac{5}{2}y$, what is the value of $\dfrac{y}{x}$?

20. If there are 30 students at a meeting of the Forum Club, and 20 are wearing white, 17 are wearing black and 14 are wearing both black and white, how many are wearing neither black nor white?

21. If a ❑ b means $a \cdot b + (a - b)$, find the value of 4 ❑ 2.

22. A drawer contains 4 red socks and 4 blue socks. Find the least number of socks that must be drawn from the drawer to be assured of having a pair of red socks.

23. How many 2-inch squares are needed to fill a border around the edge of the shaded square with a side of 6" as shown in the figure below?

24. If $3x + 3x - 3x = 12$, what is the value of $3x + 1$?

25. If $ab = 10$ and $a^2 + b^2 = 30$, what is the value of $(a + b)^2$?

PRACTICE TEST B
Answer Sheet

Section 1

1. Ⓐ Ⓑ Ⓒ Ⓓ Ⓔ   8. Ⓐ Ⓑ Ⓒ Ⓓ Ⓔ   15. Ⓐ Ⓑ Ⓒ Ⓓ Ⓔ   22. Ⓐ Ⓑ Ⓒ Ⓓ Ⓔ
2. Ⓐ Ⓑ Ⓒ Ⓓ Ⓔ   9. Ⓐ Ⓑ Ⓒ Ⓓ Ⓔ   16. Ⓐ Ⓑ Ⓒ Ⓓ Ⓔ   23. Ⓐ Ⓑ Ⓒ Ⓓ Ⓔ
3. Ⓐ Ⓑ Ⓒ Ⓓ Ⓔ   10. Ⓐ Ⓑ Ⓒ Ⓓ Ⓔ   17. Ⓐ Ⓑ Ⓒ Ⓓ Ⓔ   24. Ⓐ Ⓑ Ⓒ Ⓓ Ⓔ
4. Ⓐ Ⓑ Ⓒ Ⓓ Ⓔ   11. Ⓐ Ⓑ Ⓒ Ⓓ Ⓔ   18. Ⓐ Ⓑ Ⓒ Ⓓ Ⓔ   25. Ⓐ Ⓑ Ⓒ Ⓓ Ⓔ
5. Ⓐ Ⓑ Ⓒ Ⓓ Ⓔ   12. Ⓐ Ⓑ Ⓒ Ⓓ Ⓔ   19. Ⓐ Ⓑ Ⓒ Ⓓ Ⓔ
6. Ⓐ Ⓑ Ⓒ Ⓓ Ⓔ   13. Ⓐ Ⓑ Ⓒ Ⓓ Ⓔ   20. Ⓐ Ⓑ Ⓒ Ⓓ Ⓔ
7. Ⓐ Ⓑ Ⓒ Ⓓ Ⓔ   14. Ⓐ Ⓑ Ⓒ Ⓓ Ⓔ   21. Ⓐ Ⓑ Ⓒ Ⓓ Ⓔ

Section 2

1. Ⓐ Ⓑ Ⓒ Ⓓ Ⓔ   6. Ⓐ Ⓑ Ⓒ Ⓓ Ⓔ   11. Ⓐ Ⓑ Ⓒ Ⓓ Ⓔ
2. Ⓐ Ⓑ Ⓒ Ⓓ Ⓔ   7. Ⓐ Ⓑ Ⓒ Ⓓ Ⓔ   12. Ⓐ Ⓑ Ⓒ Ⓓ Ⓔ
3. Ⓐ Ⓑ Ⓒ Ⓓ Ⓔ   8. Ⓐ Ⓑ Ⓒ Ⓓ Ⓔ   13. Ⓐ Ⓑ Ⓒ Ⓓ Ⓔ
4. Ⓐ Ⓑ Ⓒ Ⓓ Ⓔ   9. Ⓐ Ⓑ Ⓒ Ⓓ Ⓔ   14. Ⓐ Ⓑ Ⓒ Ⓓ Ⓔ
5. Ⓐ Ⓑ Ⓒ Ⓓ Ⓔ   10. Ⓐ Ⓑ Ⓒ Ⓓ Ⓔ   15. Ⓐ Ⓑ Ⓒ Ⓓ Ⓔ

Note: Only the answers entered on the grid are scored. Handwritten answers at the top of the column are *not* scored.

PRACTICE TEST B

SECTION 1

25 QUESTIONS

Time: 30 minutes

$C = 2\pi r$ $A = lw$ $V = lwh$ $V = \pi r^2 h$ $A = \frac{1}{2}bh$ $a^2 + b^2 = c^2$
$A = \pi r^2$

The number of degrees of arc in a circle is 360.
The measure in degrees of a straight angle is 180.
The sum of the measures in degrees of the angles of a triangle is 180.

1. A musical instrument depreciates by 20% of its value each year. What is the value, after 2 years, of a piano purchased new for $1200?

   (A) $768   (B) $912   (C) $675   (D) $48   (E) $1152

2. Which of the following has the largest numerical value?

   (A) $\dfrac{3}{5}$ (B) $\left(\dfrac{2}{3}\right)\left(\dfrac{3}{4}\right)$ (C) $\sqrt{.25}$ (D) $(.9)^2$ (E) $\dfrac{2}{.3}$

3. $\dfrac{1}{4}\%$ written as a decimal is

   (A) 25   (B) 2.5   (C) .25   (D) .025   (E) .0025

4. Which of the following fractions is equal to $\dfrac{1}{4}\%$?

   (A) $\dfrac{1}{25}$ (B) $\dfrac{4}{25}$ (C) $\dfrac{1}{4}$ (D) $\dfrac{1}{400}$ (E) $\dfrac{1}{40}$

5. Roger receives a basic weekly salary of $80 plus a 5% commission on his sales. In a week in which his sales amounted to $800, the ratio of his basic salary to his commission was

   (A) 2:1   (B) 1:2   (C) 2:3   (D) 3:2   (E) 3:1

6. The value of $\dfrac{\dfrac{1}{2}}{\dfrac{1}{3} - \dfrac{1}{4}}$ is

   (A) 6   (B) $\dfrac{1}{6}$ (C) 1   (D) 3   (E) $\dfrac{3}{2}$

7. The sum of Alan's age and Bob's age is 40. The sum of Bob's age and Carl's age is 34. The sum of Alan's age and Carl's age is 42. How old is Bob?

   (A) 18   (B) 24   (C) 20   (D) 16   (E) 12

8. On a map having a scale of $\frac{1}{4}$ inch : 20 miles, how many inches should there be between towns 325 miles apart?

   (A) $4\frac{1}{16}$ (B) $16\frac{1}{4}$ (C) $81\frac{1}{4}$ (D) $32\frac{1}{2}$ (E) $6\frac{1}{4}$

9. In Simon's General Score, there are m male employees and f female employees. What part of the staff is men?

   (A) $\dfrac{m+f}{m}$ (B) $\dfrac{m+f}{f}$ (C) $\dfrac{m}{f}$ (D) $\dfrac{m}{m+f}$ (E) $\dfrac{f}{m}$

10. If the angles of a triangle are in the ratio 2:3:4, the triangle is

    (A) acute   (B) isosceles   (C) right   (D) equilateral   (E) obtuse

11. If the length and width of a rectangle are each multiplied by 2, then

    (A) the area and perimeter are both multiplied by 4
    (B) the area is multiplied by 2 and the perimeter by 4
    (C) the area is multiplied by 4 and the perimeter by 2
    (D) the area and perimeter are both multiplied by 2
    (E) the perimeter is multiplied by 4 and the area by 8

12. Paul needs m minutes to mow the lawn. After he works for k minutes, what part of the lawn is still unmowed?

    (A) $\dfrac{k}{m}$ (B) $\dfrac{m}{k}$ (C) $\dfrac{m-k}{k}$ (D) $\dfrac{m-k}{m}$ (E) $\dfrac{k-m}{m}$

13. Mr. Marcus earns $250 per week. If he spends 20% of his income for rent, 25% for food, and 10% for savings, how much is left each week for other expenses?

    (A) $112.50   (B) $125   (C) $137.50   (D) $132.50   (E) $140

14. What is the area of the shaded portion if the perimeter of the square is 32? (The four circles are tangent to each other and the square and are congruent.)

    (A) $32 - 16\pi$ (B) $64 - 16\pi$ (C) $64 - 64\pi$ (D) $64 - 8\pi$ (E) $32 - 4\pi$

15. How far is the point (-3, -4) from the origin?

    (A) 2   (B) 2.5   (C) $4\sqrt{2}$ (D) $4\sqrt{3}$ (E) 5

16. The product of 3456 and 789 is exactly

    (A) 2726787   (B) 2726785   (C) 2726781   (D) 2726784   (E) 2726786

17. Susan got up one morning at 7:42 A.M. and went to bed that evening at 10:10 P.M. How much time elapsed between her getting up and going to bed that day?

    (A)   18 hrs. 2 min.   (B)   14 hrs. 18 min.   (C)   15 hrs. 18 min.   (D)   9 hrs. 22 min.
    (E)   14 hrs. 28 min.

18. Find the perimeter of right triangle *ABC* if the area of square *AEDC* is 100 and the area of square *BCFG* is 36.

    (A)   22   (B)   24   (C) $16 + 6\sqrt{3}$ (D) $16 + 6\sqrt{2}$ (E)   cannot be determined from information given

19. Find the number of degrees in angle 1 if *AB = AC*, *DE = DC*, angle 2 = 40°, and angle 3 = 80°.

    (A)   60   (B)   40   (C)   90   (D)   50   (E)   80

20. If *p* pencils cost 2*D* dollars, how many pencils can be bought for *c* cents?

    (A) $\dfrac{pc}{2D}$ (B) $\dfrac{pc}{200D}$ (C) $\dfrac{50pc}{D}$ (D) $\dfrac{2Dp}{c}$ (E) $200pcD$

21. Two trains start from the same station at 10 A.M., one traveling east at 60 m.p.h. and the other west at 70 m.p.h. At what time will they be 455 miles apart?

    (A)   3:30 P.M.   (B)   12:30 P.M.   (C)   1:30 P.M.   (D)   1 P.M.   (E)   2 P.M.

22. If *x* < 0 and *y* < 0, then

    (A)   *x* + *y* > 0   (B)   *x* = -*y*   (C)   *x* > *y*   (D)   *xy* > 0   (E)   *xy* < 0

23. Which of the following is the product of 4327 and 546?

   (A) 2362541   (B) 2362542   (C) 2362543   (D) 2362546   (E) 2362548

24. If a classroom contains 20 to 24 students and each corridor contains 8 to 10 classrooms, what is the minimum number of students on one corridor at a given time, if all classrooms are occupied?

   (A) 200   (B) 192   (C) 160   (D) 240   (E) 210

25. If the area of each circle enclosed in rectangle $ABCD$ is 9π, the area of $ABCD$ is

   (A) 108   (B) 27   (C) 54   (D) 54π (E) 108π

SECTION 2

25 QUESTIONS

Time: 30 minutes

PART I

> *Directions:* For each of the following questions, two quantities are given—one in Column A, the other in Column B. Compare the two quantities and mark your answer sheet as follows: **(A)** if the quantity in Column A is greater **(B)** if the quantity in Column B is greater **(C)** if the quantities are equal **(D)** if the relationship cannot be determined from the information.

EXAMPLES

Column A	Column B

$$a > 0$$
$$x > 0$$

E1. $a - x$ $a + x$

Ⓐ ● Ⓒ Ⓓ

E2.   The average of   The average of
         17, 19, 21, 23   16, 18, 20, 22

● Ⓑ Ⓒ Ⓓ

Notes: (1) Information concerning one or both of the compared quantities will be centered above the two columns for some items.

(2) Symbols that appear in both columns represent the same thing in Column A as in Column B.

(3) Letters such as x, n, and k are symbols for real numbers.

DO NOT MARK CHOICE (E) FOR THESE QUESTIONS. THERE ARE ONLY FOUR ANSWER CHOICES.

Column A	Column B

$$4 \cdot a \cdot 4 \cdot 4 = 3 \cdot 3 \cdot 3 \cdot 3$$

1. a 3

___

$$X > Y$$
$$W < Z$$

$$X > 0 \quad Y > 0$$
$$W > 0 \quad Z > 0$$

2. $\dfrac{Y}{Z}$ $\dfrac{X}{W}$

___

$$-3 < a < -1$$

3. $\dfrac{1}{a^4}$ $\dfrac{1}{a^7}$

___

Column A	Column B

4. $18 \cdot 563 \cdot 10$ $12 \cdot 563 \cdot 16$

___

5. $100 - \dfrac{100}{.1}$ -900

___

6. The number of   10 posts
    posts needed for a fence
    100 feet long if the posts
    are placed 10 feet apart

___

7. A single discount   Two successive
    of 10%   discounts of 5% and 5%

Questions 8-11 refer to the diagram below.

ABCD is a parallelogram
AB + AD = 20

8.	DC	AB

9.	DC	DA

10.	Area ABCD	200

11.	40	Perimeter ABCD

Questions 12-15 refer to the diagram below.

OA = AB

12.	Area of larger circle	Twice the area of smaller circle

13.	Area of smaller circle	Area of shaded portion

14.	Diameter of smaller circle	Radius of larger circle

15.	Twice the circumference of smaller circle	Circumference of larger circle

PART II

> *Directions:* Solve each of the following problems. Write the answer in the corresponding grid on the answer sheet and fill in the ovals beneath each answer you write. Here are some examples

Answer: 3/4 (-.75; show answer either way)   *Answer :* 325

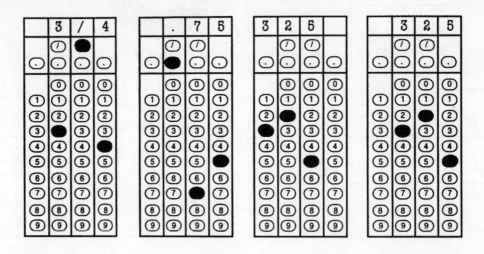

Note: A mixed number such as 3 1/2 must be gridded as 7/2 or as 3.5. If gridded as "3 1/2," it will be read as "thirty-one halves."

Note: Either position is correct.

16. Simplified as a fraction to simplest form, what part of a dime is a quarter?

17. Marion is paid $24 for 5 hours of work in the school office. Janet works 3 hours and makes $10.95. How much more per hour does Marion make than Janet?

18. If the outer diameter of a cylindrical oil tank is 54.28 inches and the inner diameter is 48.7 inches, what is the thickness of the wall of the tank, in inches?

19. What number added to 40% of itself is equal to 84?

20. If $r = 25 - s$, what is the value of $4r + 4s$?

21. A plane flies over Denver at 11:20 A.M. It passes over Coolidge, 120 miles from Denver, at 11:32 A.M. Find the rate of the plane in miles per hour.

22. 53% of the 1000 students at Jackson High are girls. How many boys are there in the school?

23. How many digits are there in the square root of a perfect square of 12 digits?

24. In May, Carter's Appliances sold 40 washing machines. In June, because of a special promotion, the store sold 80 washing machines. What is the percent of increase in the number of washing machines sold?

25. Find the value of $\left(3\sqrt{2}\right)^2$.

PRACTICE TEST C
Answer Sheet

Directions: For each question, darken the oval that corresponds to your answer choice. Mark only one oval for each question. If you change your mind, erase your answer completely.

Section 1

1. Ⓐ Ⓑ Ⓒ Ⓓ Ⓔ   8. Ⓐ Ⓑ Ⓒ Ⓓ Ⓔ   15. Ⓐ Ⓑ Ⓒ Ⓓ Ⓔ   22. Ⓐ Ⓑ Ⓒ Ⓓ Ⓔ
2. Ⓐ Ⓑ Ⓒ Ⓓ Ⓔ   9. Ⓐ Ⓑ Ⓒ Ⓓ Ⓔ   16. Ⓐ Ⓑ Ⓒ Ⓓ Ⓔ   23. Ⓐ Ⓑ Ⓒ Ⓓ Ⓔ
3. Ⓐ Ⓑ Ⓒ Ⓓ Ⓔ   10. Ⓐ Ⓑ Ⓒ Ⓓ Ⓔ   17. Ⓐ Ⓑ Ⓒ Ⓓ Ⓔ   24. Ⓐ Ⓑ Ⓒ Ⓓ Ⓔ
4. Ⓐ Ⓑ Ⓒ Ⓓ Ⓔ   11. Ⓐ Ⓑ Ⓒ Ⓓ Ⓔ   18. Ⓐ Ⓑ Ⓒ Ⓓ Ⓔ   25. Ⓐ Ⓑ Ⓒ Ⓓ Ⓔ
5. Ⓐ Ⓑ Ⓒ Ⓓ Ⓔ   12. Ⓐ Ⓑ Ⓒ Ⓓ Ⓔ   19. Ⓐ Ⓑ Ⓒ Ⓓ Ⓔ
6. Ⓐ Ⓑ Ⓒ Ⓓ Ⓔ   13. Ⓐ Ⓑ Ⓒ Ⓓ Ⓔ   20. Ⓐ Ⓑ Ⓒ Ⓓ Ⓔ
7. Ⓐ Ⓑ Ⓒ Ⓓ Ⓔ   14. Ⓐ Ⓑ Ⓒ Ⓓ Ⓔ   21. Ⓐ Ⓑ Ⓒ Ⓓ Ⓔ

Section 2

1. Ⓐ Ⓑ Ⓒ Ⓓ Ⓔ   6. Ⓐ Ⓑ Ⓒ Ⓓ Ⓔ   11. Ⓐ Ⓑ Ⓒ Ⓓ Ⓔ
2. Ⓐ Ⓑ Ⓒ Ⓓ Ⓔ   7. Ⓐ Ⓑ Ⓒ Ⓓ Ⓔ   12. Ⓐ Ⓑ Ⓒ Ⓓ Ⓔ
3. Ⓐ Ⓑ Ⓒ Ⓓ Ⓔ   8. Ⓐ Ⓑ Ⓒ Ⓓ Ⓔ   13. Ⓐ Ⓑ Ⓒ Ⓓ Ⓔ
4. Ⓐ Ⓑ Ⓒ Ⓓ Ⓔ   9. Ⓐ Ⓑ Ⓒ Ⓓ Ⓔ   14. Ⓐ Ⓑ Ⓒ Ⓓ Ⓔ
5. Ⓐ Ⓑ Ⓒ Ⓓ Ⓔ   10. Ⓐ Ⓑ Ⓒ Ⓓ Ⓔ   15. Ⓐ Ⓑ Ⓒ Ⓓ Ⓔ

Note: Only the answers entered on the grid are scored. Handwritten answers at the top of the column are *not* scored.

Grid-in answer boxes numbered 16, 17, 18, 19, 20, 21, 22, 23, 24, 25.

PRACTICE TEST C

SECTION 1

25 QUESTIONS

Time: 30 minutes

Circle: Rectangle: Rectangular Solid: Cylinder: Triangle:

$C = 2\pi r$
$A = \pi r^2$ $A = lw$ $V = lwh$ $V = \pi r^2 h$ $A = \frac{1}{2}bh$ $a^2 + b^2 = c^2$

The number of degrees of arc in a circle is 360.
The measure in degrees of a straight angle is 180.
The sum of the measures in degrees of the angles of a triangle is 180.

1. $8 \cdot 8 = 4^x$ Find x

   (A) 2   (B) 3   (C) 4   (D) 5   (E) 6

2. If $a > 2$, which of the following is the smallest?

   (A) $\dfrac{2}{a}$ (B) $\dfrac{a}{2}$ (C) $\dfrac{a+1}{2}$ (D) $\dfrac{2}{a+1}$ (E) $\dfrac{2}{a-1}$

3. Which of the following has the greatest value?

   (A) $\dfrac{1}{2}$ (B) $\sqrt{.2}$ (C) .2   (D) $(.2)^2$ (E) $(.02)^3$

4. If $\dfrac{a}{b} = \dfrac{3}{4}$, then $12a =$

   (A) $3b$ (B) b (C) $9b$ (D) $12b$ (E) $16b$

5. If $a = b$ and $\dfrac{1}{c} = b$, then $c =$

   (A) a (B) $-a$ (C) b (D) $\dfrac{1}{a}$ (E) $-b$

6. If a building B feet high casts a shadow F feet long, then, at the same time of day, a tree T feet high will cast a shadow how many feet long?

   (A) $\dfrac{FT}{B}$ (B) $\dfrac{FB}{T}$ (C) $\dfrac{B}{FT}$ (D) $\dfrac{TB}{F}$ (E) $\dfrac{T}{FB}$

7. The vertices of a triangle are (3,1) (8,1) and (8,3). The area of this triangle is

   (A) 5   (B) 10   (C) 7   (D) 20   (E) 14

8. Of 60 employees at the Star Manufacturing Company, x employees are female. If $\frac{2}{3}$ of the remainder are

    married, how many unmarried men work for this company?

    (A) $40-\frac{2}{3}x$ (B) $40-\frac{1}{3}x$ (C) $40+\frac{1}{3}x$ (D) $20-\frac{2}{3}x$ (E) $20-\frac{1}{3}x$

9. A circle whose center is at the origin passes through the point whose coordinates are (1,1). The area of the circle is

    (A) π (B) 2π (C) $\sqrt{2\pi}$ (D) $2\sqrt{2\pi}$ (E) 4π

10. In triangle ABC, $AB = BC$ and AC is extended to D. If angle BCD contains $100°$, find the number of degrees in angle B.

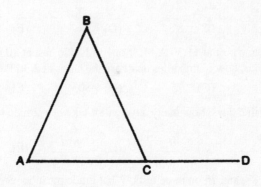

    (A) 50   (B) 80   (C) 60   (D) 40   (E) 20

11. $\dfrac{4\frac{1}{2}}{10\frac{1}{8}}$

    (A) $\dfrac{2}{5}$ (B) $\dfrac{4}{9}$ (C) $\dfrac{4}{81}$ (D) $\dfrac{3}{7}$ (E) $\dfrac{15}{23}$

12. Which of the following is greater than $\frac{1}{3}$?

    (A) .33   (B) $\left(\dfrac{1}{3}\right)^2$ (C) $\dfrac{1}{4}$ (D) $\dfrac{1}{.3}$ (E) $\dfrac{.3}{2}$

13. What percent of a half dollar is a penny, a nickel, and a dime?

    (A) 16   (B) 8   (C) 20   (D) 25   (E) 32

14. If $\dfrac{1}{a}+\dfrac{1}{b}=\dfrac{1}{c}$ then $c =$

    (A) $a+b$ (B) ab (C) $\dfrac{a+b}{ab}$ (D) $\dfrac{ab}{a+b}$ (E) $\dfrac{1}{2}ab$

15. What percent of a is b?

    (A) $\dfrac{100b}{a}$ (B) $\dfrac{a}{b}$ (C) $\dfrac{b}{100a}$ (D) $\dfrac{b}{a}$ (E) $\dfrac{100a}{b}$

16. The average of two numbers is A. If one of the numbers is x, the other number is

    (A) $A - x$ (B) $\dfrac{A}{2} - x$ (C) $2A - x$ (D) $\dfrac{A + x}{2}$ (E) $x - A$

17. If $a = 5b$, then $\dfrac{3}{5}a =$

    (A) $\dfrac{5b}{3}$ (B) $3b$ (C) $\dfrac{3b}{5}$ (D) $\dfrac{b}{3}$ (E) $\dfrac{b}{5}$

18. A rectangular door measures 5 feet by 6 feet 8 inches. The distance from one corner of the door to the diagonally opposite corner is

    (A) 9'4"   (B) 8'4"   (C) 8'3"   (D) 9'6"   (E) 9'

19. Two ships leave from the same port at 11:30 A.M. If one sails due east at 20 miles per hour and the other due south at 15 miles per hour, how many miles apart are the ships at 2:30 P.M.?

    (A) 25   (B) 50   (C) 75   (D) 80   (E) 35

20. If m men can paint a house in d days, how many days will it take $m + 2$ men to paint the same house?

    (A) $d + 2$ (B) $d - 2$ (C) $\dfrac{m+2}{md}$ (D) $\dfrac{md}{m+2}$ (E) $\dfrac{md+2d}{m}$

21. Ken received grades of 90, 88, and 75 on three tests. What grade must he receive on the next test so that his average for these 4 tests is 85?

    (A) 87   (B) 92   (C) 83   (D) 85   (E) 88

22. There is enough food at a picnic to feed 20 adults or 32 children. If there are 15 adults at the picnic, how many children can still be fed?

    (A) 10   (B) 8   (C) 16   (D) 12   (E) 4

23. In parallelogram $ABCD$, angle A contains 60°. The sum of angle B and angle D must be

    (A) 120°   (B) 300°   (C) 240°   (D) 60°   (E) 180°

24. The area of circle O is 64π. The perimeter of square $ABCD$ is

    (A) 32   (13) 32π (C) 64   (D) 16   (E) 64π

25. If a train covers 14 miles in 10 minutes, then the rate of the train in miles per hour is

    (A) 140   (B) 112   (C) 84   (D) 100   (E) 98

SECTION 2

25 QUESTIONS

Time: 30 minutes

PART I

> *Directions:* For each of the following questions, two quantities are given—one in Column A, the other in Column B. Compare the two quantities and mark your answer sheet as follows: (A) if the quantity in Column A is greater (B) if the quantity in Column B is greater (C) if the quantities are equal (D) if the relationship cannot be determined from the information

EXAMPLES

	Column A	**Column B**

$$a > 0$$
$$x > 0$$

E1. $a - x$ $a + x$

Ⓐ ● Ⓒ Ⓓ

E2.   The average of   The average of
           17, 19, 21, 23   16, 18, 20, 22

● Ⓑ Ⓒ Ⓓ

Notes: (1) Information concerning one or both of the compared quantities will be centered above the two columns for some items.

   (2) Symbols that appear in both columns represent the same thing in Column A as in Column B.

   (3) Letters such as x, n, and k are symbols for real numbers.

DO NOT MARK CHOICE (E) FOR THESE QUESTIONS. THERE ARE ONLY FOUR ANSWER CHOICES.

Column A	**Column B**

$$a > b > c > 0$$

1. $\dfrac{a}{b}$ $\dfrac{a}{c}$

$$r > 0, s > 0$$

$$\frac{1}{r} > \frac{1}{s}$$

2. r s

Column A	**Column B**

3. $\sqrt{49} + \sqrt{16}$ $\sqrt{65}$

$$2^{x-3} = 32$$

4.   5 x

The average age of Alan, Bob, and Carl is 17.

5.   The sum of   The sum of
     Alan's age and   Alan's age and
     Bob's age   Carl's age

The following diagram refers to problems 6 - 9.

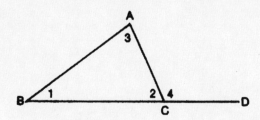

	Column A	Column B

Jack's salary is $\dfrac{3}{4}$ of Jim's salary and

Joe's salary is $\dfrac{3}{2}$ of Jack's salary.

6.	$m \angle 4$ $m \angle 1$	
12.	Jim's salary Joe's salary	

$A > 0, B > 0$
$.4A = .04B$

7.	$m \angle 1 + m \angle 3$ $m \angle 4$	
13.	A B	

8.	AB BC	

9.	$m \angle 1 + m \angle 2 + m \angle 3$ $m \angle 2 + m \angle 4$	

10.	$.5\%$ $\dfrac{1}{2}$	

$AB = AC$
$m \angle A = 60^\circ$

14.	AB BC	

$4 < a < 6$
$4 \le b \le 6$

11.	a b	

$m \angle 5 = 90^\circ$

15.	$\angle 1 + \angle 2 + \angle 3 + \angle 4$ 360°	

PART II

Directions: Solve each of the following problems. Write the answer in the corresponding grid on the answer sheet and fill in the ovals beneath each answer you write. Here are some examples.

Answer: 3/4 (-.75; show answer either way)   *Answer :* 325

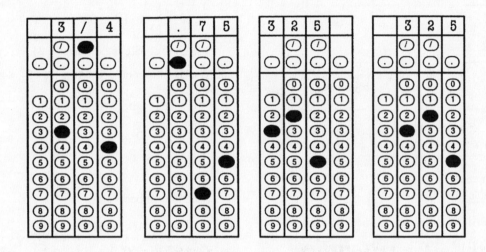

Note: A mixed number such as 3 1/2 must be gridded as 7/2 or as 3.5. If gridded as "3 1/2," it will be read as "thirty-one halves."

Note: Either position is correct.

16. If $\dfrac{8}{8}$ of $\dfrac{3}{8}$ is added to $\dfrac{3}{8}$, what is the result?

17. If $2^{n-3} = 32$ what is the value of n?

18. In a group of 40 students, 25 applied to Columbia and 30 applied to Cornell. If 3 students applied to neither Columbia nor Cornell, how many students applied to both schools?

19. If $x^2 - y^2 = 100$ and $x - y = 20$, what is the value of $x + y$?

20. A gallon of water is added to 6 quarts of a solution that is 50% acid. What percent of the new solution is acid?

21. A gasoline tank is $\dfrac{1}{4}$ full. After adding 10 gallons of gasoline, the gauge indicates that the tank is $\dfrac{2}{3}$ full.

    Find the capacity of the tank in gallons.

22. If $(x - y)^2 = 40$ and $x^2 + y^2 = 60$, what is the value of xy?

23. If 2.5 cm = 1 in. and 36 in. = 1 yd., how many centimeters are in 1 yard?

24. How much more is $\dfrac{1}{4}$ of $\dfrac{1}{3}$ than $\dfrac{1}{3}$ of $\dfrac{1}{4}$?

25. If the average of 5 consecutive even integers is 82, what is the largest of these integers?

SOLUTIONS TO PRACTICE TESTS

PRACTICE TEST A

SECTION 1

1. (B)
$$\frac{1}{5}x = 8$$
$$x = 40$$
$$\frac{1}{4}(40) = 10$$

2. (E) Multiples of 3 are 3 apart x is 3 below $x + 3$. $x + 6$ is 3 above $x + 3$. $6x + 18 = 6(x + 3)$, $2x + 6 = 2(x + 3)$. $3x + 5$ does not have a factor of 3, nor can it be shown to differ front $x + 3$ by a multiple of 3.

3. (C) Angle $C = 40°$ (Congruent angles.)

    Angle $BAC = 100°$ (Sum of the angles in a triangle is 180∞.)

    Angle $x = 100°$ (Vertical angles are congruent.)

4. (E)
$$\frac{2}{5} \cdot \frac{3}{5} = \frac{3}{5}$$
$$\frac{1}{2} - \frac{1}{10} = \frac{10 - 2}{20} = \frac{8}{20} = \frac{2}{5}$$
$$\frac{3}{5} + \frac{2}{5} = 1$$

5. (C) Basic toll $1.00.

    Extra toll $2.25, which is 3($.75).

    Therefore, the car holds a driver and 3 extra passengers, for a total of 4 persons.

6. (C) Divide by y^2 : $y = 2$.

7. (C) $x = y + 1$

    Using the largest negative integers will give the smallest product. Let $y = -2$, $x = -1$, then $xy = 2$.

8. (C) Side of square = 12 = diameter of semicircle.

    Remaining 2 sides of triangle add up to 16.

    Perimeter of semicircle =
$$\frac{1}{2}\pi d = \frac{1}{2} \cdot \pi \cdot 12 = 6\pi$$

    2 sides of square in perimeter = 24

    Total perimeter of park = $16 + 6\pi + 24 = 40 + 6\pi$

9. (A)
$$80\% = \frac{4}{5} \quad \frac{4}{5} \cdot 45 = 36$$
$$\frac{1}{3} \cdot 45 = 15$$

    Used in October = 36 - 15 = 21

10. (E) Angle $AOD = 50°$

    Angle $COB = 50°$

    Arc $CB = 50°$

    Angle CAB is an inscribed angle = 25°

11. (B)
$$\frac{a}{b} \cdot \frac{b}{c} \cdot \frac{c}{d} \cdot \frac{d}{e} \cdot x = 1$$
$$\frac{a}{e} \cdot x = 1$$
$$x = \frac{e}{a}$$

12. (B)
$$\frac{m + n + p}{3} = q$$
$$m + n + p = 3q$$
$$\underline{x + y = z}$$
$$m + n + p + x + y = 3q + z$$

13. (C) Side of square = 2

    If $BE = 2$, $EA = 1$, then by the Pythagorean theorem, BA and AC each equal $\sqrt{5}$.

    Perimeter of triangle $ABC = 2 + 2\sqrt{5}$.

14. (A) Multiply every term by a.
$$\frac{1}{2a - 2}$$

15. (C) There are 30° in each of the 12 even spaces between numbers on the clock. At 3:30, the minute hand points to 6 and the hour hand is halfway between 3 and 4. The angle between the hands is $2\dfrac{1}{2}(30°) = 75°$.

16. (A) $320 is 125% of his former salary.

$$320 = 1.25x$$
$$32000 = 125x$$
$$\$256 = x$$

17. (A) Area of each square $= \dfrac{1}{5} \cdot 125 = 25$

Side of each square = 5

Perimeter is made up of 12 sides. 12(5) = 60

18. (C) $\dfrac{1}{2} \cdot \dfrac{3}{5} = \dfrac{3}{10} = 30\%$

19. (D) Circumference is 5 times arc.

$$5(2\pi) = 10\pi = \pi d$$
$$d = 10 \qquad r = 5$$

20. (D) The sum of any two sides of a triangle must be greater than the third side. Therefore, x must be less than 7 ($4 + 3 > x$); however, x must be greater than 1, as $3 + x > 4$.

21. (E) x can be negative as $(-2)^2 = 4$, which is less than 5.

22. (D) The two children's tickets equal one adult ticket. Mr. Prince pays the equivalent of 3 adult tickets.

$$3a = 12.60$$
$$a = 4.20$$

Child's ticket $= \dfrac{1}{2}(4.20) = \$2.10$

23. (A)

$$\begin{pmatrix} 3 & \\ 4 & 5 \end{pmatrix} = 12 - 5 = 7$$

$$\begin{pmatrix} 5 & \\ 6 & 7 \end{pmatrix} = 30 - 7 = 23$$

$$7 + 23 = 30$$

24. (C) If the linear ratio is 1:1.5, then the area ratio is $(1)^2 : (1.5)^2$ or 1:2.25. The increase is 1.25 or 125% of the original area.

25. (B) $\dfrac{3}{4}$ of $\dfrac{1}{3}$ will go on to college next year.

$$\dfrac{3}{4} \cdot \dfrac{1}{3} = \dfrac{1}{4} = 25\%$$

SECTION 2

PART I

1. (B) Angle 2 contains the same number of degrees as the intercepted arc. Angle 1 contains $\dfrac{1}{2}$ as much.

2. (C) Solving the equations, $x = 1$, $y = 1$.

3. (D) Without an indication of which is greater, x or y, it is impossible to tell.

4. (A) Subtracting a negative increases a quantity. Adding a negative decreases it.

5. (C) Solving for x, $x = 12$

$$\dfrac{4}{12} = \dfrac{1}{3}$$

6. (D) If $x > 0$, A is greater.

If $x < 0$, B is greater.

If $x = 0$, A and B are equal.

7. (A) 60 seconds = 1 minute

60 minutes = 1 hour

24 hours = 1 day

Seconds in 1 day $= 60 \cdot 60 \cdot 24$

There are 30 days in April.

Number of minutes in April $= 60 \cdot 24 \cdot 30$

Without any computation, A has the greater factors.

8. (D) x and y can take on values so that A is greater, B is greater, or they are both equal.

9. (B) Area of triangle $= \dfrac{1}{2} \cdot 5 \cdot 7$

Twice area of rectangle $= 2 \cdot 5 \cdot 7$

10. (A)   A   B

$$9^2 + 10^2 = h^2$$

$$81 + 100 = h^2 \qquad s^2 = 180$$

$$181 = h^2 \qquad s = \sqrt{180}$$

$$\sqrt{181} = h$$

11. (A)   Area of a cube is the sum of 6 equal squares.

A   B

$6 \cdot 6^2 \quad 6 \cdot 6 \cdot 2^2$

The factors are greater in *A*.

12. (C)   Opposite sides of a parallelogram are congruent.

13. (D)   Not enough information is given.

14. (C)   If two parallel lines are cut by a transversal, the corresponding angles are congruent.

15. (C)   Opposite angles of a parallelogram are congruent.

PART II

16. $\sqrt{4^2 + 9} = \sqrt{25} = 5$ **(answer)**

17. The number must be an even number, as there is no remainder when divided by 2. If division by 4 does give a remainder, it must be 2, since even numbers are 2 apart. 2 **(answer)**

18. $\left(\sqrt{8}\right)^2 = 8$ **(answer)**

19. $\dfrac{y}{x} = \dfrac{\frac{2}{5}}{\frac{5}{2}} = \dfrac{2}{5} \cdot \dfrac{2}{5} = \dfrac{4}{25}$ **(answer)**

20. Illustrate the given facts as follows.

This accounts for 23 students, leaving 7. **(answer)**

21. $4 \,\square\, 2 = 4 \cdot 2 + (4 - 2) = 8 + 2 = 10$ **(answer)**

22. It is possible for the first four to be blue, but then the next two must be red. Of course it is possible that two red socks could be drawn earlier, but with 6 we are *assured* of a pair of red socks. 6 **(answer)**

23.

16 **(answer)**

24. $3x = 12$ **(answer)**

$x = 4$

$3x + 1 = 13$

25.

$$(a+b)^2 = a^2 + 2ab + b^2$$
$$a^2 + b^2 = 30$$
$$\underline{2ab = 20}$$
$$a^2 + 2ab + b^2 = 50 \qquad \textbf{(answer)}$$

PRACTICE TEST B

SECTION 1

1. (A) $20\% = \dfrac{1}{5}$

$\dfrac{1}{5} \cdot 1200 = \$240$ depreciation first year.

$\$1200 - \$240 = \$960$ value after 1 year.

$\dfrac{1}{5} \cdot 960 = \$192$ depreciation second year.

$\$960 - \$192 = \$768$ value after 2 years.

2. (E)

$\dfrac{3}{5} = .6$

$\left(\dfrac{2}{3}\right)\left(\dfrac{3}{4}\right) = \dfrac{1}{2} = .5$

$\sqrt{.25} = .5$

$(.9)^2 = .81$

$\dfrac{2}{.3} = \dfrac{20}{3} = 6.\overline{6}$

3. (E) $\dfrac{1}{4} = .25$

$\dfrac{1}{4}\% = .25\% = .0025$

4. (D) $\dfrac{1}{4}\% = \dfrac{1}{4} \div 100 = \dfrac{1}{4} \cdot \dfrac{1}{100} = \dfrac{1}{400}$

5. (A) $.05\,(800) = \$40$ commission

$80\!:\!40 = 2\!:\!1$

6. (A) Multiply every term by 12.

$\dfrac{6}{4-3} = 6$

7. (D) $A + B = 40$

$B + C = 34$

$A + C = 42$

Subtract second equation from third.

$A - B = 8$

Subtract from first equation.

$2B = 32$

$B = 16$

8. (A) Use a proportion comparing inches to miles.

$\dfrac{\frac{1}{4}}{20} = \dfrac{x}{325}$

$20x = \dfrac{325}{4}$

$x = \dfrac{325}{4} \cdot \dfrac{1}{20} = \dfrac{325}{80} = 4\dfrac{5}{80} = 4\dfrac{1}{16}$

9. (D) There are $m + f$ people on the staff. Of these, m are men.

$\dfrac{m}{m + f}$ of the staff is men.

10. (A) Represent the angles as $2x$, $3x$, and $4x$.

$9x = 180$

$x = 20$

The angles are $40°$, $60°$, and $80°$, all acute.

11. (C) The linear ratio stays constant, so the perimeter is also multiplied by 2. The area ratio is the square of the linear ratio, so the area is multiplied by 2^2 or 4.

12. (D) In k minutes, $\dfrac{k}{m}$ of the lawn is mowed.

Still undone is $1 - \dfrac{k}{m}$ or $\dfrac{m - k}{m}$

13. (A)   55% of his salary is spent. 45% is left.

There is only one answer among the choices

less than $\dfrac{1}{2}$ of his salary.

14. (B)   Each side of square = 8

Radius circle = 2

Area of square = $8^2 = 64$

Area of 4 circles = $4\pi\, r^2 = 4 \cdot \pi \cdot 2^2 = 16\pi$

Shaded area = $64 - 16\pi$

15. (E)   Plotting the point shows a 3, 4, 5 triangle.

16. (D)   Since 6 times 9 is 54, the product must end in 4.

17. (E)   Figure the time elapsed on either side of 12 noon. From 7:42 A.M. to 12 noon is 4 hrs. 18 min. From 12 noon, to 10:10 P.M. is 10 hrs. 10 min. The sum of the two is 14 hrs. 28 min.

18. (B)   Each side of square *AEDC* is 10.

Each side of square *BCFG* is 6.

Triangle *ABC* is a 6, 8, 10 triangle, making the perimeter 24.

19. (C)

There are 90° left for angle 1 since angle *BCD* is a straight angle.

20. (B)   Use a proportion comparing pencils to cents. Change 2*D* dollars to 200*D* cents.

$$\frac{p}{200D} = \frac{x}{c}$$

$$\frac{pc}{200D} = x$$

21. (C)   Distance of first train = 60*x*

Distance of second train = 70*x*

$$60x + 70x = 455$$
$$130x = 455$$
$$x = 3\frac{1}{2}$$

In $3\dfrac{1}{2}$ hours, the time will be 1:30 P.M.

22. (D)   When two negative numbers are multiplied, their product is positive.

23. (B)   Since 7 times 6 is 42, the product must end in 2.

24. (C)   The minimum is 20 students in 8 classrooms.

25. (A)   The radius of each circle is 3, making the dimensions of the rectangle 18 by 6, and the area (18)(6), or 108.

SECTION 2

PART I

1. (B)   If 64*A* = 81, then *A* = a little more than 1.

2. (B)   The larger numerator with the smaller denominator will give the larger fraction.

3. (A)   Since *a* is negative, *A* will be positive while *B* is negative.

4. (B) $18 \text{ times } 10 = 180$

$12 \text{ times } 16 = 192$

5. (C) $$\frac{100}{.1} = 1000$$

$$100 - 1000 = -900$$

6. (A)   Since a post is needed at the very beginning as well as at the end, A requires 11 posts.

7. (A)   Column A represents a greater discount since the full 10% is taken from the original price.

8. (C)   Opposite sides of a parallelogram are congruent.

9. (D)   Not enough information is given.

10. (B)   Maximum area would be if ABCD were a square with AB = AD = 10. This area would be 100.

11. (C)   If AB + AD = 20, then DC + CB is also 20.

12. (A)   Let $OA = AB = x$

   Area larger circle = $\pi(2x)^2 = 4\pi x^2$

   Twice area smaller circle = $2 \cdot \pi x^2 = 2\pi x^2$

13. (B)   See solution 12

   Area smaller circle = πx^2

   Area shaded portion = $4\pi x^2 - \pi x^2 = 3\pi x^2$

14. (C)   Since $OA = AB = x$, radius of larger circle $= 2x$, diameter of smaller circle $= 2x$

15. (C)   Let $OA = OB = x$ $C = \pi d$

   Circumference larger circle $= \pi(4x) = 4\pi x$

   Twice circumference smaller circle $= 2 \cdot \pi(2x)$ $= 4\pi x$

PART II

16. $\dfrac{25}{10} = \dfrac{5}{2}$ **(answer)**

17. Marion's hourly wage is $\dfrac{\$24}{5}$ or $4.80.

   Janet's hourly wage is or

   $\dfrac{\$10.95}{3}$ or $3.65.   **(answer)**

   $4.80 - 3.65 = 1.15$

18. The difference of 5.58 must be divided between both ends. The thickness on each side is 2.79. **(answer)**

19. $x + .40x = 84$

   $1.40x = 84$

   $14x = 840$ **(answer)**

   $x = 60$

20. $r + s = 25$

   $4(r + s) = 4(25) = 100$ **(answer)**

21. The plane covers 120 miles in 12 minutes or $\dfrac{1}{5}$ hour. In $\dfrac{5}{5}$ or 1 hour, it covers 5(120), or 600 miles. 600 **(answer)**

22. 47% of 1000 are boys.

   $(.47)(1000) = 470$ boys **(answer)**

23. For every pair of digits in a number, there will be one digit in the square root. 6 **(answer)**

24. Increase of 40

   $$\text{Percent of Increase} = \frac{\text{Amount of increase}}{\text{Original}} \cdot 100\%$$

   $$\frac{40}{40} \cdot 100\% = 100\%$$
   (answer)

25. $\left(3\sqrt{2}\right)\left(3\sqrt{2}\right) = 9 \cdot 2 = 18$ **(answer)**

PRACTICE TEST C

SECTION 1

1. (B) $64 = 4^x$

   $x = 3$ $(4 \cdot 4 \cdot 4 = 64)$

2. (D) B and C are greater than 1. A, D, and E all have the same numerator. In this case, the one with the largest denominator will be the smallest fraction.

3. (A) $\dfrac{1}{2} = .5$ $\sqrt{.2} = .45$

   $(.2)^2 = .04$ $(.02)^3 = .000008$

4. (C)   Cross multiply.

   $4a = 3b$

   Multiply by 3.

   $12a = 9b$

5. (D)

   $a = b = \dfrac{1}{c}$

   $a = \dfrac{1}{c}$

   $ac = 1$

   $c = \dfrac{1}{a}$

6. (A)   The ratio of height to shadow is constant.

   $\dfrac{B}{F} = \dfrac{T}{x}$

   $Bx = FT$

   $x = \dfrac{FT}{B}$

7. (A)

   Right triangle area $= \frac{1}{2} \cdot 5 \cdot 2 = 5$

8. (E) $60 - x$ employees are male

   $\dfrac{1}{3}$ of these unmarried

   $\dfrac{1}{3}(60 - x) = 20 - \dfrac{1}{3}x$

9. (B)

   $1^2 + 1^2 = r^2$

   $2 = r^2$

   Area $= \pi r^2 = 2\pi$

10. (E)   Angle BCA = Angle BAC = 80°

    There are 20° left for angle B.

11. (B) $\dfrac{9}{2} \div \dfrac{81}{8} = \dfrac{9}{2} \cdot \dfrac{8}{81} = \dfrac{4}{9}$

12. (D) $\dfrac{1}{.3} = \dfrac{10}{3} = 3\dfrac{1}{3}$

13. (E) $\dfrac{16}{50} = \dfrac{32}{100} = 32\%$

14. (D)   Multiply by abc.

    $bc + ac = ab$

    $c(b + a) = ab$

    $c = \dfrac{ab}{b + a}$

15. (A) $\dfrac{b}{a} \cdot 100 = \dfrac{100b}{a}$

16. (C)

    $\dfrac{x + y}{2} = A$

    $x + y = 2A$

    $y = 2A - x$

17. (B) $\dfrac{3}{\cancel{5}} \cdot \cancel{5}b = 3b$

18. (B) 5 feet = 60 inches

    6 feet 8 inches = 80 inches

    This is a 6, 8, 10 triangle, making the diagonal 100 inches, which is 8 feet 4 inches.

19. (C) In 3 hours, one ship went 60 miles, the other 45 miles. This is a 3, 4, 5 triangle as $45 = 3(15)$, $60 = 4(15)$. The hypotenuse will be $5(15)$, or 75.

20. (D) This is inverse variation.

    $$m \cdot d = (m + 2) \cdot x$$

    $$\frac{md}{m+2} = x$$

21. (A) He must score as many points above 85 as below. So far he has 8 above and 10 below. He needs another 2 above.

22. (B) If 15 adults are fed, $\dfrac{3}{4}$ of the food is

    gone. $\dfrac{1}{4}$ of the food will feed $\dfrac{1}{4} \cdot 32$, or 8,

    children.

23. (C) If angle $A = 60°$, then angle $B = 120°$. Angle B = Angle D. Their sum is $240°$.

24. (C) Area of circle $= 64\pi = r^2$

    Radius of circle = 8

    Side of square = 16

    Perimeter of square = 64

25. (C) 10 minutes $= \dfrac{1}{6}$ hour

    In one hour, the train will cover $6(14)$, or 84 miles.

SECTION 2

PART I

1. (B) Since the numerators are the same, the fraction with the smaller denominator will be larger.

2. (B) The larger fraction has the smaller denominator.

3. (A) $\sqrt{49} + \sqrt{16} = 7 + 4 = 11$

    $\sqrt{65}$ is a little more than 8.

    $$2^{x-3} = 2^5$$

4. (B) $x - 3 = 5$

    $x = 8$

5. (D) There is no information about the age of each.

6. (A) An exterior angle of a triangle is greater than either remote interior angle.

7. (C) An exterior angle of a triangle is equal to the sum of two remote angles.

8. (D) No information is given.

9. (C) Each of these is $180°$.

10. (B) $\dfrac{1}{2} = .5$

    $.5\% = .005$

11. (D) a and b can take on values to make either one greater or to make them equal.

12. (B) If Jim's salary $= 8x$

    then Jack's salary $= 6x$

    and Joe's salary $= 9x$

13. (B) $40A = 4B$

    $$A = \frac{1}{10}B$$

14. (C) There are $120°$ left between angle B and angle C. Since they must be congruent, they are each $60°$ and the triangle is equilateral.

15. (A) The sum of the angles in a polygon is $(n - 2)180$.

    $3(180) = 540°$

    If angle $5 = 90°$, there are $450°$ left for the other angles.

PART II

16. $\dfrac{3}{8} + \dfrac{3}{8} = \dfrac{6}{8}$ or $\dfrac{3}{4}$ **(answer; both acceptable)**

17. $2^{n-3} = 2^5$

$n - 3 = 5$

$n = 8$ **(answer)**

18.

$25 - x + x + 30 - x = 37$

$55 - x = 37$

$18 = x$

18 **(answer)**

19. $x^2 - y^2 = (x - y)(x + y)$

$100 = 20(x + y)$

$5 = (x + y)$

5 **(answer)**

20.

	No. of quarts	% acid	=	Amount of acid
Original	6	.50		3
Added	4	0		0
New	10			3

$\dfrac{3}{10} = 30\%$ **(answer)**

21. 10 gallons is $\dfrac{2}{3} - \dfrac{1}{4}$ of the tank.

$\dfrac{2}{3} - \dfrac{1}{4} = \dfrac{8-3}{12} = \dfrac{5}{12}$ **(answer)**

$\dfrac{5}{12}x = 10$

$5x = 120$

$x = 24$

22. $(x - y)^2 = x^2 - 2xy + y^2$ **(answer)**

$40 = 60 - 2xy$

$2xy = 20$

$xy = 10$

23. $36(2.5)$ $= 90$ **(answer)**

24. $\dfrac{1}{4} \cdot \dfrac{1}{3} = \dfrac{1}{12}$ $\dfrac{1}{3} \cdot \dfrac{1}{4} = \dfrac{1}{12}$

0 **(answer)**

25. The average is the middle integer. If 82 is the third, 86 is the last.

86 **(answer)**

NOTES

NOTES

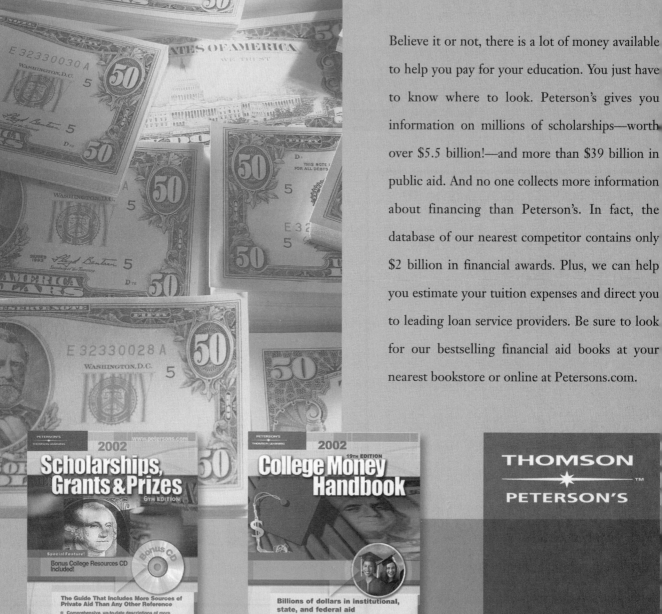